JEWISH-POLISH COEXISTENCE, 1772–1939

RECENT TITLES IN
BIBLIOGRAPHIES AND INDEXES IN WORLD HISTORY

Iran Media Index
Hamid Naficy, compiler

Serial Bibliographies and Abstracts in History: An Annotated Guide
David Henige, compiler

An Annotated Bibliography of the Holy Roman Empire
Jonathan W. Zophy, compiler

War Crimes, War Criminals, and War Crimes Trials: An Annotated Bibliography and Source Book
Norman E. Tutorow, compiler

JEWISH-POLISH COEXISTENCE, 1772–1939

A Topical Bibliography

Compiled by
George J. Lerski
and Halina T. Lerski

Foreword by Lucjan Dobroszycki

Bibliographies and Indexes in World History, Number 5

GREENWOOD PRESS
New York • Westport, Connecticut • London

LIBRARY OF CONGRESS CATALOGING-IN-PUBLICATION DATA

Lerski, Jerzy J. (Jerzy Jan), 1917-
  Jewish-Polish coexistence, 1772-1939.

  (Bibliographies and indexes in world history,
ISSN 0742-6852 ; no. 5)
  Bibliography: p.
  Includes index.
  1. Jews—Poland—Bibliography. 2. Poland—Ethnic
relations—Bibliography. I. Lerski, Halina T.
II. Title. III. Series.
Z6373.P7L47   1986   016.9438'004924   86-12119
[DS135.P6]

ISBN 0-313-24758-7 (lib. bdg. : alk. paper)

Copyright © 1986 by George J. Lerski and Halina T. Lerski

All rights reserved. No portion of this book may be
reproduced, by any process or technique, without the
express written consent of the publisher.

Library of Congress Catalog Card Number: 86-12119
ISBN: 0-313-24758-7
ISSN: 0742-6852

First published in 1986

Greenwood Press, Inc.
88 Post Road West, Westport, Connecticut 06881

Printed in the United States of America

The paper used in this book complies with the
Permanent Paper Standard issued by the National
Information Standards Organization (Z39.48-1984).

10 9 8 7 6 5 4 3 2 1

Contents

Foreword by Lucjan Dobroszycki/vii
Introduction/ix
List of Abbreviations/xv

1. Selected Reference Works/3
2. Historiography/6
3. General Works/8
4. The Late Eighteenth Century/14
5. In the Partitioned Commonwealth and in Exile/17
6. Jewish Participation in Poland's Struggle for Freedom/24
7. Jews in Independent (Interwar) Poland/29
8. Demography and Statistics/36
9. Economics/39
10. Legal Status and Minority Rights/45
11. Autonomy (Kehillots)/49
12. Religion (Orthodoxy and Reform - Haskalah)/52
13. Hasidism/57
14. Culture, Arts, Press and Folklore/63
15. Literature and Linguistics/69
16. Jews in Polish Literature/76
17. Theatre/82
18. Frankism and Neophytes/84
19. Assimilation and Emancipation/87
20. Sociology and Social Welfare/90
21. The Labor Movement and Class Struggle/95
22. Bund and Jewish Socialism/98
23. Zionism and Revisionism in Poland/102

24. Emigration/107
25. Foreign Relief and Philanthropy/111
26. Jews in the Polish Socialist Party (PPS)/113
27. Philo-Semitism/115
28. Jews in Polish Public Life/119
29. Reform Projects/123
30. Communism/126
31. Anti-Semitism/128
32. Autobiographies, Memoirs and Correspondence/137
33. Biographies and Biographical Materials/145
34. Town Communities and Shtetls/161

Author and Editor Index/211

Foreword

In the past few years, there has been a notable growth in interest in the study of Polish Jewry. The history and culture of the Jews of Poland, which came to an abrupt end during World War II, have intrigued ever-wider circles of scholars, writers, and journalists as well as the descendants of a people who, for almost a millenium, lived on Polish soil and created there a civilization of its own.

The extent of this revived interest in Polish-Jewish studies is evidenced in many endeavors and in many places: in Israel, Poland, England, France, and particularly, in the United States. We have seen a proliferation of books, articles, essays, doctoral theses, and films on the subject. Classes and seminars on the Jewish experience in Poland now appear in the course offerings of many American colleges and graduate schools. International conferences on the topic attracting Jewish and non-Jewish scholars alike -- at Columbia University, Oxford, Indiana University, and Brandeis, for example -- have become almost commonplace. This increased attention is best indicated, perhaps, by the many bibliographies on the subject published in the last ten years. Though some overlapping is unavoidable, these surveys differ from one another in the subject matter and the time span they cover. Yet for the serious researcher, there can never be too many bibliographies, for one can always find additional citations which may have previously escaped even the most scrupulous compiler.

The new bibliography by George J. and Halina T. Lerski, <u>Jewish-Polish Coexistence, 1772-1939</u>, is an important contribution to the subject because of its emphasis, for the first time in a listing of the literature, on the relations, good and bad, between two peoples on both sides of the Vistula. The Lerskis understand, as we all must, that the experience of Jews in the Diaspora cannot be studied in isolation from the history and culture of the lands in which they lived. Among the nearly 3,000 entries in their bibliography one can find numerous references to interactions between Jews and Poles, and of Jews with the other ethnic groups of multinational Poland: Germans, Ukrainians, Belorussians. From now on, any scholar or layperson seeking to portray Jewish life in Poland from the time of partition until the eve of the Nazi invasion cannot afford to overlook the Lerskis' work.

Few people are better equipped for preparing a bibliography of this kind than George Lerski. For the past ten years, as a professor at the Jesuit University of San Francisco, Mr. Lerski has been teaching and writing on the subject of Polish-Jewish history. This is not to suggest, however, that the topic is of only recent interest to him. Before World War II, he worked for the brotherhood of the two groups, defending the Jews whenever they were abused or attacked. Following the German invasion, he was a courier for the Polish government-in-exile, flying more than once on secret missions from occupied Warsaw to London carrying messages for the Resistance as well as seeking to arouse concern about the catastrophe facing Europe's largest Jewish community.

For this, in 1985 he was awarded a medal of honor as one of the "Righteous Among Nations" by the Yad Vashem Institute in Jerusalem. Mr. Lerski well understands that the history of the Jews of Poland is, in a sense, tragically complete. What he now seeks to do is to assure that this history is studied in all of its richness and complexity.

--Lucjan Dobroszycki

Introduction

> In no other country did such a proportion of Jewish children receive a Jewish education as in Poland ... Polish Jewry was the strongest fortress of our national Jewish values ... Polish Jewry, according to its tradition, its stubbornness, and its devotion was called upon to serve as an example for all other Jewish communities.
>
> --Dr. Abraham Gordon Duker

Most of the world's Jewry shared a homeland with the Polish nation during the last five centuries. While developing their own cultural existence in this post-medieval "haven of refuge," naturally the Jews also contributed substantially to the growth of Polish and Lithuanian cultures. Protected since the mid-thirteenth century by princely privileges, the Jews were able to establish almost a state within a state, commonly known as the "Council of the Four Lands" (Waad Arba Avazoth in Hebrew). This was the basis of the Jewish self-government, with its kehillots (consistories) even at the lowest shtetl (townlet) level. The prominent Jewish historians Simon M. Dubnow, Salo Wittmeyer Baron, and, recently, Bernard Weinryb devoted their great works, or at least important parts of them, to the historical background of that rich Jewish life and to manifold aspects of Jewish-Polish coexistence.

Professor Lucy S. Dawidowicz, in the introduction to her important collection The Golden Tradition: Jewish Life and Thought In Eastern Europe (1967), claims that

> in the sixteenth century, the center of world Jewry moved to Eastern Europe, which until 1939 remained the region of greatest Jewish population and density. Eastern Europe was the cradle of almost every important Jewish cultural, religious and national movement, and the area where Jewish faith, thought and culture flourished unsurpassed. Thence came the impetus and vitality that preserved the Jewish people intact in prosperity and adversity. East European Jewry became a reservoir of manpower and from the nineteenth century on, provided the overwhelming bulk of migrants to the United States, to Israel and many far-flung communities.

The above assessment, while correct, requires some clarification; namely, until the first partition of the Polish-Lithuanian Commonwealth in 1772, the bulk of Eastern Jewry lived in the Polish-Lithuanian lands and constituted approximately one-tenth of its population of ten million. Actually, by the eighteenth century more than 75 percent of the world's Jewish community was living in the Polish-Lithuanian Commonwealth, while as late as the outbreak of World War II, the Jewish community in Poland was the second largest in the world, after that in the United States, with Warsaw being the largest Jewish community in Europe. The succession of partitions in 1772, 1793, and 1795 formed a crucial turning point for Jews and Poles alike. The latter lost their national independence for 123 years; the former found themselves under three new masters and were put in the so-called "Pale of Settlement" in Czarist Russia. Their remnants in the Soviet Union remain the third largest concentration of Jewish people after America and Israel.

This bibliography attempts to cover the entire field of relations between the two nations from the first partition in 1772 up to the outbreak of World War II on September 1, 1939, with Germany's unprovoked attack on Poland. The six-year-long war coincided with the Nazi Holocaust, which took the lives of almost six million European Jews on Polish soil. The war also claimed some three million non-Jewish Polish lives, and resulted again in the destruction of Poland's independence.

The entire 167-year period has never yet been covered by a comprehensive bibliography, although the late Professor Meir Balaban made an ambitious attempt. In 1939 he published, mainly in the Polish language, the first volume of a major reference work, Bibliography of the History of Jews in Poland and Adjacent Countries, 1900-1930. It proved so valuable to scholars that it was reprinted in Israel in 1975. Another recent work is the analytical bibliography, primarily in English, by Professors Gershon David Hundert and Gershon C. Bacon, The Jews in Poland and Russia, published in 1984 by Indiana University Press. Though very helpful indeed, it only partially covers the tremendous richness of Jewish life in Poland. As aptly stated recently by the Polish professor of philosophy Leszek Kolakowski of Oxford University: "Good or bad, the centuries long experience of Jewish life in Poland was crucial in the cultural formation of modern Jewry, and it was of great importance in the history not of Poland only, but of European civilization. Nobody can doubt that systematic study of Polish-Jewish history is of highest scholarly interest." (1985 blurb for Polin, forthcoming Oxford journal).

As prevailing misconceptions, often based on emotional, mutual recriminations, serve to undermine serious research efforts, it is of vital importance to show, by the accumulated "dry material," the enormous scope of Polish-Jewish coexistence. That the vital part of the modern history of both nations was lived jointly and in mutual interrelationships during these times of trial is recorded in almost 3,000 sources listed. While no bibliography can ever be definitive, it is hoped that no major works have been left out.

Besides the 1772 and 1939 time limits for the presented material, the main criterion in the selection of entries concerned was whether a given publication devotes at least half of its material to the main topic of the bibliography. Hence, even important sources that may contain very valuable information about the subject matter but that deal primarily with other concerns are not to be found here. Only books, brochures, pamphlets, and articles in learned journals and other significant periodicals were considered; there are no entries from daily newspapers, encyclopaedias, biographical dictionaries, book reviews, or press obituaries, or from unpublished dissertations. Because an intent of this bibliography is also to demonstrate the immensity of the writings dedicated to Jewish-Polish coexistence during the last two centuries and to record them in one volume for the convenience of reference libraries and their patrons, it was decided to forgo what would necessarily be superficial, arbitrary annotations added at the expense of imposing a higher degree of selectivity.

The sources have been entered topically under thirty-four distinct chapter headings. While space considerations precluded narrative introductions to the respective topics and a separate, detailed subject index, it is hoped that the chapter headings will provide adequate designation of the subject matter. Except in the last two long chapters on biographies and on specified Jewish communities, and in chapter nine on economics, all entries are listed alphabetically by authors' family names within each chapter. Biographical sources are first organized alphabetically by the names of the personalities discussed and then, in case of more than one source, by actual author. The final chapter on Jewish organized communities in larger cities and the so-called shtetls again lists these various localities alphabetically; sources are then entered alphabetically by respective author or editor. The chapter on economics is subdivided into short sections on the general situation; agriculture; banking, commerce, and cooperatives; and crafts and industry. Very often an entry could well have been listed in at least two chapters; in assigning it to what seemed its most logical place the geographical location generally prevailed, which should explain the disproportionate length of the last chapter. A detailed index of authors and editors provides an alternative means of access.

An abbreviation key to the main periodicals and collective book sources is given directly following this introduction together with a list of symbols representing the original language of publication. In view of the large number of entries and the fact that this reference book is being published in the United States, it was decided to translate all titles from the eleven languages represented into English and to indicate the original language of the given publication after each respective entry only in parenthesis, for example: (H) for Hebrew or (P) for Polish. Where the language of publication was English, there is no parenthetical code. If a book or article was also published in English translation from the original text, this will be indicated by the name of the translator; when a work has been published in two or more languages, preference is given consistently to the English version without mention that the same work was published earlier or simultaneously in another language. Professional bibliographers may question these decisions of the authors, but the options were taken to complete this bibliography in one not over-large volume.

This work being published in English, the authors decided to avoid confusion by standardizing the spelling of names of personalities, authors, and localities according to the Encyclopaedia Judaica or the National Union Catalog rather than to preserve the original spelling as given with each source. With respect to the localities, preference was given to their official Polish names, although these often differ from their German or Yiddish counterparts, which are indicated in parenthesis. The same two sources were also consulted for birth and death dates of the authors, which are given whenever possible in the author index.

The geographical coverage here may be controversial. Establishing geographical boundaries for Poland and Jews in Poland is difficult first because of the breaking up of the old Polish-Lithuanian Commonwealth and also in view of the fact that some of the old Jewish communities never returned to the reborn Polish state after World War I or World War II, while others existed under German rule in what is now, in the post-World War II era, considered by the Poles to be "Regained Territories." It was therefore decided to focus the coverage on the territorial boundaries of interwar (1918-1939) Poland with inclusion of northern and western 1945 acquisitions such as Gdansk (Danzig) or Wroclaw (Breslau). Even if somewhat inconsistent, such an extensive coverage seems justified from the viewpoint of deep-rooted historical aspects of Jewish-Polish relations. A major exception from strict territorial coverage had to be made for Jewish-Polish relations in West European exile or American emigration, mainly due to their continuous strong impact on the overall Jewish-Polish relationship in Poland.

A prominent Lwow member of Shomer Israel, Dr. Emil Byk, stated in 1899 that "_Polonia Judaeorum paradisus_." According to him, Palestine was only a religious and historical memory, while Poland was the true homeland for the Jews. And immediately after the outbreak of World War II, Vladimir Zhabotinskii (the guru of recent Israeli Prime Ministers Begin and Shamir) cabled, in the name of the New Zionist Organization, to President Ignacy Moscicki of Poland: "I humbly call God's blessing upon your country, her president, her marshall, her soldiers of all creeds, united in loyalty and service."

The continuously updated _National Union Catalog_ must serve as the best source of information on availability of books and pamphlets in the main libraries on this continent, while the archival sources and old periodicals specializing in Jewish history are to be tapped by interested scholars in such rich collections as those of the YIVO Institute for Jewish Research--which was providently moved before World War II from the place of its origin in Wilno to New York City--or the Jewish Historical Institute in Warsaw. The main Polish publication of this institute, _Biuletyn Zydowskiego Instytutu Historycznego_, was a valuable source for this bibliography. Increasingly important also are the growing collections of the _Gal Ed_ Diaspora Research Institute in Israel.

Work on this project was initiated some ten years ago when George Lerski began developing materials for academic instruction. Lerski has had a lifelong interest in working for Jewish-Polish brotherhood and in the improvement of mutual relations. But it was only in the mid-1970s that he was able to introduce the upper division survey course on "History of Jews in Europe" at the Jesuit University of San Francisco. Also beginning to appear at about that time, the growing number of book reviews written for learned journals in the United States greatly helped in amassing the bibliographical data. Simultaneously, a much younger scholar, Dr. Tadeusz Wojnicki, originally of the Catholic University of Lublin (KUL), was doing research at the Hebrew Union College Archives in Cincinnati. The original intention was a joint publishing venture, but for personal reasons Dr. Wojnicki left the project in 1980, retaining sources for the introductory chapter on the "Bibliography of Bibliographies," which he intended to publish separately. For this reason, we have decided to limit the entries in the first chapter to "Selected Reference Works." Dr. Wojnicki contributed substantially to the last chapter on town communities and shtetls with his valuable collection of Memorial Book entries, which constitute more than half of that chapter. We are therefore grateful for the contributions he provided, and for suggestions he was able to make during the early stage of this project.

At that time the authors appealed, through Jerzy Giedroyc, editor-in-chief of the Polish literary monthly Kultura in Paris, and through other journals, for twenty dollar subscriptions to support the project. Over one hundred people responded, but the collected money proved insufficient. Now that Greenwood Press has published the work, any of the original subscribers who have not already been contacted by Dr. Lerski should write to him in care of the publisher to determine how they can be reimbursed. Again, all the subscribers are to be thanked for their kind support of the initial project. Also to be thanked is our dear friend Professor Jan Karski, who always shared our views concerning the need for better Jewish-Polish understanding. This war hero, who recently retired from Georgetown University, once more underscored his friendship and gave credence to his ideas by contributing funds toward the purchase of a computer to finalize the project.

As bibliographical work is to a large extent a sophisticated technical effort, especially in its final stages, coauthor Halina T. Lerski undertook special computer-cum-word-processing training and devoted hundreds of late hours to that meticulous joint endeavor during the last four years.

We are both very grateful to our Israeli friend Shoshana Korthamar-Kowalski and her husband Artur Kowalski of San Jose, California, who helped immensely in the translation of hundreds of Hebrew and Yiddish titles. The authors also wish to thank Professor Jerzy Krzyzanowski of Ohio State University for his generous assistance in the chapter "Jews in Polish Literature," an important vehicle for demonstrating the varied aspects of Jewish-Polish coexistence. The foremost Polish exile bibliographer Jan Kowalik of San Jose helped by guiding us in the general skills of bibliographical writing. Wlada Grycz of the University of San Francisco's Gleason Library and Dr. Maciej Siekierski of the Hoover Institute on War, Revolution and Peace at Stanford University were very resourceful in finding material on the subject. Expert secretarial help was provided by Sandra Gamble and Ksenya Zavarin; the former was particularly meticulous in her research assistance, the latter, in the editing of translated titles. The author of the foreword, Dr. Lucjan Dobroszycki of the YIVO Institute for Jewish Research-Max Weinreich Center in New York City, deserves special gratitude for his kind support and penetrating remarks. Last, but not least, we wish to thank wholeheartedly Marilyn Brownstein of Greenwood Press for her friendly guidance in completing this publication.

We believe that all these people contributed to an endeavor, the need for which was outlined by Sir Isaiah Berlin of Oxford University as follows: "The history of Polish-Jewish relations is of cardinal importance in the history of the Jews since the late Middle Ages, and scarcely less so in the history of Poland in more modern times. The story is often painful, at all times complex, and at times of high achievement; and it deserves ... objective and illuminating treatment."

While this statement was made to inaugurate the new journal of Polish-Jewish studies <u>Polin</u>, to be started in 1986 by the Institute for Polish-Jewish Studies in Oxford, England, it applies as well, we think, to our bibliography.

List of Abbreviations

MOST-CITED SOURCES

BZIH	--	Biuletyn Zydowskiego Instytutu Historycznego (Warsaw).
GGZ	--	Glos Gminy Zydowskiej (Warsaw).
GT	--	The Golden Tradition: Jewish Life and Thought in Eastern Europe. Edited by Lucy S. Davidowicz. New York: Schocken Books, 1984.
JSS	--	Jewish Social Studies (New York).
J.St.	--	Jewrejskaia Starina (St. Petersburg).
KZP	--	Kwartalnik Poswiecony Badaniu Przeszlosci Zydow w Polsce (Warsaw).
MSC	--	Materialy do Dziejow Sejmu Czteroletniego. vol. VI. Edited by Artur Eisenbach, et al. Warsaw: Instytut Historii Polskiej Akademii Nauk, 1969.
M.Zyd.	-	Miesiecznik Zydowski (Warsaw).
SPJ	--	Studies on Polish Jewry, 1919-1939. Edited by Joshua A. Fishman. New York: YIVO Institute for Jewish Research, 1974.
YIVO	--	Yiddish Scientific Institute (Wilno and New York).
ZPO	--	Zydzi w Polsce Odrodzonej. Edited by Ignacy Schiper, et al. Warsaw: 2 vol. 1932-1933.

ORIGINAL LANGUAGE OF PUBLICATION

The language of the non-English publications is indicated by letter symbol in parenthesis at the end of the entry. Those in English are not indicated by a letter symbol.

- (E) -- Esperanto
- (F) -- French
- (G) -- German
- (H) -- Hebrew
- (L) -- Latin
- (Li) - Lithuanian
- (P) -- Polish
- (R) -- Russian
- (S) -- Spanish
- (U) -- Ukrainian
- (Y) -- Yiddish

JEWISH-POLISH
COEXISTENCE, 1772–1939

1
Selected Reference Works

1   Alsberg, P.A. Guide to the Archives in Israel. Jerusalem: Israel Archives Association, 1973. 257p.

2   Bacon, Gershon C. "East European Century Jewry from the First Partition of Poland to the Present." In The Jews in Poland and Russia: Bibliographical Essays, edited by Gershon David Hundert and Gershon C. Bacon, pp.121-276. Bloomington: Indiana University Press, 1984.

3   Bałaban, Majer. A Bibliography of Jewish History in Poland and Neighboring Countries. 1900-1930. Part 1. Warsaw: Towarzystwo Szerzenia Wiedzy Judaistycznej w Polsce, 1939. 112p. (P)

4   Cutter, Charles and Oppenheim, Mika Falk. Jewish Reference Sources: A Selective Annotated Bibliographic Guide. New York: Garland, 1982. xiii, 180p.

5   Farmer, Kenneth C. and Crowe, David. "Jews." In "National Minorities in Poland, 1919-1980," Chapter 2 in Eastern European National Minorities, 1919-1980: a Handbook, edited by Stephan M. Horak, pp. 79-92. Littleton, Colorado: Libraries Unlimited, Inc., 1985.

6   Gilbert, Martin. Jews History Atlas: Cartography by Arthur Banks. London: Weidenfelt & Nicolson, 1968. 112p.

7   Glikson, Paul. Preliminary Inventory of the Jewish Daily and Periodical Press Published in the Polish Language, 1823-1982. Jerusalem: The Hebrew University Institute of Jewish Studies: Center for Research on Polish Jewry, 1983. pp. 69.

8   Gunzenhäuser, Max von, ed. A Bibliography for the Nationality Question and for the Jewish Question in the Polish Republic. 1919-1939. Stuttgart: Weltkriegsbücherei Institut für Weltpolitik, 1941. 76p. (G)

9   Guterman, Józef. "Jews in the Polish Biographical Dictionary." BZIH 2/82 (1972): 121-126. (P)

10 Harvard University Library. Slavic Judaica Pamphlets. Cambridge:

Harvard University Library, 1981. 107p.

11   Hochberg, Leo, ed.   "Memorial Books of Polish Jews."   BŻIH   2/90 (1974): 103-129.   (P)

12   Hoffman, Zygmunt.   "Archives of the Jewish Historical Institute in Poland."   BŻIH   4/112 (1979): 101-114.   (P)

13   Kaplan, Jonathan, ed.   International Bibliography of Jewish History and Thought.   Jerusalem: Magnes Press, 1984.   xviii, 483p.

14   Lange, Nicholas D.   Atlas of the Jewish World.   New York: Facts on File, 1984.   240p.

15   Merowitz, Morton J.   "'Once a Jew, Always a German': An Annotated Bibliography of English Language Materials on Polish-Jewish Relations and History prior to 1939."   The Polish Review, 30, no.2 (1985): 185-202.

16   Morawski, Karol.   "Photographic Collections of the Jewish Historical Institute in Poland."   BŻIH, 1-2/129-130 (1984):   169-173. (P)

17   Rajzen, Zalman.   Lexicon of Yiddish Literature, Press & Philology. 4 vols.   Wilno: YIVO, 1927-1929.   (Y)

18   Roth, Cecil and Wigoder, Geoffrey, eds.   Encyclopaedia Judaica. 16 vols.   Jerusalem: Keter, 1972; New York: Macmillan.

19   Segal, Aryen.   Guide to Jewish Archives (Preliminary Edition). Jerusalem: World Council on Jewish Archives, 1981.   90p.

20   Shayn, Israel.   "Materials for a Bibliography of Jewish Periodicals in Independent Poland (prepared for publication with an introduction by Ezra Mendelsohn)."   In Studies on Polish Jewry, 1919-1939, edited by Joshua A. Fishman, pp.422-483.   New York: Yivo Institute for Jewish Research, 1974.   (Y)

21   Shunami, Shlomo.   Bibliographies of Jewish Bibliographies.   2d ed., enl.   Jerusalem: The Magnes Press, Hebrew University, 1965.   xxiv, 992p.

22   Shunami, Shlomo.   Bibliographies of Jewish Bibliographies: Supplement to Second Edition Enlarged 1965.   Jerusalem: The Magnes Press, Hebrew University, 1975.   xxvi, 464p.

23   Trunk, Isaiah S.   Poland.   3 vols.   New York: Farlag Unser Tsait, 1944-1946.   (H)

24   Uchitelle, Daniel J.   "New Sources of Information on Eastern European Jewish Life, 1875-1920."   East European Quarterly (Boulder, Colo.) 19, no.2 (Summer 1985): 161-174.

25   Weinreich, Uriel and Weinreich, Beatrice.   Yiddish Language and Folklore: A Selective Bibliography for Research.   The Hague: Mouton, 1959.   66p.

26   Wigoder, Geoffrey, ed.   *Encyclopedic Dictionary of Judaica*.
Jerusalem: Keter Publishing House, 1974. xi, 673p.

2
Historiography

27   Abramsky, Chimen. "The Jewish Labour Movement: Some Historiographical Problems." Soviet Jewish Affairs 1 (1971): 45-51.

28   Bałaban, Majer. A Review of Literature for Jewish History in Poland 1899-1907. Lwów: Drukarnia Ludowa, 1908. 35p. (P)

29   Bałaban, Majer. "Tasks and Needs of Jewish Historiography in Poland." Pamiętnik V Zjazdu Historyków Polskich (Lwów) 2 (1931): 225-228. (P)

30   Balaban, Majer. "The Problem of Jewish Historiography in Regard to the History of Jews in Poland." M. Zyd. 2 (1939): 369-382. (P)

31   Biderman, Israel M. Mayer Balaban, Historian of Polish Jewry: His Influence on the Younger Generation of Jewish Historians. New York: I. M. Biderman Book Committee, 1976. xxv, 334 p. illus.

32   Dubnov, Semen Markovich. Jewish History: An Essay Philosophy of History. Philadelphia: The Jewish Publication Society of America, 1903. xv, 184p.

33   Frank, M. Z. "Poland in Jewish History." In Polish Jewish 11th Yearbook, pp.33-40. New York: American Federation of Polish Jews, 1944.

34   Friedman, Philip. "Polish Jewish Historiography Between the Two Wars, 1918-1939." JSS 11 (October 1949): 373-408.

35   Johnpoll, Bernard K. "A New View of Polish Jewish History". Midstream, 25(7). (August-September, 1979): 62-63.

36   Junger Historiker. vol.2 Warsaw: YIVO, 1929. 138p. (Y)

37   Kaznelson, Mejer. Problems of Jewish History and Philosophy of History. Berlin: Judischer Verlag, 1929. 127p. (G)

38   Lerski, Jerzy "Jur". "The Post War Research on Polish-Jewish Relations." In Symposiones, edited by A. Żaki, pp.225-229. Vol.I. London: Universitas Polonorum In Exteris, 1981. (P)

39   Mishkinsky, Moshe, ed.   In Commemoration of The History of Jews in Poland. 2 vols. Tel-Aviv: Gal Ed Diaspora Research Institute and The World Federation of Polish Jews, 1978. xxx, 749p.

40   Sadykiewicz, Lucja.   "Jewish Topics in Masters' Theses."   BŻIH 4/80 (1971): 75-86. (P)

41   Shatzky, Jacob.   "Balance Sheet of a Jewish Historian."   In the Golden Tradition: Jewish Life and Thought in Eastern Europe, edited by Lucy S. Dawidowicz, pp.263-269. New York: Holt, Rinehart & Winson, 1967.

42   Sommerfeldt, Joseph.   "Development of Historical Writings about Jews in Poland." Die Burg (Kraków, 1940): 64-69. (G)

43   Stein, E.   "The Roads and Pathless Tracts of Learning on Jews in Reborn Poland." GGŻ. 2, no. 10-11 (October-November, 1938): 285-287. (P)

44   Szulkin, Michal.   "Creation of the Department of History of Jews in Poland at the Hebrew University in Jerusalem." BŻIH   no.2/106 (1978): 27-32. (P)

45   Tartakower, Arieh.   "The Institute for Jewish Studies in Warsaw." In Studies in Memory of Moses Schorr, edited by L. Ginzberg and A. Weiss, pp.163-176. New York: 1944.

46   Tomaszewski, Jerzy.   "A Few Remarks Concerning Works About the Recent History of Polish Jews." Przegląd Historyczny, (Warsaw) 75, no.1 (1984): 137-141.

47   Trunk, Isaiah.   Studies in Jewish History in Poland.   Buenos Aires: 1963. 328p. (Y)

48   Trunk, Isaiah.   "How to Study the History of the Liquidated Communities in Poland." Yiddish Almanac (New York, 1961): 275-286. (Y)

49   Yiddish Scientific Institute.   YIVO: Yiddish Scientific Institute, an Outlook on its Goals and Achievements.   Wilno: 1931. 32p.

3
General Works

50   Agnon, Samuel.   The Book about Polish Jews.   Berlin: Ydischer Verlag, 1916.   270p.   (G)

51   Avidan, Moshe.   "Poland."   Encyclopaedia Judaica   (Jerusalem) 13 (1972): 709-787.

52   Bader, Gershom.   Thirty Generations of Jews in Poland.   New York: 1927, xvi, 495p.   (Y)

53   Bałaban, Majer.   From the History of Jews in Poland: Sketches and Studies.   Warsaw: B-cia Lewin-Epstein i S-ka, 1920.   238p.   (P)

54   Bałaban, Majer.   Jews in Poland.   Vienna: Habrit Verlags-Gesellschaft, 1927.   91p.   (G)

55   Bernfeld, Simon.   Jews and Jewishness in the Nineteenth Century. Berlin: S. Cronbach, 1898.   167p.   (G)

56   Boleski, Andrzej.   The Polish Question and the Jews.   Warsaw: E. Wende, 1911.   16p.   (P)

57   Borwicz, Michal Maksymilian, ed.   1000 Years of Jewish Life in Poland.   Paris: Centre D'études Historiques, 1955.   440p.

58   Brückner, Aleksander.   "The Jews."   Dzieje Kultury Polskiej, vol. 2, pp.413-424.   Warsaw: Książka i Wiedza, 1958.   (P)

59   Bujak, Franciszek.   The Jewish Question in Poland.   Paris: Impr. Levé, 1919.   50p.   (F)

60   Chicherin, Boris Nikolaevich.   Polish and Jewish Problems. Berlin: G. Steinitz, 1901.   64p.   (R)

61   Czyński, Jan.   Israel in Poland: Letters Addressed to Jewish Archives.   Paris: Aux Bureaux Des Archives Israelites, 1861.   54p.   (F)

62   Czyński, Jan.   The Question of Polish Jews Seen as a European Question.   Paris: Guillaume, 1833.   29p.   (F)

63   Datner, Szymon.   From Jewish History in Poland.   Warsaw: Interpress, 1983. 38p. (P)

64   Davies, Norman.   "Zydzi-The Jewish Community."   In his God's Playground: A History of Poland, pp.240-266.   New York: Columbia University Press, 1982.

65   Dawidowicz, Lucy S.   "Introduction: The World of East European Jewry."   In The Golden Tradition, edited by Lucy S. Dawidowicz, pp.5-90. New York: Beacon Press, 1967.

66   Dubnov, Semen Markovich.   History of the Jews in Russia and Poland, From the Earliest Times Until the Present Day.   Translated from Russian by I. Friedlaender. 3 vols.   Philadelphia: The Jewish Publication Society of America, 1916-1920.

67   Duker, Abraham Gordon.   The Situation of the Jews in Poland.   New York: American Jewish Congress, 1936. 31p.

68   Dzwonkowski, Władysław.   Comments on the Peasant, Ruthenian and Jewish Question Caused by Recent Events.   Paris: L. Martinet, 1862. 77p. (P)

69   Efrosy, Ch.   Jewish History in Eastern Europe (Lithuania, Poland and Russia) From the End of the 18th till Beginning of the 20th Century. Warsaw: Chmurner-Fond bay der jid. szulorganizacje in Pojln, 1938. 214p. (Y)

70   Eisenbach, Artur.   From the History of the Jewish Population in 18th and 19th Century Poland: Studies and Sketches.   Warsaw: Państwowy Instytut Wydawniczy, 1983. 241p. (P)

71   Feinkind, M.   History of Jews in Poland from Several Centuries Before to Present. Piotrków: 1928. 31p. (Y)

72   Feldman, Wilhelm.   "The Jewish Question in Poland."   Krytyka 10, no.2   (Kraków, 1908): 307-308. (P)

73   Feldstejn, Herman.   The Poles and the Jews: An Appeal, with an Introduction by Joseph Sare.   Kraków: Supreme Polish National Committee, 1915. 23p.

74   Frenk, Ezriel Nathan.   Burghers and Jews in Poland: Historical Study. Warsaw: 1921. 164p. (H)

75   Frenk, Ezriel Nathan. Jews in Poland.   Warsaw: 1912. 55p. (Y)

76   Friedlander, Israel.   The Jews of Russia and Poland: A Bird's-Eye View of their History and Culture.   New York and London: G.P. Putnam's Sons, 1915. xiv, 214p.

77   Fuks, Marian.   "As they were ..." Mówią Wieki no. 9 (1983): 10-13. (P)

78   Fuks, Marian, et al.   Polish Jewry: History and Culture.   Warsaw: Interpress Publishers, 1982. 196p.

79   Grunbaum, Isaac.   **Struggles of Polish Jews**.   Jerusalem: 1941. 474p.   (H)

80   Halpern, Israel.   **Eastern European Jewry**.   Jerusalem: Magnes Press, 1968.   435p.

81   Halpern, Israel, ed.   **The House of Israel in Poland**.   2 vols. Jerusalem: Youth Department of Zionist Organization, 1948-1953.   (H)

82   Hirschhorn, Samuel.   **History of Jews in Poland: from the Four Years Diet up to the European War, 1788-1914**.   Warsaw: B-cia Lewin-Epstein, 1921.   376p.   (P)

83   Hollaenderski, Leon.   **The History of the Israelites of Poland**. San Francisco: P. Jacoby's English & German Printing Office, 1865.   vi, 43p.

84   Hollaenderski, Leon.   **The Jews of Poland**.   Paris: Dagetau,   1846. xvi, 342p.   (F)

85   Horwitz, Max H.   **On the Jewish Question**.   Krakow: Drukarnia Narodowa, 1907.   viii, 100p.   (P)

86   Iranek-Osmecki, Kazimierz.   "The Jews in the Poland of Old".   In his **He who saves one life**,   pp.1-16.   New York: Crown Publishers, Inc., 1971.

87   Janowsky, Oscar Isaiah.   **People at Bay: The Jewish Problem in East-Central Europe**.   New York & London: Oxford University Press, 1938. 193p.

88   Jastrow, Markus.   **The Situation of Jews in Poland**.   Hamburg: Hoffman und Campe, 1859.   133p.   (G)

89   Jeske-Choinski, Teodor.   **History of Jews in Poland**.   Warsaw: Gebethner i Wolff, 1919.   350p.   (P)

90   "Jews in Poland".   **Polish Facts & Figures**.   no.6,   pp.1-15.   New York: Polish Government Information Center, July 1944.

91   **The Jews in Poland and in the World: Catholicism and Judaism**. Warsaw: Znak, 1983.   vol. 35, no.2-3.   574p, 50 illus.   (P)

92   Kaplun-Kogan, Wladimir Wolf.   **Jews in Poland: A Historical Outlook**.   Berlin: 1915.   19p.   (G)

93   Katz, Ben-Zion.   **History of Jews in Russia, Poland & Lithuania**. Berlin: 1899.   64p.   (H)

94   Kirszrot, Jan, ed.   **Collective Work dedicated to Jewish Problems**. Warsaw: "Safrus", 1905.   335p.   (P)

95   Kraushar, Aleksander.   **History of the Jews in Poland**.   2 Vols. Warsaw: Drukarnia Gazety Polskiej, 1865-1866.   (P)

96   Kutrzeba, Stanislaw.   **The Jewish Question in Poland: Historical**

Essay. Lwów: Księgarnia Polska Bernarda Połonieckiego, 1918. 76p. (P)

97   Lauer, Bernard. The Polish Jewish Question according to a Polish Jew. Paris: Lévé, 1916. 20p. (F)

98   Lew, Myer S. The Jews of Poland. London: E. Goldston, 1944. 191p.

99   Lewin, Isaac. The Jewish Community in Poland: Historical Essays. New York: Philosophical Library, 1985. xiii, 247p.

100   Lubliner, Ludwig Osias. The Jews in Poland: Review of Their Conditions from the Historical, Legislative and Political Viewpoints. Bruxelles: by the author, 1839, iii, 237p. (F)

101   Mahler, Raphael. History of Jews in Poland. Merhavia, Israel: 1946. 502p. (H)

102   Mahler, Raphael. A History of Modern Jewry, 1780-1815. New York: Schocken Books, 1971, xxiii, 742p.

103   Margolin, Arnold. The Jews of Eastern Europe. New York: T. Seltzer, 1926, xii, 292p.

104   Mark, Bernard. History of Jews in Poland. Warsaw: 1957. 447p. (Y)

105   Marylski, Antoni. History of the Jewish Question in Poland. Warsaw: Gebethner i Wolff, 1912. 144p. (P)

106   Meisl, Josef. History of the Jews in Poland and Russia. 3 vols. Berlin: A. Schwetscke und Sohn, 1921-1925. (G)

107   Meisl, Josef. Jews in the Polish Kingdom: A Historical Overview. Bonn: A. Marcus und E. Weber, 1916, vi, 78p. (G)

108   Mendes-Flohr, Paul R. and Reinharz, Jehuda, eds. The Jew in the Modern World: A Documentary History. New York: Oxford University Press, 1980. 576 p. tables.

109   Merunowicz, Teofil. Jewish National Policy of the Present Era: (Die Ostjudenfrage). Lwów: N. Gubrynowicz i Synowie, 1917. 156p. (P)

110   Merunowicz, Teofil. The Jews. Lwów: Księgarnia Polska, 1879. 222p. (P)

111   Modras, Ronald. "Jews and Poles: A Relationship Reconsidered". America (Chicago) 146, no.1 (January 2-9, 1982): 5-8.

112   Nissenbaum, Salomon Baruch. History of Jews in Poland. Warsaw: 1908. 88p. (G)

113   Nussbaum, Hilary. The Jews of Poland. Warsaw: I. Majzner, 1890. (P)

114   Papajski, Leon. The Role of the Jews in Polish History. Krakow:

"Samodzielność", 1937. 66p. (P)

115 Peter, Egon. "The Largest Jewish State in the World", Raubstaat Polen, pp.87-110 Berlin-Leipzig: Nibelungen Verlag, 1939. (G)

116 Piotrowski, Nicholas L. The Jews in Poland. Chicago: Naród Polski Publishing Co., 1919. 16p.

117 Polish Association in Great Britain, Jews in Poland: Yesterday and Today. London: The White Eagle Press, 1968. 88p.

118 Ringel, Michał. On the Platform and Before the Tribunal: On the Jewish Question. Warsaw: F. Hoesick, 1927. vii, 130p. (P)

119 Rosenfeld, Max. Poles and Jews: Contemporary Considerations. Vienna: R. Lowitt, 1917. 63p. (G)

120 Rosenfeld, Max. The Polish Jewish Question: Problem and Solution. Vienna: R. Lowitt, 1918. 266p. (G)

121 Rosenthal, Judah M. "The History of Jews in Poland in Light of the Responsa of the MaHaRaM of Lublin." In Studies and Texts in Jewish History vol.2, pp. 479-512. Jerusalem: R. Mass, 1967. (H)

122 Rubin, Elias. 700 Years of Jewish Life in Poland: Illustrated. London: W. & G. Foyle Ltd., 1944. 79p.

123 Sawicki, M. P. The Jews: Their History from the Viewpoint of the Current Status of Poland's Inhabitants of Mosaic Faith. Warsaw: J. Blaskowski, 1865. 355p. (P)

124 Schall, Jakób. History of Jews in Poland, Lithuania and Russia. With 25 Illustrations. Lwów: Polska Niepodległa, 1934. viii, 320p. (P)

125 Schall, Jakób. A Jewish History in Polish Lands: Textbook for Highschools. Lwów: A. Bardach, 1926. 129. (P)

126 Scharf, Rafael. "Poles and Jews: Summary of a Discussion". Kultura 11/386 (Paris, 1979): 115-123. (P)

127 Schiper, Ignacy; Tartakower, Arieh and Hafftka, Aleksander, eds. Jews in Reborn Poland: Social-Economic, Educational and Cultural Activity. (Żydzi w Polsce Odrodzonej: Działalność Społeczna, Gospodarcza, Oświatowa i Kulturalna - ŻPO) 2 vols., illus. Warsaw: 1932-1933. Volume I, 574p.; Volume II, 617p. (P)

128 Segel, Benjamin Wolf. The Polish Jewish Question. Berlin: Nibelungen Verlag, 1916. 160p. (G)

129 Shulman, Abraham. The Old Country. New York: Charles Scribner's Sons, 1974. x, 210p. illus.

130 Simonson, Emil. The Jewish Polish Problem. Berlin: L. Lamm, 1916. 16p. (G)

131 Skierko, Adam. The Jews and the Polish Question. Paris: Carlos-Courmont, 1919. 37p. (F)

132 Stecka, Marja. The Jews in Poland. Warsaw: Niklewicz, 1921. 191p. (P)

133 Stępień, Marian. "The Jewish Themes." Zdanie 10/31, (Warsaw, October 1984): 8-13. (P)

134 Studnicki, Władysław. The Polish-Jewish Question. Wilno: J. Zawadzki, 1936. 123p. (P)

135 Szczypiorski, Andrzej. "Poles and Jews." Kultura 5/380 (Paris, 1979): 3-13. (P)

136 Szerer, Emanuel. Poland and the Jews. New York: The American Representation of General Jewish Workers, Union of Poland, 1942. 88p. (P)

137 Tenenbaum, Joseph. In Search of a Lost People: The Old and The New Poland. New York: Beachhurst Press, 1948. viii, 312p.

138 Tenenbaum, Joseph. The Jewish Question in Poland. Paris: Comité des délégations juives d'auprès de la Conference de la Paix, 1919. 61p. (F)

139 Turowski, Stanisław. "Poland - Paradise for the Jews." Kwartalnik dla Historii Zydow w Polsce 3 (Warsaw, 1913): 73-100. (P)

140 Tyloch, W., ed. From the History of Jews in Poland. Warsaw: Interpress, 1983. 40p. (P)

141 Vago, Bela & Mosse, George, eds. Jews and Non-Jews in Eastern Europe, 1918-1945. New York: Wiley, 1974. xvii, 334p.

142 Wandycz, Piotr. "The Jewish Issue." In his The United States and Poland, pp. 157-169. Cambridge: Harvard University Press, 1980.

143 Wańkowicz, Melchior. De Profundis. Tel-Aviv: Przez Lady i Morza, 1943. 158p. (P)

144 Weinryb, Bernard D. "East European Jewry since the Partition of Poland ", In Louis Finkelstein's (ed.) The Jews: Their History, Culture and Religion. 1, pp. 343-398. New York: Macmillan Co., 1970.

145 Wendel, Jerzy. "Polish Jews" in Henryk Paszkiewicz's ed. Polska i jej Dorobek Dziejowy w Ciągu 1000 lat Istnienia: Zarys i Encyklopedia Spraw Polskich. pp. 549-561. London: Księgarnia Polska Orbis-Polonia, 1956. (P)

146 Wettstein, Feivel Hirsch. History of Jews in Poland. Jerusalem: 1968. 82p. (H)

147 Zamoyski, Adam. "The Jews in Poland, Part II, 1795-1939." History Today. (London, March 1976): 194-200.

4
The Late Eighteenth Century

148   Balaban, Majer. Herz Homberg and Jewish Schools of During the Era of Joseph II in Galicia, 1787-1809: Historical Study. Lwow: Kadimah, 1906. 40p.

149   Balaban, Majer. The History of the Jewish People and its Literature: With Special Consideration of the History of Jews in Poland. Vol.III. (From the Expulsion of Jews from Spain until the French Revolution: From Sigismund the Old to the Third Partition of Poland.) Lwow: Zaklad Narodowy Im. Ossolinskich, 1925. 448p. (P)

150   Balaban, Majer. "The Educational System in the Old Republic." ZPO 1 (1932): 337-344. (P)

151   Balaban, Majer. "The Passage of Polish Jews under Austrian Rule: Galician Jews under Maria Theresa and Joseph II." J.St. (1913): 289-307. (R)

152   Bartoszewicz, Kazimierz. Antisemitism in Polish Literature of the XV-XVIII Centuries. Warsaw: Gebethner i Wolff, 1914. 143p. (P)

153 Behr, Isachar Falkensohn. The Story of One of the Polish Jews. Leipzig: J. F. Hinz, 1772. 77p. (G)

154   Bersohn, Mathias. Official Collection of Documents Pertaining to the Jews in Old Poland: Based on Archival Sources (1388-1782). Warszawa: E. Nicz i S-ka, 1910. xxxvii, 266p. (P)

155   Butrymowicz, Mateusz. The way to form Polish Jews into useful Citizens of the Country. Warsaw: 1789. 20p. (P)

156   Deiches, Ernest. The Jewish Question During the Great Diet. Lwow: Towarzystwo "Przymierze Braci", 1891. 87p. (P)

157   Dubnow, Semen Markovich. "Jewish Poland During the Last Partitions." J.St. St. Petersburg (1911): 441-463. (R)

158   Eisenbach, Artur, et al. Materials on the History of the Four Years Diet. Volume VI. Wroclaw-Warszawa-Krakow: Zaklad Narodowy im. Ossolinskich; Wydawnictwo Polskiej Akademii Nauk, 1969. 547p. (P)

159   Eisenbach, Artur.   "To the Question of the Class Struggle Among the Jewish Population in Poland in the Second Half of the XVIII Century." BŻIH 19-20 (1956): 60-113. (P)

160   Frenk, Ezriel Nathan. "The Jews and Burghers in Poland by the end of the 18th Century", Hacefira 5 (Warsaw, 1919): 21-31. (H)

161   Gelber, Nathan Michael.   "Father Piattoli and the Jewish Question in the Great Diet", Nowe Życie. Warszawa: 1924, pp.20-34. (P)

162   Gelber, Nathan Michael.   "Foreign Travelers about Polish Jews in the XVIII Century", Historisze Szriftn. Wilno: YIVO, (1929): 231-252. (Y)

163   Glatman, Ludwik.   "How the Jews Used to Break Diet Meetings", Szkice Historyczne z XVIII wieku. (Kraków, 1906): 103-117. (P)

164   Goldberg, Jakub.   "The Baptized Jews in Poland-Lithuania in XVI-XVIII Centuries: Baptism, Social Adaptation and Integration". Jahrbücher für Geschichte Osteuropas. Neue Folge, München, 1982. 1, pp.54-99. (G)

165   Goldberg, Jakub. "Poles and Jews in the 17th and 18th Centuries. Rejection or Acceptance", Jahrbücher für Geschichte Osteuropas. Neue Folge, vol.22 (1974): 248-283. (G)

166   Goldberg, Jakub. "Toward a History of Polish-Jewish Relations in Old Poland during the 16th-18th Centuries", New York: Yearbook of the World Federation of Jews from Poland 3 (1970): 14-32. (Y)

167   Jacobsohn, Jacobi. "The Attitude of the Jews in 1793 and 1795 in the Polish Provinces taken by Prussia at the time of the Occupation." Monatschrift für Geschichte und Wissenschaft des Judentums vol. 64, pp. 209-226 et 282-304; vol. 65, pp. 42-70 et 151-163 et 221-245. (G)

168   "The Jews to the Representatives of the Cities of Poland, May 30, 1790." Journal Hebdomadaire de Varsovie 22, (May, 1790): 171-176. (F)

169   Mościcki, Henryk.   "The Jews in Poland under the Sceptre of Catherine II". In his Pod Znakiem Orła i Pogoni: Szkice Historyczne. Lwów: 1923, pp.25-37. (P)

170   Penkalla, A.   "The Jewish Question in Poland during the Great Diet". Więź 10, (Warsaw, 1967): 130-146. (P)

171   Ptaśnik, Jan. "The Deluge of Polish Towns by the Jews from the XVI to XVIII centuries." Przegląd Warszawski, 25, (Warsaw:1924). (P)

172   Ringelblum, Emanuel.   "Economic and Social Conditions of Jews in Poland in the second half of the XVIII Century". M. Żyd. 3, no.2 (1933): 227-235. (P)

173   Ringelblum, Emanuel. "From the History of Jewish Books and Printing in Poland of the Second Half of the XVIII Century." BŻIH 41, (1962): 20-44. (P)

174   Ringelblum, Emanuel. "The Jews in the Light of the Warsaw Press of the XVIII Century". M. Żyd. 2, (1932) no.1, 489-518 et no.2, 42-85 et no.7-8, 79-85. (P)

175   Ringelblum, Emanuel. Projects and Attempts to Regroup the Jews in the Era of King Stanislaw.   Warsaw: Instytut Badań Spraw Narodowościowych, 1934. 82p. (P)

176   Ringelblum, Emanuel. To the History of the Yiddish Book. Wilno, 1936. 64 p. (Y)

177   Smoleński, Władysław.   The Situation and the Problem of Polish Jews in XVIII Century. Warsaw: Lewicki i S-ka, 1876. 95p. (P)

5
In the Partitioned Commonwealth and in Exile

178   Adler-Rudel, S.   Eastern Jews in Germany, 1880-1940; Together with the History of Organizations which Represented Them.   Lwd. Schr.: Leo Baeck Institute, 1959. XII, 169p. (G)

179   Alexandrow, H. B.   "Jewish Population in Byelorussia During the Partitions of Poland."   Cajtszrift   (Minsk, 1930): 37-84. (Y)

180   Askenazy, Szymon.   "From the History of Polish Jews in the Period of the Duchy of Warsaw."   KZP   1 (Warsaw, 1912): 1-14. (P)

181   Askenazy, Szymon.   "From the Jewish Problems in the Congress Era."   KZP, 3 (1913): 1-38. (P)

182   Balaban, Majer.   "Correspondence Between Lubliner and Lelewel."   M.Zyd. 1 (1933): 289-321. (P)

183   Balaban, Majer.   The History of Jews in Galicia and in the Krakow Commonwealth, 1772-1868.   Lwow: Ksiegarnia Polska B. Polonieckiego, 1916. 238p. (P)

184   Balaban, Majer.   The Jews in Austria Under the Rule of Franz Joseph I, (1848-1908).   Stanislawow: A.Staudacher i Syn,1909. 32p. (P)

185   Balaban, Majer.   "The School System in Galicia and Teaching of the Mosaic Religion."   Haor   Lwow. no. 2 (1905): p. 1-4; no. 3 (1905): p. 3-5; no. 4 (1906): p. 9-12. (H)

186   Bershadskii, Sergei Aleksandrovich.   Lithuanian Jews.   Petersburg: 1883. vii, 431p. (R)

187   Bielecki, Tadeusz.   The Polish-Jewish Dispute of 1815.   Warsaw: by the author: 1933, 18p. (P)

188   Brozek, Andrzej.   "Attempts to Employ Jewish Workers in High Silesia before the First World War: (A Contribution to the Origin of German Racism)."   Studia i Materialy z Dziejow Slaska   9 (Katowice - Wroclaw, 1968): 133-166. (P)

189   Carmoly, E.   "The Situation of Jews in Poland."   Revue Orientale

2   (Paris, 1842):   418-428.   (F)

190   Czyński, Jan.   An Enquiry into the Political condition of Polish Jews, considered in Relation to the General Interests of Europe. London: 1834.   34p.

191   Czyński, Jan.   Israel in Poland: Letters addressed to Archives Israelites.   Paris: Aux Bureau des Archives Israélites, 1861.   54p.   (F)

192   Danielewicz, J.   "Polish Jews among Revolutionary Patriots of the Great Emigration."   BŻIH   2-3.   (1953)   (P)

193   "Discussion Concerning Agitatio among Jews during the XI Congress of Galicia and Silesia."   Przedświt   8-9 (Kraków, 1908):   336-342.   (P)

194   Dubanowicz, Edward.   The Attitude of the Jewish Population in Galicia to the Election of the Vienna Parliament.   Lwów: Drukarnia Polonia, 1907.   40p.   (P)

195   Duker, Abraham G.   "Hollaenderski's Letter of Inquiry to Lelewel." Studies in Bibliography and Booklore, 1, pp.161-166.   Cincinnati: Library of Hebrew Union College, 1954.

196   Duker, Abraham G.   "Leon Hollaenderski's Statement of Resignation: A Document of the Polish Great Emigration."   JSS   15   (1953):   293-302.

197   Duker, Abraham G.   "Polish Democratic Society and the Jewish Problem, 1832-1846."   JSS   19, no.3-4 (July-October, 1957):   99-112.

198   Duker, Abraham G.   "The Polish Political Emigres and the Jews in 1848."   Proceedings of the American Academy for Jewish Research   24 (1955): 69-102.

199   Duker, Abraham G.   "Polish Political Emigres in the United States and the Jews, 1833-1865."   Publications of the American Jewish Historical Society vol.39. part 2 (New York, December 1949):   143-167.

200   Duker, Abraham G.   "Polish Emigre Christian Socialists on the Jewish Problem." JSS   14   (1952): 317-342.

201   Duker, Abraham G.   "Prince Czartoryski: The Emigre on the Jewish Problem." in The Joshua Bloch Memorial Volume: Studies in Booklore and History, edited by Abraham Berger et. al., pp.165-179. New York: New York Public Library, 1960.

202   Dzwonkowski, Władysław.   Commentary on the Peasant, Ruthenian and Jewish Question Caused by Recent Events.   Paris, 1862, 77 p.   (P)

203   Eisenbach, Artur.   The Great Emigration on the Jewish Question, 1832-1849.   Warsaw: Państwowe Wydawnictwo Naukowe, 1976.   472p.   (P)

204   Eisenbach, Artur.   "The Great Emigration's Attitude Towards the Jewish Question in the Era of the Post-Sebastopol Thaw."   BŻIH   no.4/112 (1979):   3-24.   (P)

205   Eisenbach, Artur.   "The Hotel Lambert Towards the Jewish Question

on the Eve of the Spring of Nations." Przegląd Historyczny no.3 (1976): 369-398. (P)

206 Eisenbach, Artur. "Jewish Immigration to the Kingdom of Poland." Bleter far Geszichte 17 (1966): 26-60. (Y)

207 Eisenbach, Artur. "Materials to the History of Jewish Departamental Dietines and Attempts to Organize a Central Jewish Diet in the Duchy of Warsaw." Bleter far Geszichte. 2 (Warsaw, 1930): 127-149. (Y)

208 Eisenbach, Artur. Memorial on the Situation of the Jewish Population in the Kingdom of Poland. BŻIH 4/100 (1976): 35-62. (P)

209 Everett, Leila P. "The Rise of Jewish National Politics in Galicia, 1905-1907" in Andrei S. Markovitz and Frank E. Syssyn, eds. Nationbuilding and the Politics of Nationalism: Essays on Austrian Galicia, pp.149-177. Cambridge: Harvard University Press, 1982.

210 Fajnhauz, Dawid. "Jews in Lithuania and Byelorussia in the XIX century." BŻIH 4/52 (1964): 3-15. (P)

211 Feldman, Wilhelm. "The Jewish Question" in his Geschichte den politischen Ideen in Polen seit dessen Teilungen, (1795-1914), pp.195-200 et 423-430. München und Berlin: Verlag von R. Oldenburg, 1917. (G)

212 Feldman, Wilhelm. "The Jews" in his Stronnictwa i Programy Polityczne w Galicyi, 1846-1906, 2, pp.265-314. Kraków: Spółka Nakł. "Książka", 1907. (P)

213 Frenk, Ezriel Nathan. "To the History of Jews in the Duchy of Warsaw." Hatkufa 4 (Warsaw, 1919): 451-488. (H)

214 Friedman, Filip. "History of Jews in Galicia, (1772-1914)." in ŻPO 1 (1932): pp.337-412. (P)

215 Friedman, Filip. "The Jewish Question in Galicia's Parliament, 1861-1868." Monatschrift für Geschichte und Wissenschaft des Judentums (1928): 379-390 et 457-497. (G)

216 Gąsiorowska, Natalia. "Jewish Censorship in the Congress Kingdom." KŻP 1 (1912): 55-59. (P)

217 Golczewski, Frank. Polish-Jewish Relations, 1881-1922. Wiesbaden: Franz Steiner Verlag, 1981. 391 p. (G)

218 Haesler, Wolfgang. Galician Jewry in the Habsburg Monarchy: In Light of Contemporary Journalism and Travelogues from 1772 till 1848. Vienna: Verlag für Geschichte und Politik, 1979. 90p. (G)

219 Hagen, William W. Germans, Poles and Jews: the Nationality Conflict in the Prussian East, 1772-1914. Chicago: University of Chicago Press, 1980. ix,406p.

220 Handelsman, Marceli. "The Jewish Petition to Frederick August." KŻP. 1, no.3 (1912): 174-176. (P)

221 Hasman, R. et al., eds. Lithuanian Jewry. Vol.III.Tel-Aviv: Association for Mutual Help of Former Residents of Lithuania in Israel, 1967. 369p. (H)

222 Heppner, Aaron. From the Past and Present Situation of Jews and Jewish Communities in Poznan Lands: Based on printed and unprinted Sources of A. Heppner and J. Herzberg. Koshmin: 1909. 1034p., illus. (G)

223 Hessen, J. "In an Ephemeral State: Jews in the Duchy of Warsaw, 1807-1812." J. St. 2, no.3. (Petersburg, 1910): 1-38. (R)

224 Hirszhorn, S. "Jewish History in the Congress Kingdom of Poland from 1864 until 1918." ŻPO 1 (1932): 472-503. (P)

225 Horowitz, Leon. What Could We Do to Help Our Coreligionists in Galicia in their Dire Need? Vienna: Viertel-jahr - Berichte d. Bnei-Brith fur Ostereich, 1899. 21p. (G)

226 Janulaitis, Augustinas. Lithuanian Jews. Kaunas: by the author, 1923. 174p. (Li)

227 Jastrow, Marcus. Explanation of Government's Statement Concerning the Jewish Situation in the Kingdom of Poland: Caused by Imperial Will and Bureaucratic Licence. Hamburg und Campe, 1859. 133p.

228 Kandel, Dawid. "The Jews in 1812." Biblioteka Warszawska, 70 no.2 (1910): 157-175. (P)

229 Kandel, Dawid. "Jews in the Era of the Creation of Congress Kingdom." KZP. 1, no.2 (1912): 95-113. (P)

230 Kandel, Dawid. "Jews in the Polish Kingdom after 1831." Biblioteka Warszawska 70, no.3 (1910): 542-558. (P)

231 Kandel, Dawid. "Nowosilcow and the Jews." Biblioteka Warszawska 31, no.2 (1911): 141-155. (P)

232 Kandel, Dawid. "Józef Berkowicz in Exile." KŻP, 1, no.1 (1912): 125-131. (P)

233 Kieniewicz, Stefan. "Poles and Jews in the XIX Century." Polityka 50/1441 (Warsaw, December 15, 1984). (P)

234 Laubert, Manfred. "Correspondence Concerning the Jewish Question in the Poznan Province (1829)." Historische Monatsblätter für die Provinz Posen 8 (Poznań, 1909): 125-129. (G)

235 Laubert, Manfred. "Last Municipal Privileges de non tolerandis Judaeis in the Poznan Province." Zeitschrift der historischen Gesellschaft für die Provinz Posen (Poznań, 1906): 145-158. (G)

236 Lech, Marian J. "Attempts of Jewish Booksellers to Form Unions in the Kingdom of Poland." BŻIH 2/106 (1978): 19-25. (P)

237 Lelewel, Joachim. "Appeal to the Israelite People." In his

Polska, Dzieje i Rzeczy Jej. 20 (Poznań, 1864): 117-131. (P)

238   Lerski, George J.   "Jewish-Polish Amity in Lincoln's America."
The Polish Review   18, no.4   (1973): 34-51.

239   Lewin, Louis.   The Land Council of Jewry in Great Poland.
Frankfurt a/M: 1926. 126p. (G)

240   Lewin, Louis.   "One Jewish Day in South and New East Prussia."
Monatschrift für Geschichte und Wissenschaft des Judentums   59   (1915):
180-192 et 278-300. (G)

241   Lipszic, S.   "Lithuanian Jews: Eastern Jews."   Süddeutsche
Monatshefte   (München, February 1916): 829-934. (G)

242   Lozynskyj, M.   "The Jewish Question in Galicia and the Austrian
Social Democracy."   Ukrainische Rundschaue   6   (Lwów, 1906): 208-214.
(G)

243   Moszczeńska, Izabella.   "The Jewish Question in the Polish
Kingdom."   Izraelita   nos.1-8   (Warsaw, 1906): 40-41, 52-53, 62-63, 75-
76, 89-90.   (P)

244   Neubach, Helmut.   Banishment of Poles and Jews from Prussia, 1885-
1886.   Wiesbaden: O. Harrassowitz, 1967.   293p.   (G)

245   Piłsudski, Józef.   "The Jewish Question in Lithuania."   In his
Pisma Zbiorowe   2, pp.223-227.   Warsaw: Instytut Józefa Piłsudskiego
Poświęcony Badaniu Najnowszej Historii Polski, 1937.   (P)

246   Polish National Committee "Appeal to the Israelite People."   In
Łukasiewicz, Witold and Lewandowski Władysław eds.   Postępowa
Publicystyka Emigracyjna 1831-1846: Wybór Źródeł, pp.41-48.   Wrocław:
Ossolineum, 1961.   (P)

247   Rabinowicz, Sara.   "Concerning the Jewish Question in Galicia."
Woschod   11 (1903): 125-142, et 12 (1904): 37-54.   (R)

248   Rosenberg, Leo.   The Jews in Lithuania: History, Population and
Economy.   Berlin: Neue Jüdische Monatshefte, 1918.   48p.   (G)

249   Schiper, Ignacy.   "The Galician Jewry from the Economic and
Statistical Viewpoint."   Neue Jüdische Monatshefte   (Berlin, 1918):
223-233.   (G)

250   Schiper, Ignacy.   "History of the Jews in the Duchy of Warsaw and
Kingdom of Poland, 1795-1863."   ŻPO, 1 (1932): 423-471.   (P)

251   Schiper, Ignacy.   "Jews in the Prussian Sector, 1772-1807 and
1815."   ŻPO   1   (1932):   551-562. (P)

252   Schiper, Ignacy.   Jews of the Polish Kingdom in the Era of the
November Uprising.   Warsaw: F.Hoesick, 1932. 217p. illus.   (P)

253   Schiper, Ignacy.   "Jews in Northern and Eastern Borderlands after
the Partitions." ŻPO. 1 (1932): 563-574 et 2 (1933): 5-23.   (P)

254   Shatzky, Jacob. "An Attempt at Jewish Colonization in the Kingdom of Poland." YIVO Annual. 1 (New York, 1946): 44-63.

255   Shatzky, Jakób. Jewish Educational Policies in Poland from 1806 to 1866. New York: YIVO Scientific Institute, 1943. 272 p. (Y)

256   Shatzky, Jacob. "Jewish Ideologies in Austria during the Revolution of 1848." In Baron, Sal W. and Pinson, Koppel S., eds. Freedom and Reason: Studies in Philosophy and Jewish Culture in Memory of Morris Raphael Cohen. (Glencoe, Ill., 1951): 413-417.

257   Shmeruk, Chone. "Young Men from Germany in the Yeshivot of Poland." In Sepher Yobel La-Yidzak Baer. (Jerusalem, 1960): 304-317. (H)

258   Tatarzanka, W. "Contributions to History of Jews in the Congress Kingdom, 1815-1830: Economic and Cultural Situation of Jewish Community in Congress Kingdom from 1815 till 1830." Przegląd Judaistyczny 4-6 (Warsaw, 1922): 279-294. (P)

259   Tenenbaum, Joseph. Galicia, My Old Home. Buenos Aires: 1952. 319p. (Y)

260   Tokarz, Wacław. "From the History of the Jewish Question in the Duchy of Warsaw." Kwartalnik Historyczny (Lwów, 1902): 262-276. (P)

261   Tyrowicz, Marian. "The Jewish Question in the History of the Great Emigration: Review of American Studies of Abraham G. Duker." Studia Historyczne 2 (Kraków. 1968): 259-265. (P)

262   Warschauer, A. "The Education of Jews in the Poznań Province through the Elementary School Level." Zeitschrift für Geschichte der Juden in Deutschland (Neue Folge) 3 (1889): 29-43. (G)

263   Warszawski, Isaiah. "The Jews in Congress Poland, 1815-1831." YIVO Historishe Shriftn. 2 (Wilno, 1937): 322-354. (Y)

264   Wasilewski, Leon. The Jewish Question in Congress-Poland: Its Complications and Solution. Vienna: Verlag der Wochenschrift "Polen", 1915. 45p.

265   Wasiutyński, Bohdan. The Jewish Population in the Polish Kingdom. Warsaw: 1911. 99p. (P)

266   Wassermann, Rudolf. "Development of Jewish Population in the Poznań Province and the Problem of Eastern Marks." Zeitschrift für Demographie und Statistik der Juden 6 (Berlin, 1910): 65-76. (G)

267   Weinstejn, L. "The Polish-Jewish Problem in Galicia." Woschod. 35 (1910): 30-33. (R)

268   Wolf, G. "Teachers' Seminars in Galicia." Zeitschrift für Geschichte der Juden in Deutschland (Neue Folge) 5 (1982):146-153. (G)

269   Zarchin, Michael Moses. Jews in the Province of Posen: Studies in the Communal Records of the XVIII & XIX Centuries. Philadelphia: The

Dropsie College for Hebrew and Cognate Learning, 1939. 115p.

270 Zucker, Nechemias, ed. <u>Memorial Book of Galicia</u>. Buenos Aires: Former Residents of Galicia in Argentina, 1945. 638p. (Y)

6
Jewish Participation in Poland's Struggle for Freedom

271   Almi, A. (pseud. of Sheps, Elias). <u>Jewish Legends about the 1863 Insurrection</u>. Translated from Yiddish by S. Hirszhorn. Warsaw: E. Gitlin, 1929. 87p. (P)

272   Bałaban, Majer. <u>Album to Commemorate and Honor Berek Joselewicz, Colonel of the Polish Army, on the 125th Anniversary of His Heroic Death, 1809-1934</u>. Warsaw: Wydawnictwo Komitetu Wileńskiego ku Uczczeniu Pamięci Berka Joselewicza, 1934. 208p. (P)

273   Bałaban, Majer. "Galician Jews in the Time of the 1848 Revolution." <u>J. St.</u> (1912): 423-452. (R)

274   Bałaban, Majer. "From My Archives." <u>Historysze Szryftn</u>. 1 (Warsaw, 1929): 737-750. (Y)

275   Bałaban, Majer. "A Jew from Bendzin as an Officer in the Polish Legions of Napoleon." <u>Pinkas Bendin</u>. Tel-Aviv, 1959): 33. (Y)

276   Bałaban, Majer. "Jews in the 1863 Uprising: An Attempt at Reasoned Bibliography." <u>Przegląd Historyczny</u> 34, no.2 (Kraków, 1934): 564-599. (P)

277   Bałaban, Majer. "Polish Jews and World War I." <u>Hatkufa</u> 14-15 (Warsaw, 1922): 754-763. (H)

278   Beilin, Asher. <u>1863 - Uprising</u>. Warsaw: Groshn - Bibliotek, 1934. 63p. (Y)

279   Bender, Ryszard. "Jewish Population in the Lublin District during Pre-insurrectionary Action, 1861-1862." <u>BŻIH</u> 35 (1960): 47-54. (P)

280   Bloch, Philip. "Jewish Combatants in Polish Army." <u>Historische Monatsblätter fur die Provinz Posen</u>. 1, no.2 (Poznań, 1900): 21-24. (G)

281   Blum, E. "Jews in the Polish November Uprising." <u>Literarisze Bleter</u> (Warsaw, 1930): 941-943. (Y)

282   Brandstaetter, Roman. <u>The Jewish Legion of Adam Mickiewicz:</u>

History and Documents. Warsaw: "Menora", 1932. 70p. (P)

283 Cederbaum, Henryk. The January Uprising: Sentences of Field Auditors from the years 1863-1866. Warsaw: Gebethner i Wolff, 1917. 439p. (P)

284 Chankowski, Stanisław. "The Jewish Population in the Augustow Region and its Attitude to the January Uprising." BŻIH 64 (1967): 55-68. (P)

285 Christiani, W. "Trzemeszno Expedition of 1863." Historische Monatsblätter für die Provinz Posen (1913): 81-87. (Y)

286 Cynberg, J. "A Yiddish Popular Song about a Polish Insurrectionist." Cajtschrift. 2-3 (Mińsk, 1928): 783-786. (Y)

287 Datner, Szymon. "Jews in the National-Liberation Struggles for Integrity and Independence of Poland: From their Contributions on behalf of the Country's Defense up to the Insurrection of the Warsaw Getto." BŻIH. 1/109 (1979): 17-40. (P)

288 Duker, Abraham G. "Jewish Participants in the Polish November (1830-31) Insurrection: A List of Seventeen Names Hitherto Not Recorded." In The Abraham Weiss Jubilee Volume. (New York, 1964): 81-87.

289 Duker, Abrahanm G. "Jewish Participants in the Polish Insurrection of 1863 - Thirty-Eight Newly Identified Names." In Ben-Horin, Meir et al., eds., pp.144-153. Studies and Essays in Honor of Abraham A. Neuman, President, Dropsie College for Hebrew and Cognate Learning. Philadelphia and London: 1962.

290 Duker, Abraham G. "Jewish Volunteers in the Ottoman-Polish Cossack Units during the Crimean War." JSS 16, no.3 (July, 1954): 203-218.

291 Duker, Abraham G. "The Polish Insurrection's Missed Opportunity: Mochnacki's Views on the Failure to Involve the Jews in the Uprising of 1830/31." JSS. 28, no.4 (October, 1966): 212-232.

292 Eile, Henryk. "The Jewish Question in the Era of the November Uprising." Gazeta Administracji i Policji Państwowej. 7 (Warsaw, 1932): 226-235 et 14 (Warsaw, 1932): 481-494. (P)

293 Eisenbach, Artur. "The Jewish Population of the Kingdom and the November Insurrection." BŻIH 1/97 (1976): 3-30. (P)

294 Eisenbach, Artur et al. eds. Jews and the January Uprising: Materials and Documents. Warsaw: Państwowe Wydawnictwo Naukowe, 1963. 237p. illus. (P)

295 Fajnhauz, Dawid. "Jewish Population in Lithuania and Byelorussia and the January Uprising." BŻIH 27 (1961): 3-34 et 38 (1961): 39-68. (P)

296 Familien-bibliotek. Jews in the Polish 1863 Insurrection.

Warsaw: 1914. 32p. (Y)

297   Gelber, Natan Michael.   "Acts of the Polish-Jewish Brotherhood before the 1863 Uprising." Almanach Żydowski na r. 5678/1918, edited by Z.F. Finkelstein. (Vienna): 101-109. (P)

298   Gelber, Natan Michael.   "A Jewess' Memoirs of the Polish Uprising of 1863." YIVO Annual. 13 (New York, 1965): 243-263.

299   Gelber, Natan Michael. The Jews and the Polish 1863 Insurrection. Vienna und Leipzig: R. Löwit, 1923. 235p. (G)

300   Grunwald, M. "Jewish Military Purveyor of Napoleon I (1812-1813)." Revue des Études Juives. 57 (Paris, 1909): 79-92. (F)

301   Grzybowski, Konstanty.   "Jews and the Fight for Poland's Independence." Poland. no.9/109 (Warsaw, September 1963). 28-29.

302   Herzberg, J. "The Polish Insurrection of 1848 and the Jews in the Poznań Region." Allgemeine Zeitung des Judentums. 74 (1910): 475-477. (G)

303   Hirszhorn, S.   "The Kościuszko Insurrection and the Jews." Almanach Żydowski. (Vienna,1918): 59-63. (P)

304   Jastrow, Marcus. Homilies Delivered During Last Events in 1861 in Warsaw. Poznań: L. Merzbach, 1862. 108p. (P)

305   "Jews in the Polish Army in 1831." KŻP 3 (1913): 3-184. (P)

306   Kahan, Jacob. Three Years in the Polish Army, 24.10.1919 - 22.11.1922. Białystok: 1930. 101p. (Y)

307   Kandel, Dawid.   "Elegy on the Death of Prince Józef." KŻP 2 (1912): 127-133. (P)

308   Kandel, Dawid. "The Jewish Warsaw Appeal in 1861." KŻP 3 (1913): 143-147. (P)

309   Kempiński, Israel. "Memoirs of a Jew Kempinski, witness of the Sammo-Sierra Charge." KŻP 2 (1912): 176-180. (P)

310   Kon, Pinchas. In Berek's Era in Lithuania. Warsaw: 1934. 122p. illus. (P)

311   Konic, Władysław. "Jews in Legions, 1914-1917." ŻPO 1 (1932): 542-550. (P)

312   Konic, Władysław. "Jews in the Legions of Józef Piłsudski." GGŻ 2, no.10-11 (October-November 1938):   239-242. (P)

313   Korobkow, Chaim. "Polish-Jewish Relations in 1861-1863: Lüders' Report to the Tsar about Jewish Behavior on the Eve of the January Uprising." J.St. 8 (1915) 147-152. (R)

314   Korobkow, Chaim. "Jews in the North-East Land during the Polish

Revolution of 1963." J.St. 9 (1916): 330-332. (R)

315 Kowalczyk, K. "The Story Told by Bajrach Harc, Participant in the 1863 Insurrection." BŻIH 1/93 (1975): 83-95. (P)

316 Kulka, Erich. "Jewish Refugees from Czechoslovakia in Poland and Their Recruitment to Military Units." Yad Vashem Studies 12 (Jerusalem, 1976): 74-83. (H)

317 Lewandowski, W. "Materials to Jewish Participation in National Guard and Security Militia in the November Uprising, 1830-1831." BŻIH 19/20 (1956): 114-133. (P)

318 Lewin, Jacob Ha-Levi. Jews in the Polish Insurrection of 1830-1831. Jerusalem: 1953. 150p. illus. (H)

319 Liwerant, Elia Boruch. "The Adventures of a Jew During the Polish Insurrection of 1863." J.St. 2 (1910): 278-390. (R)

320 Łuniński, Ernest. Berek Joselewicz. Kock: Obywatelski Komitet Budowy Pomnika-Szkoły Zawodowej i Powszechnej im. Pułk. Berka Joselewicza, 1928. 47p. (P)

321 Merwin, Bertold. Jews in the 1863 Insurrection: In Commemoration of the 50th Anniversary of the Uprising. Lwów: Koło T.S.L. im. Goldmana, 1913, 54p.ill. (P)

322 Mieses, Mateusz. "Jews in the Liberation Struggle for Poland." GGŻ 2, no.10-11 (October-November 1938): 235-238. (P)

323 Mstislawskaja, S. "Jews in the Polish Uprising of 1831." J.St. (1910): 61-80 et 235-252. (R)

324 Nadel, Beniamin. The Jewish Attitude to the January Uprising in the Wilno Region." BŻIH 28 (1958): 44-48. (P)

325 Polish Jewry to their Bretheren who Fought for Independence and Freedom of Poland, 1905-1918: Memorial Book to Commemorate Jewish Fighters for the Cause of Poland. Warsaw: 1936. 90p. (P)

326 Raphael, P. "Polish-Jewish Relations and the 1830-1831 Insurrection." La Revolution de 1848 et les Revolutions du XIX-e siécle 1830-1848-1870. 23 (Paris, 1926): 778-793. (F)

327 Ringelblum, Emanuel. Jews in the Kościuszko Insurrection. Warsaw: Księgarnia Popularna, 1938. 190p. (P)

328 Rosenstadt, B. "Jewish Losses in the Polish 1863 Insurrection." J.St. (1913): 484-492. (R)

329 Schiper, Ignacy. Jews of the Polish Kingdom in the Era of the November Uprising. Warsaw: F. Hoesick, 1932. 217p. ill. (P)

330 Schiper, Ignacy. "Jews in the January Uprising." ŻPO. 1 (1932): 468-471. (P)

331　Schiper, Ignacy. "Participation of the Jews in the November Uprising." Sprawy Narodowościowe 5-6 (Warsaw, 1930): 695-699. (P)

332　Segel, Harold B. "Mickiewicz and the Jewish Legion in the Memoirs of Sadyk Pasha." 10 no.3 Polish Review (Summer 1965): 78-81.

333　Shatzky, Jacob. "American Jews and the 1863 Uprising." YIVO Bleter 4-5 (Wilno, 1932): (Y)

334　Shatzky, Jacob. Jews and the Polish Uprising of 1831. Wilno: YIVO, 1937. 380p. (Y)

335　Shatzky, Jacob. Kościuszko and the Jews: Historical Notes. Warsaw: F.Hoesick, 1917. 15p. (P)

336　Shatzky, Jacob. "New Materials about Jewish Participation in the War of 1812." J. St. (1914): 495-499. (R)

337　Shatzky, Jacob. "Towards History of Jewish Participation in the Polish 1863 Uprising." J. St. (1915): 29-37. (R)

338　Skarbek, Jan. "Lublin District Jews in the November Insurrection." BŻIH 1/93 (1975): 63-81. (P)

339　Stocki, Edward. "Jews in the Health Service of the November Uprising." BŻIH 21 (1957): 104-114. (P)

340　Stocki, Edward. "Participation of Jewish Physicians in the Poznania Insurrection of 1848." BŻIH 11-12 (1954): 109-122. (P)

341　Tugenhold, Jakob. Reveries of an Israelite on Sentinel Duty in the first Days of December 1830. Warsaw: I. Tugenhold, 1831. 12p. (P)

342　Urbach, Janusz Konrad. Jewish Participation in the Struggle for Poland's Independence. Łódź: Związek Żydów Uczestników Walk o Niepodległość, 1938. ix, 206p. illus. (P)

343　Warmiński, Jan. "Jewish Participation in Podlasie District in Providing Shoes and Sheepskins for the Polish Army during the November Uprising, 1830-1831." BŻIH 2/94 (1975): 41-48. (P)

344　"Warsaw Jews' Appeal to their Co-religionists of February 13, 1861." KŻP 2 (1912): 143-147. (P)

345　Ziołek, Jan. "Jewish Voluntary Cavalry Squadron in the November Uprising." BŻIH 80 (1971): 43-50. (P)

346　Zubrzycki, Tadeusz. Jews in Polish Ranks from 1913 till 1920. Lwów: 1924. 15p. (P)

347　Zubrzycki, Tadeusz. "Jews in the Ranks of the 1863 Insurrection." Jedność. no.5 (Lwów, 1909): (P)

7
Jews in Independent (Interwar) Poland

348   Ainsztein, Reuben.   "The Sikorski Affair." The Jewish Quarterly 17 no.1 (London, Spring, 1969)

349   Aisene, Benjamin.   The Polish Jews, 1918-1944:   Or the Dead Accuse. Paris: Pensée Universelle, 1980, 185p. (F)

350   American Committee on Religious Rights and Minorities. Statement Regarding Poland's Treatment of the Jews. New York: 1937. 12p.

351   Bierzanek, Remigiusz.   "Jews Population in Eastern Lands." Rocznik Ziem Wschodnich. 5 (Warsaw, 1939): 63-72. illus. (P)

352   Buchweitz, R.   "Jewish Vocational School System in Reborn Poland." GGŻ 2, 10-11 (1938): 294-296. (P)

353   Buell, Raymond Leslie.   "The Minorities: The Jewish Question." Poland: Key to Europe: Third Edition, pp.308-319. New York and London: Alfred Knopf, 1939.

354   Cang, Joel.   "The Opposition Parties in Poland and their Attitude Towards the Jews and the Jewish Question." JSS 1. no.2 (1939): 241-256.

355   Chmielewski, Samuel.   "The State of the Educational System of the Jews in Poland." Sprawy Narodowościowe 1-2 (Warsaw, 1937): 32-74 (P)

356   Chojnowski, Andrzej.   "National Minorities in Polish Government Politics in the 1921-1926 Years." Przegląd Historyczny 67, no.4 (1976): 593-616. (P)

357   Chołoniewski, Antoni. Us, The Jews and the Congress towards Galician Disturbances. Kraków: Towarzystwo im. Stefana Buszczyńskiego, 1919. 58p. (P)

358   Ciołkosz, Adam.   "The Jewish Quarter in the Jablonna Camp." Zeszyty Historyczne 20 (1971): 177-199. (P)

359   Cohen, Israel.   "Documents - My Mission to Poland, 1918-1919." JSS 13, no.2 (April 1951): 149-172.

360   Cohen, Israel. "The Jews in Poland." Contemporary Review 40 (London, 1936): 716-723.

361   Czerniakow, Adam. "Jewish Participation in the Rebuilding of Destruction by the War." GGŻ 2 no.10-11 (1938): 276-278.

362   Davies, Norman. "Great Britain and the Polish Jews. Journal of Contemporary History. 8 no.2 (London, April 1973): pp.119-142.

363   Drymmer, Wiktor Tomir. "The Jewish Question in Poland in the 1935-1939 Years." Zeszyty Historyczne 13 (1968): pp.55-77. (P)

364   Duker, Abraham Gordon. The Situation of the Jews in Poland. New York: American Jewish Congress, 1936. 31p.

365   Dzwonkowski, Władysław. "The Jewish Question in Reborn Poland." GGZ 2 no.10-11 (1938): 264-268. (P)

366   Eck, Nathan. "The Educational Institutions of Polish Jewry, 1921-1939." JSS 9, no. 1 (January 1947): 3-32.

367   Eden, S. "Institute for Higher Jewish Learning." In Mosdot Torah B'Eiropa B'Vinyanim Uve'hurbanam edited by Samuel Kalman Mirsky. New York: 1956, 561-584. (H)

368   Eisenstein, A.E. "State Loyalty - Reflections." GGŻ 2 no.10-11 (1938): 234-235. (P)

369   Eisenstein, Miriam. Jewish Schools in Poland, 1919-1939: their Philosophy and Development. New York: King's Crown Press, 1950. 112p.

370   Ettinger, Shmuel. "Jews and Non-Jews in Eastern and Central Europe between the Wars: An Outline." In Vago, Bela and Mosse, George, eds. Jews and non-Jews in Eastern Europe. 1918-1945. pp. 1-19 New York: Willey, 1974.

371   Feldstein, H. The Poles and the Jews; an Appeal by H. Feldstejn. Kraków and Chicago: The Supreme Polish National Committee, 1915. 23p.

372   "The First Yiddish Teachers' Conference." Szul un Leben 10-11 (March 1924): 12-37. (Y)

373   Fishman, Joshua A. (ed.) Studies on Polish Jewry, 1919-1939: The Interplay of Social, Economic and Political Factors in the Struggle of a Minority for its Existence. New York: YIVO Institute for Jewish Research, 1974, pp.x, 294 (English); 537 (Yiddish).

374   Friedman, Filip. "History of the Jews in Reborn Poland." GGŻ 2 no.10-11 (1938): 247-254. (P)

375   Fuks, Marian. "The Jewish Press in Interwar Poland." BŻIH 75 (1970): 55-73. (P)

376   Fuks, Marian. "Materials to a Bibliography of the Jewish Provincial Press, Publilshed in Poland 1918-1939." BŻIH 2/118 (1981): 65-87 et 3/119 (1981): 77-97. (P)

377   Gorewicz R.   "In the Times of Bulak Balachowicz."   Rszumot   3 (1923): 514-523. (H)

378   Groth, Alexander. "Dmowski, Piłsudski and Ethnic Conflict in Pre-1939 Poland." Canadian Slavic Studies 3 (Toronto, 1969): 69-91.

379   Grünbaum, Yitshak.   The Face of a Generation.   Jerusalem: 1957. 419p. illus. (H)

380   Grünbaum, Yitshak.   "The Jews and Their School System in Poland." In Milhamot Yehude Polin. Jerusalem/Tel-Aviv: 1941, 172-191. (H)

381   Hecht, Gedo. "Development of Jewish Elementary Schools in Reborn Poland." GGŻ 2, no.10-11 (1938): 288-290. (P)

382   Hecht, Gedo.   "Twenty Years of Jewish Schools in Poland." Almanach; Rocznik Naszego Przglądu. Warsaw: 1938. (P)

383   Heller, Celia Stopnicka.   On the Edge of Destruction: Jews in Poland between the two World Wars. New York: Columbia University Press, 1977. xx, 369p. ill.

384   Hersch, Liebman.   The Jewish Delinquent: Comparative Study Concerning the Criminality of Jewish and Non-Jewish Population of the Polish Republic. Paris: F. Alcan, 1938. 104p. (F)

385   Hersch, Liebman. "Jewish and Non-Jewish Criminality in Poland, 1932-1937." YIVO Annual 1 (1946): pp.178-194.

386   The Jews in Poland: Official Reports of the American and British Investigating Missions. Chicago: National Polish Committee of America, n.d. 64p.

387   Jews in Post War Poland, A Digest of Documents. New York: Polish Government's Information Center, 1944. 18p.

388   Kahn, Alexander.   Conditions of Jews in Poland.   New York: American Jewish Joint Distribution Committee, 1937. 12p.

389   Katz, M. "The Crisis in Poland." Jewish Life 1 no.3, (October 1937): 7-12.

390   Kazhdan, Khaim Shloyme.   The History of Jewish Schools in Independent Poland. Mexico City: Gezelschaft "Kultur un Hilf", 1947. 571p. (Y)

391   Kligsberg, Moshe. "The Jewish Youth Movement in Interwar Poland: A Sociological Study." In Fishman, Joshua A., ed. Studies on Polish Jewry. pp. 137-238. 1974. (Y)

392   Korzec, Paweł. "Agreement Between the Grabski Government and the Jewish Representation." Gal-ed. 1 (Tel-Aviv, 1973): 175-210. (H)

393   Korzec, Paweł.   Jews in Poland: the Jewish Question Between the Two Wars. Paris: Presses de La Fondation Nationale Des Sciences Politiques, 1980. 326p. (F)

394   Krevets'kyi, Ivan.   Ukrainians and Jews: Several Comments Concerning the Jewish Question.   Lwów: R. Litopysets, 1937.   87p.   (U)

395   Landau, Moshe.   "Coup d'état of May 1926 and Unfulfilled Jewish Expectations for Changes in Poland."   Gal-ed.   2   (1975): 237-286.   (H)

396   Landau, Moshe.   "The Meaning of the 1925 Agreement for Continuity of Jewish-Polish Relations."   Zion.   1-2 (Jerusalem, 1972): 66-110.   (H)

397   Landau, Moshe.   "Ugoda's (1925 Agreement's) Place in History of Jewish-Polish Relations."   Gal-ed.   2 (1975): pp.237-286.   (H)

398   Langnas, Saul.   The Jews and Higher Studies in Poland in the 1921-1931 Period: A Statistical Study.   Lwów: Centrala Żydowskiego Akademickiego Stowarzyszenia "Samopomoc" Środowiska Lwowskiego, 1923. 23p. (P)

399   Lestchinsky, Jacob.   On the Eve of the Destruction of Jewish Life in Poland, 1935-1937.   Buenos Aires: 1951.   255p. (Y)

400   Lichten, Joseph L.   "Jews of Poland Between the Two World Wars."   Polish Review   22 no.3, (1977): 101-106.

401   Lifschutz, Ezekiel.   "Selected Documents Pertaining to Jewish Life in Poland, 1919-1939 (31 reproductions with an introduction and annotations)."   In Fishman Joshua A., ed.   Studies on Polish Jewry. (New York, 1974): 277-294.

402   Mahler, Raphael.   "Jews in Public Service and Liberal Professions in Poland, 1918-1939."   JSS   6 no 4, (October, 1944): 291-350.

403   Mahler, Raphael.   The Jews of Poland between the Two World Wars: a Socio-Economic History Based on Statistics.   Tel-Aviv: Dviv, 1968. 195p. (H)

404   Mahler, Raphael.   The March 17, 1921 Constitution: Article 109. New York: American Jewish Committee, 1941. 74p.

405   Mahler, Raphael.   Polish Jews in the Interwar Period.   Tel-Aviv: 1968.   195p. (H)

406   Marcus, Joseph.   Social and Political History of the Jews in Poland, 1919-1939.   New York: Mouton Publishers,1983. xviii, 569p.

407   Mauersberg, Stanisław.   The Elementary School System for National Minorities in Poland, 1918-1939.   Wroclaw: Zaklad Narodowy im. Ossolinskich, 1968.   230p. (P)

408   Mayzel, Maurycy.   "Twenty Years of Polish Independence."   GGZ 2 no.10-11 (1938): 227-228.   (P)

409   Meltser, Emanuel.   "Polish-German Relations in 1935-1938 and its Impact on Jewish Life in Poland."   Yad Va-shem, Kovets Mekharim. Jerusalem. 12 (1977): 145-170.   (H)

410   Memorandum On the Jewish Question.   Warszawa: Federation des

Association Polonaises pour la Societe des Nations, 1938. 15p. (F)

411 Mendelsohn, Ezra. The Jews of East-Central Europe: Between the World Wars. Bloomington: Indiana University Press, 1983. xi, 300p.

412 Mendelsohn, Ezra. "The Politics of Agudah Yisrael in Inter-War Poland." Soviet Jewish Affairs. 2 no.2 (London, 1972): 47-60.

413 Mendelsohn, Ezra. "Reflections on the Ugoda." In Yeivin, Sh., ed. Studies in Jewish History Presented to Raphael Mahler. pp.87-102. Merharya, Israel: 1974.

414 Merunowicz, Teofil. Jewish National Policy of the Present Era. Warsaw: Kasa Przezorności i Pomocy Warszawskich Pomocników Księgarskich, 1919. ii, 87p. (P)

415 Mirkin, Menahem. "Jewish Students in Polish High Schools." Yidishe Ekonomik 4-5 (1939): 205ff. (Y)

416 Morgenthau, Henry. "My Mission to Poland." In his All in a Lifetime. New York: 1922, 348-384 et "Report of the Mission of the United States to Poland." ibid., Appendix: 405-437.

417 Mozes, Samuel R. "Jewish Telegraphic Agency in Poland." BZIH 1/97 (1976): 109-121. (P)

418 Nossig, Alfred. Poles and Jews: Polish-Jewish Understanding for Regulation of the Jewish Question in Poland. Vienna: Internationaler Verlag "Renaissance", 1921. 72p. (G)

419 Noylens, Joseph. "The Jewish Question." Report of the Inter-Allied Committee for Polish Affairs. Reprint in Najnowsze Dzieje Polski, 1918-1939. 16 (Warsaw, 1939): 215-219. (P)

420 Orlicki, Józef. Essays from the History of Polish-Jewish Relations, 1918-1939. Szczecin: Krajowa Agencja Wydawnicza, 1983. 271p. (P)

421 Ormian, Haim. "The Hebrew Grammar School in Poland Between the Two World Wars." Gal-ed 4-5 (1978): 231-261. (H)

422 Rabinowicz, Harry. The Legacy of Polish Jewry: A History of Polish Jews in the Inter-war Years, 1919-1939. New York: T.Yoseloff, 1965. 256p.ill.

423 Radt, Jenny. The Jews in Poland. Berlin: Schocken-Verlag, 1935. 35p. (G)

424 Samuel, Sir Stuart Montagu. Report by Sir Stuart Samuel on his Mission to Poland, (Presented to Parliament. Miscellaneous Nr.10). London: His Majesty's Stationary Office, 1920. 14p.

425 Schorr, Moses. "Our Desires." GGŻ 2, no 10-11 (1938): 232-233. (P)

426 Schwartzbard, Ignacy. During the Interwar Period. Buenos Aires:

Tsentral Farband fun Poilische Yidden, 1953. 385p. (Y)

427   Segal, Simon. The New Poland and the Jews. New York: Lee Furman Inc., 1938. xiii, 223 p.

428   Seraphim, Peter Heinz. The Jewry in the Eastern European Area. Essen: Essener Verlags-Anstalt, 1938. 736p. illus. (G)

429   Shatzky, Jacob. "Struggle Concerning the Planned Jewish Periodicals in Poland." YIVO-Bleter 6, no. 1 (1934): 61-83. (Y)

430   The Situation of Polish Jewry: Text of a Memorandum Submitted to the Secretary of State of the United States on July 12, 1937. New York: American Jewish Congress, 1937. 14p.

431   Skierko, Adam. The Jews in Poland. Lausanne: Imprimeries reunies, 1920. 41p. (F)

432   Sopicki, Stanisław. Jewish Question in Poland from the Viewpoint of the Polish Christian Democratic Party. Krakow: 1926, 40p. (P)

433   Stańczyk, Jan. "The Status of Jews in Free Poland: Declaration presented on behalf of the Polish Government by the Minister of Labor and Social Welfare, December 1941." In Olszer, Krystyna M., ed. For Your Freedom and Ours: Polish Progressive Spirit from the 14th Century to the Present. pp. 267-269. New York: Frederick Ungar Publishing Co., 1981, 267-269.

434   Stendig, S. "The Jewish High Schools in Reborn Poland." GGŻ 2, 10-11 (1938): 290-292. (P)

435   Strobel, Georg W. Polish-Jewish Relations: The Jews, The Polish State and the Polish Public up to 1945. Cologne: Bundesinstitut fur Ostwissen-Schaftliche und Internationale Studien, 1968. (G)

436   Studnicki, Władysław. The Polish Jewish Question. Wilno: J. Zawadzki, 1935. 24p. (P)

437   Szajn, Izrael. "Bibliography of Jewish Dailies and Periodicals published in Poland between 1918-1939 in the Polish Language." BŻIH 2/78 (1971): 107-132. (P)

438   Szajn, Izrael. "Bibliography of the Jewish Youth Press Published in Poland in 1918-1939 in Polish." BŻIH 2/94 (1975): 103-113. (P)

439   Szajn, Izrael and Fuks, Marian. "Bibliography of Irregular Publications Concerning Jewish Social Institutions and Organizations which acted in Poland in the Years 1918-1939 in the Polish Language." BŻIH 3/95 (1975): 105-112. (P)

440   Szajn, Izrael. Bibliography of Publications of Jewish Labor Parties in Poland between 1918-1939. Warsaw: Idish Buch, 1963. 183p. (Y)

441   Szulkin, Michał. "Palestinian Jews in Light of Polish Diplomatic Service Reports: Part I, 1923-1935." BŻIH 4/116 (1980): 127-143. (P)

442   Szulkin, Michał.   "Palestinian Jews in Light of Polish Diplomatic Service Reports: Part II, 1936-1939." BŻIH 1/117 (1981): pp.63-82. (P)

443   Szwalbe, Natan.   "The Jewish Question in Newborn Poland." Kalendarz Naszego Przeglądu. (Warsaw, 1928): 103-110. (P)

444   Tamir, Nachman, ed.   The Polish Jews Before the Holocaust.   Tel-Aviv: 1983, 215p.

445   Tartakower, Arieh.   "Jewish Life in Reborn Poland."   GGŻ 2, 10-11 (1938): 255-263. (P)

446   Tartakower, Arieh.   "The Problem of Jewish Education in Poland." Almanach Szkolnictwa Żydowskiego w Polsce 1, (Warsaw, 1928): 25-30. (P)

447   Tartakower, Arieh.   "Professional and Social Structure of Jews in Reborn Poland." ZPO. 2 (1933): 363-394. (P)

448   Thon, Ozjasz.   "Introduction."   In Schiper, Ignacy et al., eds. Żydzi w Polsce Odrodzonej (Jews in Reborn Poland).   pp.7-18.   Warsaw: 1936, (P)

449   Tomaszewski, Jerzy.   "Diplomatic Report Concerning Situation of Polish Jews in Germany in Early 1936." BŻIH 2/106 (1978): 101-109. (P)

450   Tomaszewski, Jerzy.   "Polish Diplomatic Service Regarding the Situation of Polish Jews in the Third Reich in the Beginning of 1936." BŻIH 1/125 (1983): 91-107. (P)

451   Urbański, Zygmunt.   National Minorities in Poland.   Warsaw: Instytut Mniejszości Narodowych, 1932. 375p. (P)

452   Waldman, Morris David.   Conditions up to Date in Poland: Report Delivered at the Constructive Relief Conference of the Joint Distribution Committee and the United Jewish Campaign.   Chicago: October 22-23, 1927. 24p.

453   Wasserman, P.   "To Commemorate the Twentieth Anniversary of the Act of Historical Justice." GGŻ 2, 10-11 (1938): 229-231. (P)

454   Wójcicki, Mieczysław.   Poland and the Jewish State.   Lwów: Księgarnia Polska Bernarda Połonieckiego, 1919. 40p. (P)

455   Zaleski, Władysław Józef.   "Retrospective View: Treaty Obligations Concerning Protection of Minorities During the 20-Years of Independence." Niepodległość. (London-New York, 1972): 88-132. (P)

456   Żmigryder-Konopka, Zdzisław.   "Value of the Past." GGŻ 2 no.10-11 (1938): 9-10. (P)

8
Demography and Statistics

457 Aleksandrova, H. "The Jewish Population in Byelorussia in the Period of the Partitions of Poland. (Historical Statistical Studies)." Cajtszrift 4 (Mińsk, 1929): 31-38. (Y)

458 Bergmann, Eugen von. Towards a History of Development of German, Polish and Jewish Population in the Poznan Province since 1824. Tübingen: H.Laupp, 1883. 365p. (G)

459 Bronsztejn, Szyja. Jewish Population in Interwar Poland: Statistical Study. Wrocław: Zakład Narodowy Im. Ossolińskich,, 1963. 295p. (P)

460 Buzek, Józef. Impact of Jewish Policy of the Austrian Government in the 1772-1778 Period on Growth of Jewish Population in Galicia. Kraków: Uniwersytet Jagielloński, 1903. 130p. (P)

461 Ćwik, Władysław. "Jewish Population of Royal Towns of Lublin Region in the 2nd Half of the 18th Century." BŻIH 59 (1966): 29-62. (P)

462 Eisenbach, Artur. "Jews in Old Poland in the Light of Numbers." Kwartalnik Historyczny no.2. (Warsaw, 1959): 511-520. (P)

463 Eisenbach, Artur. "Territorial Mobility of the Jewish Population of the Kingdom of Poland." Revue des Études Juives 126 no.1 (Paris 1967): 55-111, et ibidem, no.4, pp.435-471. (F)

464 Feldman, Eliezar. "On Statistics of the Jews in Old Poland." M.Żyd. 3 (1933): 130-135. (P)

465 Fogelson, S. "Natural Growth of the Jewish Population in Poland." Sprawy Narodowościowe 11 no.4-5 (Warsaw, 1937): 405-419. (P)

466 Frenk, Ezriel Nathan. "Numbers and Professions of Jews in the Polish Kingdom in 1843." Blätter für Jüdische Demographie Statistik un Ekonomik. 3 (Berlin, 1923): 184-193. (Y)

467 Gelber, Nathan Michael. "History of Sephardic Jews in Poland." Tesoro be Los Judios Sefardies 6 (1963): 88-99. (Ladino)

468   Gelber, Nathan Michael. "On the Statistics of Jews in Poland at the End of the 18th Century. YIVO Szriftn far Ekonomik un Statistik 1 (Berlin, 1928): 185-188. (Y)

469   Gruiński, Stanisław. Materials to the Jewish Question in Galicia. Lwów: Wydział Krajowy, 1910. 81p. (P)

470   Hekker, Helena. "Jews in Polish Towns in the Second Half of the 18th Century." J.St. (1919): 184-200 et 325-332. (R)

471   Korkis, Abraham. "Movement of the Jewish Population in Galicia." Krytyka 1 (Kraków, 1903): 306-310. (P)

472   Korobkow, Chaim. "The Statistics of Jewish Settlement in Poland and Lithuania in the Second Half of the 18th Century (On the Basis of Data in Original Registers)." J.St. 4 (1911): 541-562. (R)

473   Laubert, M. "Resettlement and Reclassification of Jewish People During the Last Centuries,"pp.570-580. In Weltwirtschaftliches Archiv. Berlin: 1930. (G)

474   Lestchinsky, Jacob. "The Jews in Cities of the Republic of Poland." YIVO Annual 1 (1946): 156-177.

475   Lewinzon, J. "Jews in Old Poland in the Light of Numbers: The Demographic Structure and Socio-Economic Status of the Jews in The Polish Crown in the Eighteen Century." Przeszłość Demograficzna Polski. 1 (Warsaw, 1967): 130-180. (P)

476   Mahler, Raphael. Jews in Old Poland in Light of Statistics. Warsaw: 1958. 201p. (Y)

477   Rosenfeld, M. "Jewish Population of Galicia, 1772-1867." Zeitschrift für Demographie und Statistik der Juden 10 (1914): 138-143. (G)

478   Ruppin, Arthur. Social Relations of Jews in Russia, Based on Official Statistical Material Arranged by the Office for Jewish Statistics in Berlin Halensee on Request of the Zionist action Committee. Berlin-Charlottenburg: Jüdischer Verlag, 1906. 68p. (G)

479   Schiper, Ignacy. "The Distribution of Jews in Poland and Lithuania." In Dubnov Semen Markovich et al., eds. Istoria Evreev v Rossii. 1 (Moscow , 1914): 105-131. (R)

480   Schiper, Ignacy. "Growth of the Jewish Population in the Former Republic." ŻPO. 1 (1932): 21-36. (P)

481   Shatzky, Jacob. "An Attempt at Jewish Colonization in the Kingdom of Poland." YIVO Annual I (1946): 44-63.

482   Sprecher, N. "Movements of Jewish Population in Galicia." Morja 2 (Kraków, 1904): 184-188. (P)

483   Sułowski, Zygmunt. "Mechanisms of Jewish Demographic Expansion in Polish Towns in the period during XV-XIX Centuries."   Zeszyty Naukowe

Katolickiego Uniwersytetu w Lublinie 17 no.3/67 (Lublin, 1974): pp. 93-110. (P)

484 Szpidbaum, Henryk. "Racial Structure of Polish Jews." ŻPO 2 (1933): 165-184. (P)

485 Tartakower, Arieh. "Numbers and Natural Growth of the Jewish Population in Poland." ŻPO 2 (1933): 185-194. (P)

486 Tomaszewski, Jerzy. "Jewish Workers in Poland, in the Years 1921-1939: A Statistical Essay." BŻIH 51 (1964): 21-39. (P)

487 Wasiutyński, Bohdan. Jewish Population in Poland in the 19th and 20th Centuries: A Statistical Study. Warsaw: Kasa im. Mianowskiego, 1930. ii, 224p. (P)

9
Economics

General Situation

488 Baskerville, Beatrice C. The Polish Jew, his Social and Economic Value. Ne York: The Macmillan Co., 1906. 336p.

489 Blumenstrauch, B. "Participation of the Jews in Economic Life of Reborn Poland." GGŻ 2 no.10-11 (1938): 269-273. (P)

490 Bornstein, I.L. "Problem of Pauperization of the Jewish Population in Poland." ŻPO, 2 (1933): 395-407. (P)

491 Cohn, Adam. Economic Relations of Jews in the Russian State. Warsaw: Drukarnia Lepperta, 1904. 77p. (P))

492 Diament, Jozef. In a Blind Alley: Economic Agony of Jews in Poland. Kraków: Spółka Wydawnicza "Nowy Dziennik", 1933. 111p. (P)

493 Eisenbach, Artur. "Materials for Economic Structure and Activity of Jewish Population in Polish Kingdom in the Eighties of the XIX century." BŻIH 29 (1959): 72-112. (P)

494 Feldstejn, Herman. Impact of Werner Sombart's Essay on the Future of the Jews. Lwów: 1912, 23p. (P)

495 Frostig, M. "Destitution of Galician Jews and Action Plan Directed towards their Ecomonic Improvement." Almanach Reicha. (Kraków) 1910, pp. 174-188. (P)

496 Glicksman, William M. In the Mirror of Literature; The Economic Life of the Jews as Reflected in Yiddish Literature, 1914-1939. New York: Living Books, 1966. 254p.

497 Gliksman, Jerzy G. Economic Aspect of the Jewish Question in Poland. Paris: Les Éditions Rieder, 1929. 126p. (F)

498 Kandel, Dawid. "The 1857 Petition." KŻP. 3 (1913): 119-121. (P)

499 Korobkow, Chaim. "The Economic Role of Jews in Poland at the End of the XVIII Century." J.St. 1910, pp.346-377. (R)

500   Korobkow, Chaim.   "Economic Role of Jews in the Congress Kingdom of Poland, 1815-1830." J.St. 1910, pp.121-136. (R)

501   Landsberger, J. "Debts of Jews in Poland." Jahrbuch der jüdischer Literarischen Gesellschaft. Frankfurt a/Main: 1908. Vol. 6, pp. 252-279. (G)

502   Lestchinsky, Jacob.   "Economic Aspects of Jewish Community Organization in Independent Poland." YIVO Annual 11 (1956/57), pp. 243-269.

503   Lestchinsky, Jacob.   The Economic Situation of Jews in Poland. Berlin: 1932, 152p. (Y)

504   Lestchinsky, Jacob.   The Economic Situation of Jews since the World War: Eastern and Central Europe. Paris: Rousseau and Compagnie, 1934, 148p. (F)

505   Lestchinsky, Jacob.   Joint Economic Collapse of the Jews in Germany and Poland.   Paris: Exekutiwe Komittee fur Judischen Welt Kongress, 1936. 55p. (G)

506   Lestchinsky, Jacob.   "The Pauperization of the Jewish Masses in Poland." YIVO Bletter 6 no.2 (Wilno, March-April, 1934): 201-228. (Y)

507   Lestchinsky, Jacob.   "Poland" in La Situation Economique des Minorités Juives. Paris: 1939. Part I, pp.185-300. (F)

508   Reich, Nathan.   "Towards a Solution of the Jewish Problem in Poland." Menorah Journal 26 no.2 (April-June, 1938): 151-172.

509   Szacki, Jerzy.   "The Role of Jews in Economic Life of Poland in the Years 1863-1896." BŻIH 30 (1959): 12-49. (P)

510   Tenenbaum, Joseph. Jewish Economic Problems in Galicia. Vienna: 1918, 129p. (P)

511   Tomaszewski, Jerzy.   "Concerning the Financial Situation of Jews in the Years 1918-1939." BŻIH 94 (1975): 93-101. (P)

512   Weinryb, Bernard Dov.   The Jews of Poland: A Social and Economic History of the Jewish Community in Poland, from 1100-1800. Philadelphia: The Jewish Publication Society of America, 1973. xvi, 424p.

513   Weinryb, Bernard Dov.   The Newest Economic History of the Jews in Russia and Poland. New York: George Olms, 1972. 282p. (G)

514   Weinryb, Bernard Dov.   Studies in the Economic and Social History of Jews in Poland. Jerusalem: R. Mass, 1939. 120p. (H)

515   Zylbersztajn, Roman. "Economic Problems of Jews in Poland." Przegląd Handlowy. 10 (Warsaw, September 15, 1936): 7-8. (P)

Agriculture

516 Antonow, M. "Abraham Muhr's Memorial of 1844 in the Matter of Organization of a Jewish Agricultural Colony in Upper Silesia." BŻIH 21 (1957): 118-124. (P)

517 Bartyś, Julian. "The Level of Farming in the Jewish Agricultural Colonies in Some Provinces of the Kingdom of Poland During The Period Preceding Enfranchisement." BŻIH 47-48 (1963): 29-52. (P)

518 Bartyś, Julian. "Numbers and Composition of Jewish Agricultural Settlers in the Kingdom of Poland during the Period Before Enfranchisement." BŻIH 43-44 (1962): 18-40. (P)

519 Bartyś, Julian. "On Jewish Agricultural Settlements in Zamoyski's Estates in the First Half of the 19th Century." BŻIH 15-16 (1955): 209ff. (P)

520 Brutzkus, Boris. Jewish Agrarian Economy in Eastern Europe. Berlin: 1926. 107p. (Y)

521 Dobrzyński, Bernard. "Jews in Agriculture in the former Congress Kingdom and Eastern Borderlands." ŻPO 2(1933): 408-423. (P)

522 Eisenbach, Artur. "Land Estates in Jewish Possession." In Kula, Witold ed. Społeczeństwo Królestwa Polskiego. 3 pp.201-294. Warsaw: 1967. (P)

523 Friedman, Filip. "Agriculture, Colonization and Land Possession by Galician Jews in the 19th Century." Junger Historiker 2 (Warsaw, 1929): 131-142. (Y)

524 Jankielewicz, Michal. "Development of Jewish Agriculture in Byelorussia in the Years 1923-1928." BŻIH 2/118 (1981): 15-36. (P)

525 Landsberger, J. "Jewish Landlords in South Prussia." Historische Monatsblätter fur die Provinz Posen 12 (1900): 177-183. (G)

526 Lapkes, Y. Lease Conditions Among Jewish Agrarian Workers in Austrian Poland. Wilno: 1921. 16p. (Y)

527 Lvavi, Jacob. "The State of Jewish Agriculture in Poland in the Years 1918-1939." Gal-Ed 2 (1975): 179-207. (H)

528 Penkalla, Adam. "The Jewish Rural Population of the Kraków Voievodship in Light of the Census of 1819." BŻIH 1/105 (1978): 83-92. (P)

529 Przedpełski, Jan. "Pioneers of Mechanization of Agriculture in Mazovia." BŻIH 1/85 (1973): 79-83. (P)

530 Schiper, Ignacy. "Jews in Agriculture in the Malopolska Region." ZPO 2 (1933): 424-431. (P)

531 Statute (By-Laws) of the Association to Spread Professional and Agricultural Work among Jews. Warsaw: Bracia Wójcikiewicz,1927. 16p. (P)

532　Str., F. "Description of the Łabędź and Ksawerów Colonies." Jutrzenka 23 (Warsaw, 1861): 184 ff. et 24, 191 ff. (P)

533　Szurowa, Bogumiła. "The Building Trade in the Jewish Farming Settlements of the Radom District in Mid-19th Century." BŻIH 1-2, 121/122 (1982): 27-49. (P)

534　Tapuach, Shimshon. "Farming among Jews in Poland, 1919-1939." In Fishman Joshua A., ed. Studies on Polish Jewry. pp.336-421. New York, 1974. (Y)

535　Tapuach, Shimshon. A Jewish Village in the Wilno Region. Warsaw: 1937. 30p. (P)

Banking, Commerce and Cooperatives

536　Caro, Leopold. The Usury. Leipzig: Duncker und Humblot, 1893. xv, 311p. (G)

537　Grynberg, Michał. "The Jewish Cooperative Movement in Interwar Poland." BŻIH 1/89 (1974): 65-81. (P)

538　Korobkov, Chaim. "Jewish Participation in the Internal Commerce of Poland." J.St. 1911, pp.19-39 at 137-220. (R)

539　Korobkov, Chaim. "Jewish Participation in Small Trade in Poland." J.St. 1911, pp.19-39 at 197-220. (R)

540　Laubert, Manfred. "Regulations of Debts of Jewish Corporations in the Poznań Province." Monatschrift für Geschichte und Wissenschaft des Judentums 68 (1924): 321-331. (G)

541　Lipp, Adolf. Traffic and Trade Relations of Galicia. Prag: C.H. Hunger, 1870. 336p. (G)

542　Marek, Lucjan. "Association for Mutual Aid of the Jewish (employee) Trade Salesman,1882-1903." BŻIH 69 (1969): 21-49. (P)

543　Parnas, H. "Paper on Perspectives of Jewish Credit-Cooperatives Given at the 10th Meeting of the Jewish Cooperatives Societies." Ruch Spółdzielczy. 12 (Warsaw, 1934): pp.148-153. (P)

544　Peretz, Adolf. "Jews in Polish Banking." ŻPO 2 (1933): 432-454. (P)

545　Perl, Leon. "Jewish Participation in the Field of Commercial Agencies and Commissions." ŻPO 2 1933): 475-478. (P)

546　Prowalski, Abraham J. The Jewish Cooperative Movement in Poland. Warsaw: Komitet dla Zbadania Potrzeb Gospodarczych Ludności Żydowskiej w Polsce, 1933. 45p. (P)

547　Prowalski, Abraham J. "Jewish Co-Operative Movement in Reborn Poland." ŻPO 2 (1933): 590-617. (P)

Economics 43

548 Schiper, Ignacy. History of Jewish Commerce on Polish Soil. Warsaw: Centralny Związek Kupców, 1937. vii, 791p. (P)

549 Schiper, Ignacy. "Jews in Banking and Credit, (Great Poland, Little Poland, Wilno Region and Eastern Borderlands)." ŻPO 2 (1933): 455-463. (P)

550 Schiper, Ignacy. "The Participation of Jews in Communications and Transport." ŻPO 2 (1933): 542-549. (P)

551 Schiper, Ignacy. "The Taxing of Jews." Istoria Jewrejskowo Naroda. 11 (Moskwa, 1914): 300-319. (R)

552 Szlamowicz, L. "The Number of Jewish and Non-Jewish Shops in Small Towns." Zagadnienia Gospodarcze 1-2 (Warsaw, 1935): pp.48-55. (P)

553 Zajdeman, M. "Jewish Participation in the Trade of Reborn Poland." ŻPO 2 (1933): 464-474. (P)

Crafts and Industry

554 Bornstein, I.L. Jewish Handcraft in Poland. Warsaw: Instytut Badań Spraw Narodowościowych, 1936. 130p. illus. (P)

555 Burchard, Przemysław. "Contributions to the Question of Jewish Folkhandicrafts in Old Poland." BŻIH 37 (1961): 66-80. (P)

556 Hafftka, Aleksander. "The Jewish Crafts Estate in Reborn Poland." ŻPO 2 (1933): 550-569. (P)

557 Heller, Eliezer. Jewish Industrial Establishments in Poland, surveyed in 1921. Warsaw: "Gloria" with the Assistance of the American Joint Distribution Committee, 1922. 6 vols. (P)

558 Jaros, Jerzy. "Information about Jews Active in the Polish Coal Industry." BŻIH 35 (1960): 87-89. (P)

559 Kremer, M. "Jewish Artisans and Guilds in Former Poland, 16th-18th Centuries." YIVO Annual (1956-1957): 211-242.

560 Rosiński, W. "The Tobacco Monopoly in the Kingdom of Poland." In L. Kronenberg's Festschrift. Warsaw (1922): 187-314. (P)

561 Schweikert, Kurt. The Russo-Polish Cotton Industry: Its Development as Main Industry and the Position of the Workers. Zürich-Leipzig: Rascher & Co., 1913. 381p. (G)

562 Schiper, Ignacy and Hafftka, Aleksander. "Jews in Polish Industry." ŻPO 2 (1933): 479-541. (P)

563 Tomaszewski, Jerzy. "The Situation of Small Jewish Tradesmen in Poland in the Years of the Great Crisis, 1929-1935." BŻIH 102 (1977): 35-54. (P)

564 Wein, Adam. "The Book of the Guild of Jewish Tailors, Furriers and Haberdashers." BŻIH 42 (1962): 128-130. (P)

565 Weinrach, B. "To the History of the Jewish role in Polish Industry." YIVO Ekonomisze Szryften (Wilno: 1932): 41-53. (Y)

566 Wischnitzer, Mark. A History of Jewish Crafts and Guilds. New York: Jonathan David, 1965. 324p.

10
Legal Status and Minority Rights

567   Aubac, Stéphane.   The Truth Concerning National Minorities in Poland.   Paris: Éditions de la Revue politique et litteraire (Revue Bleue) et la Revue scientifique, 1924, 28p. (F)

568   Bałaban, Majer. " From the Studies of the Legal System in Poland: the Jewish Judge and His Jurisdiction." in Pamiętnik Trzydziestolecia Pracy Naukowej prof. dr. Przemysława Dąbkowskiego. pp.245-280. Lwów: 1927. (P)

569   Bloch, Philipp.   General Privileges of Polish Jewry. Poznań: J. Jolowicz, 1892. 120p. (G)

570   Brandes, Leo.   "The Legal Situation of the Jews in Interwar Poland."   YIVO bleter   42 (1962): 147-186. (Y)

571   Bronisławski, Jerzy. "The Legal Status of Jews in Poland Under the Partitions and the Second Republic of 1918-1939." Wiadomości Historyczne 3 1984. (P)

572   Czechowski, Michał B.   Poland: Sketch of her History: Treatment of the Jews and Laws Concerning Them.   New York: Baker and Godwin, 1863. 58p.

573   Drozdowski, Marian Marek. "National Minorities in Poland in 1918-1939." Acta Poloniae Historica   22 (Warsaw 1970): 226-251. (P)

574   Eisenbach, Artur.   "Civic and Honour Rights of Jews, 1790-1861." in Spoleczeństwo Królestwa Polskiego: Studia o Uwarstwowieniu i Ruchliwości Społecznej,   edited by Witold Kula, pp.265-271. Vol.1, Warsaw: 1965. (P)

575   Eisenbach, Artur. "Jewish Civic Rights in the Congress Kingdom of Poland, 1815-1863." Revue des Études Juives 121 (1964): 1984. (F)

576   Eisenbach, Artur.   The Question of Equal Rights for Jews in the Kingdom of Poland.   Warsaw: Książka i Wiedza, 1972. 578p. illus. (P)

577   Feinberg, Nathan.   The Minorities Question at the Peace Conference of 1919-1920 and Jewish Action in Favor of International Protection of

Jewish Minorities. Paris: Rousseau, Comité des Delegations Juives, 1929. 167p. (F)

578   Friedman, Philip. The Galician Jews in their Struggle for Equal Rights. Frankfurt a/Main: J. Kauffmannn, 1929. viii, 215p. (G)

579   Goodhart, Arthur Lehman. Poland and the Minority Races. New York: Arno Press, 1971. 194p.

580   Grynsztejn, M. "Legislation Concerning Jewish Communities in Independent Poland." GGŻ 2, no.10-11 (1938): 322-324. (P)

581   Gumplowicz, Ludwig. Polish Legislation Concerning the Jews. Kraków: J.M. Himmelblau, 1867. 176p. (P)

582   Hafftka, Aleksander. "Legislation of Reborn Poland with Regard to the Jewish National Minority." ŻPO 2 (1933): 234-241. (P)

583   Hartglas, Apolinary. "The Law about Sunday Rest and the Jews." Natio (June 6, 1927): 2-31. (P)

584   Hirschhorn, Samuel. The Jewish Problem During the Four Years' Diet, 1788-1792): or an Answer to the question of what the May 3rd Constitution gave the Jews? At the Occasion of the 125th Anniversary. Warsaw: by the author, 1916. 26p. (P)

585   Horak, Stephan. Poland and Her National Minorities, 1919-1939: A Case Study. New York: Vantage Press, 1961. 259p. illus.

586   Janowsky, Oscar Isaiah. The Jews and Minority Rights,(1898-1919). New York: Columbia University Press, 1933. 419p.

587   Janowsky, Oscar Isaiah. Nationalities and National Minorities : with special Reference to East Central Europe. New York: The Macmillan Co., 1945. xix, 232p.

588   Kirszrot, Jakob. The Rights of Jews in the Polish Kingdom: Historical Outline. Warsaw: Zarząd Warszawskiej Gminy Starozakonnych, 1917. iv, 327p. (P)

589   Korzec, Paweł. "The Poles and the Minorities' Protection Agreement." Jahrbücher für Geschichte Osteuropas 4 (München, 1975): 1-40. (G)

590   Koźminski, Tadeusz. The Minorities Problem, based on the Treaty between Major Allied and Associated Powers and Poland, signed in Versailles, June 28, 1919. Warsaw: Perzyński, Niklewicz i S-ka, 1922. 162p. (P)

591   Kupfer, Efraim. "To the question of the legal and factual situation of Jews in Poland." Bleter far Geszychte. 5 (1952): 49-60. (Y)

592   Laserson, Max M. THe Status of Jews after the War: A Proposal for Jewish Demands at the Forthcoming Peace Conference. New York: Educational Committee, Jewish National Workers Alliance, 1940. 23p.

593   Lewin, Isaac. "The Protection of Jewish Religious Rights by Royal Edicts." In Giergielewicz, Mieczysław, ed. Polish Civilization Essays and Studies   pp.115-134. New York:1971.

594   Lichtensztejn, M.   "Legislation of Reborn Poland Concerning the Jews."   GGŻ 2, no.10-11 (1938): 326-329.   (P)

595   Lisser, Michal.   "Jewish Courts in Poland until the End of the 18th Century: Their Structure and Competence." BZIH   34 (1960): 97-130. (P)

596   Łunski, Ch.   "Book of Announcements, Decrees and Orders." Pinkas-Wilno. 1922, pp. 629-682. (Y)

597   Macartney, Carlile Aylmer.   National States and National Minorities. London: Oxford University Press, for the Royal Institute of International Affairs. 1934. ix,553p.

598   Mendelssohn, Moses.   Ritual Rules of The Jews Concerning Inheritance, Legal Custodies, Bequest and Marital Relations, as far as they Apply to Property Rights: arranged in the German Language on Instruction of the Prussian Court, translated by Jan Nepomucen Janowski. Warsaw: 1938. xvii, 176p. (P)

599   Paprocki, Stanisław J.(ed.) Poland and the Problem of Minorities: Collection of Information.   Warsaw: Instytut Spraw Narodowościowych, 1935.   173p. (F)

600   Ringel, Michał. "Fundamental Rights of the Jewish Minority in Poland and their History." ŻPO 2 (1933): 225-233. (P)

601   Ringel, Michał. "Legislation Of Reborn Poland Concerning Jewish Communities." ŻPO 2 (1933): 242-248. (P)

602   Robinson, Jacob et al.   eds.   Were the Minorities Treaties a Failure?   New York: Institute Of Jewish Affairs of the American Jewish Congress and the World Jewish Congress, 1943. xvi, 349p.

603   Rosenfeld, Max.   "Galicia's distinct Status and the Jews." Neue Jüdische Monatshefte. Berlin: 1918, pp.210-214. (G)

604   Rosenfeld, Max.   National Right for Selfdetermination of Jews in Poland. Vienna: R. Löwitt,1918. 62p. (G)

605   Rundstein, Szymon.   Polish Law of 1920 Concerning Problems of Nationality and the Versailles Treaties: Response to M. A. de Lapradelle.   Paris: Comité des delegations juives, 1924. 27p. (F)

606   Scherer, I.E.   The Legal Relations of Jews in German-Austrian Countries. Leipzig: 1901. xx, 671p. (G)

607   Schorr, Moses.   "A Kraków Compilation of Jewish Statutes and Privileges: Summary of Privileges." J.St.   (1909): 247-264 et 76-100. (R)

608   Schorr, Moses.   Legal Position and Internal Constitution of Jews

in Poland: Historical Outline. Berlin-Vienna: R. Löwitt, 1917. 36p. (G)

609 Seidman, Hillel. The Oath in Jewish Law: in Response to "Experts on Jewry. Warsaw: by the author, 1936. 61p. (P)

610 Stoeger, Michael. Presentation of the Legal Constitution of Galician Jewry. Two Volumes in One. Lwów: Kuhn and Millikowski. 1833. (G)

611 Stoiever. "Reports About Life and the Rights of West Prussian Jews, 1772-1812. Monat der Westprüssichen Geschichtsvereibes 1 (Gdańsk): 8-11. (G)

612 Wein, Adam. "About Jewish Efforts to Annul Civil Rights Limitations in the Polish Kingdom." BZIH 36 (1960): 41-61. (P)

613 Wein, Adam. "Efforts of the Jewish Bourgeoisie's Representatives for Privileges for the Prominent Citizens in the Polish Kingdom." BZIH 34 (1960). (P)

614 Wolf, Lucien. Legal Sufferings of the Jews in Russia: A Survey of their present Situation and a Summary of Laws. London: T.F. Unwin, 1912. 106p

615 Zieleniewski, L. "The Problem of National Minorities in the Constitution ." Sprawy Narodowościowe. 9 no.1-2. (1935): 1-37. (P)

11
Autonomy (Kehillots)

616 Allerhand, M. The Elections to Councils and Boards of Directors of Jewish Denominational Communities." Lwów: Ignacy Jaeger, 1928. 55p. (P)

617 Bałaban, Majer. "The Jewish Diet in Poland, or Crown's Waad and Dietines, or Regional Waads." Istoriya Jewrejskowo Naroda. 11 Moscow: 1914. pp. 165-167. (R)

618 Bałaban, Majer. "The Kahał System in Poland, 16th-18th Century." KŻP., 2 (1912): 16-54. (P)

619 Bałaban, Majer. "Organizational Problems of Polish Jewry", Studia Lwowskie. Lwów: 1932. pp.41-66. (P)

620 Bałaban, Majer. Problems Concerning Constitutional Issues of Polish Jewry. Lwów: Towarzystwo Miłośnikow Przeszłości Lwowa, 1932. 25p. (P)

621 Brafman, Iakov Aleksandrovich. The Jews and the Kahals: with Comments by Teodor Jeske-Choinski. Warsaw: Drukarnia Synów S. Niemiry, 1914. 203p. (P)

622 Cytron, Szymon L. Lobbyists, Activists and Interesting Characters (Personalities) from Recent Past. Warsaw: 1924. 376p. (Y)

623 Dawidsohn, Jozef. Jewish Communities: with the Texts of Laws and Ordinances. Warsaw: Klub Posłów Sejmowych Żydowskiej Rady Narodowej, 1931. 110p. (P)

624 Glicksman, William M. A Kehillah in Poland During the Inter-War Years; Studies in Jewish Community Organization. Translated from Yiddish by Max Rosenfeld. Philadelphia: M.E. Kalish Folkshul, 1970. xiii. 158p.

625 Goldberg, J. "The Jewish Community in a Town Owned by a Nobleman." BŻIH 59 (1966): pp.3-28. (P)

626 Jacobson, Jacobi. "General List of Alternating Privileges of Jewish Communities and Guilds in the South Prussian Poznań Division in

1797." Monatschrift für Geschichte und Wissenschaft des Judentums (1913): 62-131. (G)

627 Jeske-Choiński, Teodor. The Jews and Their Kahał- Communities. Warsaw: Drukarnia Synów S. Niemiry, 1914. 208p. (P)

628 "Kahal." Istoria Yevreyskovo Naroda, 11 (Moscow, 1914): 132-160. (R)

629 Kandel, Dawid. "Committee of Orthodox Jews." KŻP 2 (1912): 85-103. (P)

630 Kempner, R. "Agony of the Kahal." KŻP 1 (1912): 67-73. (P)

631 Kollenscher, Max. Jewish Communal Tasks. Poznań: Philipp, 1905. 12p. (G)

632 Lewin, Isaac. "The Ban as an Effective Instrument fo the Council of the Four Lands." Yearbook of the World Federation of Polish Jews 1 New York, 1964): 79-109. (Y)

633 Lisser, M. "Jewish Courts to the End of the 18th Century." BŻIH 34 (1960): 97-130. (P)

634 Marek, P. "Income Tax Collectors in Lithuanian Kahals." J.St. 1 (1909): 161-174. (R)

635 Paperna, A. "Kehillas and the Synagogue Patronage." Woschod 4 (1901): 96-114. (R)

636 Pazdro, Zbigniew. Organization and Practice of Jewish Sub-District Courts in Period 1740-1772: Based on Lwów Archival Materials. Lwów: Fundusz Konkursowy im. H. Wawelberga, 1903. 294p. (P)

637 Rappaport, Jacob. "Constitution of Jewish Religious Communities in Poland." Nation and State 3 (1929-1930): 302-315. (G)

638 Reich, Leon. "Electro-Reform and Jewish Autonomy." Moria (1906): 66-72. (P)

639 Schiper, Ignacy. "Internal Organization of the Jews in Old the Commonwealth." ŻPO 1 (1932): 81-110. (P)

640 Schiper, Ignacy. "Jewish Self-Government in Poland at the Turn of the 18th to 19th Century." M.Żyd. 1 (1931): 513-529. (P)

641 Seidman, J. "The Development of Jewish Communities in Reborn Poland." GGŻ 2 no.10-11 (1938): 324-326. (P)

642 Semiatitzki, Mordechai. "The Right of Settlement in Poland." Ha-mishpat ha-ivris (1936-1937): 199-253. (H)

643 Shefner, B. "Slamming the Door: (about our further attitude to the Jewish Commune)." Unzer Cajt 3 (Warsaw, March 1929): 32-41. (Y)

644 Walski, K. "Isn't It Too Early? Concerning Discussions about

Kahal." Unzer Cajt 4 (Warsaw, June 1929): 26-31. (Y)

645   Weinryb, Bernard Dov.   Texts and Studies in the Communal History of Polish Jewry.   New York: Proceedings of the American Academy for Jewish Research, 1951. 264p. (H)

646   Zajączkowski, Henryk.   "Waad - Jewish Parliament."   Wiadomości. 32 no 50/51 (London, December 10/17): 1978, p.4. (P)

647   Zygelboym, Shmuel Mordecai.   "In the Struggle for Secular Communities." 3 Unzer Cajt (Warsaw, April 1929): 63-70. (Y)

12
Religion
(Orthodoxy and Reform—Haskalah)

648   Ackerberg, Armand. Talmud, Bolshevism and the Project of Polish Marital Law: Response to Father Stanisław Trzeciak. Warsaw: 1952. 126p. (P)

649   Alfassi, J. "The Seer of Lublin and His Students." Sinai 59, (1966): 251-279. (H)

650   Alter, M. "Institutions of Higher Judaic Learning in Reborn Poland." GGŻ 2 no.10-11 (1938): 294-296. (P)

651   Ashkenazi, Abraham ben Shmuel. Suffering of the Community: (ed. by B. Friedberg). Lwów: 1905, 401p. (H)

652   Asz, Nachum. In Defense of Ritual Slaughter. Częstochowa: Gmina Wyznaniowa Żydowska, 1936. 60p. (P)

653   Assaf, Simhah. Contribution to the Rabbinate's History in Germany, Poland and Lithuania. Tel-Aviv: 1927, 42p. (H)

654   Bałaban, Majer. History of the Project of the School for Rabbis and Learning of Mosaic Religion in Polish Lands. Lwów: Przełożeństwo Zboru Izraelickiego, 1907, 48p. (P)

655   Bałaban, Majer. "Mysticism and Messianic Movements Among Jews of the Old Republic." ŻPO 1 (1932): 250-280. (P)

656   "Polish Translations and Edition of Mendelssohn's Writings." Zeitschrift für die Geschichte der Juden in Deutschland 1 (Berlin, 1929) 262-268. (G)

657   Buchner, Abraham. Oriental Flowers: Collection of Moral Principals, Theological Proverbs, Social Rules, Allegories and Stories taken from the Talmud and Contemporary Writings. Warsaw: W Drukarni pod Firmą M. Chmielewskiego, 1842. xxvii, 260p. (P)

658   Chanuka. Warsaw: Centralna Żydowska Komisja Historyczna w Polsce; Feniks, 1930. 95p. (P)

659   Chones, Simon Moses. History of Rabbinical Legal Decisions.

Warsaw: 1929. 635p. (H)

660   Cytron, Szymon L.   From Behind the Scenes: Converted Jews, Renegades and Heretics.   Part I. Wilno: 1924. 236p. (H)

661   Czerikower, A.   "From Russian Archives."   Historisze Szriftn (Warsaw: YIVO, 1929): 779-804.   (Y)

662   Erter, Isaac.   Oberving the Nation of Israel.   Tel-Aviv: 1951/52, 213p.   (H)

663   Feldman, E.   "Where and for Whom Were the Regulations Forbidding Work on the Sabbath of R. Meshullam Faibish of Cracow Composed."   Zion 34   (Jerusalem, 1969):   90-97.   (H)

664   Fraenkel, Jacob Emanuel.   Talmud and its Principles: Response to A. Rohling's Work entitled "Talmudic Jew" or Disastrous Principles of Talmudism....   Transl. from German by N. Landes.   Lwów: 1876. 72p. (P)

665   Frenkel, Jeremiasz.   "Importance of Teaching Religion and Reigious Education."   M. Żyd. (July-December, 1932): 238-239. (P)

666   Frenkel, Jeremiasz.   "Rabbinical Literature of Jews in the Old Commonwealth."   ZPO 1 (1932):   213-224.   (P)

667   Frydman, A.Z.   "The Aims and Purposes of the Orthodox Jewish School Organization 'Chorev.'"   Almanach Szkolnictwa Żydowskiego w Polsce 1, (Warsaw, 1938): 296-299.   (P)

668   Frydman, Ber.   Towards Freedom of the "Pesach."   Lwów: Wydawnictwo Podręczne Naftalego Shippera, 1938. 31p. illus. (P)

669   Gelber, Nathan Michael.   "The Regional Rabbinate in Galicia"   Jewish Quarterly Review   14 (1923-1924):   303-328.

670   Gottlieb, Samuel Noah.   The Tents of God.   Pińsk: 1912. xvi, 560. (H)

671   Heschel, Abraham Joshua.   The Earth is the Lord's and The Sabbath. New York: Harper Torch Books, 1966. 136p. illus.

672   Horodezky, Samuel Aba.   Mystical-Religious Currents Among Jews in Poland in XVI - XVIII Centuries.   Leipzig: G. Engel, 1914. 80p. (G)

673   Horodezky, Samuel Aba.   On the Rabbinate's History.   Warsaw: 1911. 228p.   (H)

674   Institute of Judaic Learning in Warsaw.   Warsaw: Towarzystwo dla Krzewienia Nauk Judaistycznych w Polsce,1927. 42p. (P)

675   Jacobs, N.J.   "Solomon Mainmon's Relation to Judaism."   Yearbook of the Leo Baeck Institute of Jews from Germany.   8   (London, 1963) 117-135.

676   Kahana, Sh.Z.   "Ethical Heritage of Polish Jews."   Sefer ha-shana 2 (1967):   34-70   (H)

677	Kramstück, Izaak. Eternal Truth or Principles of Mosaic Religion. Warsaw:1872. iii, 101p. (P)

678	Kraus, Samuel. "Concerning Literature of the Prayerbooks." Sonzino Blätter 2 (1927): 1-31. (G)

679	Krochmal, Abraham. Book About God's Presence in the World. Lwów: 1862/1863. 113p. (H)

680	Krochmal, Abraham. Jerusalem Rebuilt. Lwów: M.F. Poremba, 1867. 112p. (H)

681	Krochmal, Abraham. Investigation Concerning Prayer and Historical Relationship of Men to God. Lwów: 1885. 221p. (H)

682	Krochmal, Abraham. Theology of the Future: Critical-Philosphical Thesis for Justification of Religious Consciousness. Lwów: M.F. Poremba, 1872. 60p. (G)

683	Krochmal, Abraham. The Writ and Critical Letters. Lwów: 1874. viii, 239p. (H)

684	Krochmal, Nachman. Collected Works. Berlin: 1924. 224p. (H)

685	Krochmal, Nachman. Guide for the Perplexed in Various Times. (Post-Humuous Edition by Leopold Zunz). Lwów: 1851. iv, 300p. (H)

686	Kroszczor, Henryk. "Institute of Judaic Sciences in Warsaw." BŻIH 2/28 (1972): 27-39. (P)

687	Ladier, Salomon. Several Remarks Concerning Criminal Law in the Talmud. Lwów: Księgarnia Lwowska, 1934. 32p. (P)

688	Langsam, A. Ritual Slaughter, (Shehitah). Warsaw: Centrala Związku Kupcow Branży Mięsnej, 1929. 23p. (P)

689	Lebensohn, Abraham Dob Baer. Truth and Faith. Wilno: 1870. x, 286p. (H)

690	Lewin, Isaac. "Religious Judaism in Independent Poland." In his Late Summer Fruit: Essays. New York: Bloch, 1960, pp. 9-20.

691	Lewin, L. "Rabbinical Literature of Polish Jews in Post-Partitioned Times." ŻPO 2 (1933): 103-113. (P)

692	Lewinsohn, Isaac Baer. Apologetical Work Against Accusations of Ritual Murder Against the Jews. Warsaw: Samuel Lewin, 1903. 94p. (Y)

693	Lewinsohn, Isaac Baer. Mission in Israel. Warsaw: 1901. xx, 187p. (H)

694	Lewinsohn, Isaac Baer. The Sea of Yehudah. Warsaw: 1901. 2 vols. (H)

695	Lilienthal, Regina. Jewish Holidays in Past and Present. Kraków: Polska Akademia Umiejętności, Wydział Filozoficzny, 1919. 103p. (P)

696 Łastik, Salomon. From the History of Jewish Enlightment: Personalities and Facts. Warsaw: Państwowy Instytut Wydawniczy, 1961. 293p. illus. (P)

697 Majzel, E. The Truth about Jewish Ritual Slaughter. Łódź: Międzyzwiązkowa Komisja Organizacji Rzeźniczych, 1936. 30p. (P)

698 Marek, P. "Internal Jewish War in XVIII Century." 12 J.St. (1928): 102-178. (R)

699 Meisl, Josef. Haskalah: History of the Enlightment Movement Among Jews in Russia. Berlin: C.A. Schwetschke and Sohn, 1919. vii, 229p. (G)

700 Mirsky, Samuel Kalman. Jewish Institutions of Higher Learning in Europe: Their Development and Destruction. New York: 1955. 730p. (H)

701 Moskowitz, Moses. "Anti-Shehitah Legislation in Poland." Contemporary Jewish Record 2 no.3 (May-June, 1939): 32-42.

702 Nahman, Rabbi of Bracław. "On R. Nahman of Bracław's 'Hidden Book.'" Kirjath Sepher 44 (Jerusalem, 1969): 443ff. (H)

703 Newachowicz, Jehuda L. "The Cry of the Jehuda People." Heawar 2, (Petersburg, 1918): 195-281. (H)

704 Olechowski, Gustaw. Book of the New Faith. Warsaw: Kasa Przezorności i Pomocy Warszawskich Pomocników Księgarskich, 1919. 239p. (P)

705 Paperna, A. "Elementary Schools and Cheder." Woschod 11, (1901): 92-106 et 12, 75-99. (R)

706 Prayerbook Siddurim. (Transl. from Hebrew by S., Szenhak). Warsaw: I, Knaster, 1921. 543p. (P)

707 Purim. Warsaw: Biblioteka dla Dzieci i Mlodziezy, 1930. 7p, illus. (P)

708 Raisin, Jacob S. The Haskalah Movement in Russia. Philadelphia: Jewish Publication Society of America, 1913. 355p.

709 Rappaport, A. "Two Sources of R. Nahman's Journey to the Holy Land." Kirjath Sepher 46 (1970): 147-153.

710 "The Religious Educational Movement of Bejs-Jakow." Almanach Szkolnictwa Żydowskiego, 1 (Warsaw, 1938): 316-320. (P)

711 Rosenman, Gedalia. The Ritual Staughter Problem and Answer to Father Stanislaw Trzeciak. Białystok: Drukarnia "Technograf", 1936. 87p. (P)

712 Schauss, Hayyim. The Jewish Festivals: History and Observance. New York: Schocken Books,Inc. 1962. 316p.

713 Schechter, Solomon. Studies in Judaism. Philadelphia: The Jewish

Publication Society of America, 1911. xxv. 366p.

714   Schiper, Ignacy.   "Haskalah Beginnings in the Lands of Central Poland." M. Żyd. 4 (1932): 319-324. (P)

715   Scholem, Gershom Gerhard. On the Kabbalah and its Symbolism. New York: Schocken Books, Inc., 1965. v, 216p.

716   Scholem, Gershom Gerhard.   Major Trends in Jewish Mysticism. London: Thomas and Hudson, 1955. xv, 456p.

717   Scholem, Gershom Gerhard. The Messianic Idea in Judaism and Other Essays on Jewish Spirituality. New York: Schocken Books, Inc., 1971. viii, 376p.

718   Seidman, Hillel.   The Truth About Ritual Slaughter: Response to Father Stanisław Trzeciak. Warsaw: F. Hoesick, 1936. 87p. (P)

719   Shatzky, Jacob.   Cultural History of Haskalah in Lithuania. Buenos Aires: 1950. 231p. illus. (Y)

720   Shtern, Yekhel. Elementary School and Higher Religious Education. New York: YIVO Insitute for Jewish Research, 1943. (Y)

721   Shulvass, Moses Avigdor. Dates and Chronicles from the History of the "Torah-Labor" Movement in Poland. Warsaw:1935. 88o. (Y)

722   Shulvass, Moses Avigdor. "The Story of Torah Learning in Eastern Europe." Between the Rhine and the Bosphorus. Chicago:1964. pp. 70-95.

723   Statement of Jewish Clergy in Poland Concerning Ritual Slaughter. Warsaw: Omnium, 1936. 37p. (P)

724   Tishby, I.   "The Spreading of Ramhal's Kabbalistic Writings in Poland and Lithuania." Kirjath Sefer. 45, (1969), pp. 127-154. (H)

725   Trzeciak, Stanislaw.   Ritual Slaughter in Light of the Bible and Talmud. Warsaw: Księgarnia Kroniki Rodzinnej, 1935. 71p. (P)

726   Urbach, E., Werblowsky, R.J. Zwi., and Wirszubski Chaim, eds. Studies in Mysticism and Religion Presented to Gershom G. Sholem on His 70th Birthday by Pupils, Colleagues and Friends. Jerusalem: Magness Press, Hebrew University, 1967. 387 et 235p.

727   Walden, Aron.   The Name of the New Sage.   2 vols.   Warsaw:1864. (H)

728   Weissberg, Max.   The New Hebraic Enlightments Literature in Galicia: A Literary - Historical Characteristic. Leipzig und Vienna: M. Breitenstein, 1898. 88p. (G)

729   Załudkowski, Elias. Culture-Bearers of Jewish Liturgy.   Detroit, Mich.: 1930. xv, 351p. (Y))

730   Związek Rabinów Rzeczypospolitej Polskiej.   By-Laws of the Association of Rabbis of Polish Commonwealth. Warsaw:1921. 9p. (P)

13
Hasidism

731 Aescoly, Aaron Ze'ev. Introduction to the Study of Religious Heresies Among the Jews. Kabbalah, Hasidism: Critical Essay. Paris: P. Genthner,1928. 202p. (F)

732 Alfasi, Yitshak. Hasidism. Tel-Aviv: Sifriat Maariv, 1974. 269p. illus. (H)

733 Aron, Milton. Ideas and Ideals of the Hassidim. New York: The Citadel Press, 1969. 350p.

734 Bacon, I. "On the Character of the Letter Against the Besht." Zion, 32 (1967): 116-122. (H)

735 Baer, Y.F. "The Religious - Social Theory of 'Sepher Hasidim'." Zion, 3 (1937): 1-50. (H)

736 Bałaban, Majer. "Hasidism." Ha'tekufait, 18 (1923): 488-502. (H)

737 Bloch, Hayim. Hasidic Congregation: Their Growth and Their Teaching, Their Life and their Work. Berlin: B. Harz, 1920. 352p. (G)

738 Brawer, Michael. Tzaddik Zevi. Vienna: 1931. 111p. (H)

739 Buber, Martin. Ecstatic Confessions. Jena: E. Diederichs, 1909. 238p. (G)

740 Buber, Martin. For the Sake of Heaven. Philadelphia: Jewish Publication Society of America, 1953. 316p.

741 Buber, Martin. Hasidic Books (also published in English by Schocken Books in New York, 2 vols.1947-1948, as Tales of the Hasidism in translation of Olga Marx). Hellerau: J. Hegner, 1928. xxxi, 717p. (G)

742 Buber, Martin. Hasidism (trans. by Greta Hort and others). New York: Philosophical Library, 1948. 208p.

743 Buber, Martin. Hassidism and Modern Man (edited and translated by Maurice Friedman). New York: Horizon Press, 1958. 256p.

744 Buber, Martin. The Legend of the Baal-Shem (translated by Maurice Friedman). New York: Harper, 1953. 222p.

745 Buber, Martin. The Origin and Meaning of Hasidism (edited and translated by Maurice Friedman). New York: Horizon Press, 1960. 254p.

746 Buber, Martin. The Way of Man According to the Teaching of Hasidism. New York: The Citadel Press, 1966. 41p.

747 Bunam, Simha. "Hasid of Inwardness." In The Golden Tradition, edited by Lucy S. Dawidowicz, pp.96-99. New York: 1967.

748 Chajes, Chaim. "Baal Szem Tow with the Christians." M. Żyd. 4 (1934): 440-459 et 550-565. (P)

749 Dan, Joseph, ed. The Hasidic Novella. Jerusalem: Mosad Bialik, 1968. 188p. (H)

750 Dinur, Ben Zion. On the Turn of Generations. Jerusalem: 1955. 383p. (H)

751 Dresner, Samuel H. The Zaddik: The Doctrine of the Zaddik According to the Writings of Rabbi Yaakov Yosef of Polnoye. New York and London: Abelard-Schuman, 1960. 312p.

752 Dubnov, Semen Markovich. History of Hasidism. (Translated from Hebrew by A. Steinberg), Berlin: Judischer Verlag, 1931. 2 Vols. (G)

753 Dubnov, Semen Markovich. "Sources to History of Hasidism." In Geschichte des Chassidismus, (Berlin) 1 (1931) 273-312. (G)

754 Dubnov, Semen Markovich. "The Meddling of Russian Authorities in the Struggle Against Hasidism (1800-1801)." J.St. 3 (1910): 84-109 et 253-282. (R)

755 Ehrenkranz, Benjamin Wolf. Rug Beater. Przemyśl: 1869. 39p. (H)

756 Elimelech, of Leżajsk. Pentateuch Commentaries. New York: 1955/1956. 100p. (H)

757 Elimelech of Leżajsk. Speeches of Elimelech. New York: 1955/1956. 100p. (H)

758 Ettinger, S. "The Hasidic Movement, Reality and Ideals." Cahiers D'Histoire Mondiale 11 (1967): 251-266.

759 Federbush, Simon, ed. Hasidism and Zion. Jerusalem: 1963. 298p. (H)

760 Frenkel, Jeremiasz. "Growth of Hasidism Among Jews in Post-Partition Poland (1795-1918)." ŻPO 1, 504-517. (P)

761 Frenkel, Jeremiasz. "Hasidism Among Jews of the Old Commonwelth." ŻPO 1, 281-288. (P)

762 Galant, I. "From the History of the War with Zaddikism (1859-1866)." Zbirnyk Prat Jewrejskiej Istoryczno - Archeologicznoj Komisji (Kijów) (1929): 313-344. (U)

763 Gulkowitsch, Lazar. The Cultural History Aspect of Hasidism. Tartu, Estonia: Acta et Commentationes Universitatis Tartuensis (Dorpatensis), 1938. 104p. (G)

764 Gulkowitsch, Lazar. Hasidism: Religious Scientific Examination. Leipzig: E. Pfeiffer, 1927. 81p. (G)

765 Guttman, Mathias Ezekiel. The Wisemen of Hasidism. Tel-Aviv: 1952/1953. 240p. (H)

766 Horodezky, Samuel Aba. Hasidism and the Hasids. Tel-Aviv:1957. 4 Vols in 2. (H)

767 Horodezky, Samuel Aba. Religious Currents Among the Jewry, With Special Consideration of Hasidism. Bern und Leipzig: E. Birchjer, 1920. xii,260. (G)

768 Jacobs, Louis. Hasidic Prayer. New York: Schocken Books, 1973. ix,195.

769 Jacobs, Louis. "Hassidism." Judaism. 18, 1969, 337-342.

770 Jacobs, Louis. Tract on Ecstasy. London: Vallentine and Mitchell, 1963. 195p.

771 Kazis, Israel Joseph. Hasidism: A Study in the Sociology of History of Religion: From the Beginning of the Movement (1740) until 1804. Cambridge, Mass.: Harvard University Press, 1939. xi, 499.

772 Klausner, J. "The Internal Struggle of the Communities of Russia and Lithuania and the Recommendations of R. Simeon Wolfowicz." HaAvar 19 (1972): 54-73. (H)

773 Landau, Bezalel and Ortner, Natan. The Holy Rabbi from Belz. New York: 1967. 288p. illus. (H)

774 Langer, Mordecai Georgo. Nine Gates to the Chassidic Mysteries, translated by Stephen Jolly. New York: The McKay Co., 1961. 266p.

775 Löwenkopf, Anne N. The Hasidism: Mystical Adventures and Ecstatics. Los Angeles: Shelbourne Press, 1973. x, 163p.

776 Maggid, D. G. "On History of the War with Hasidism." Perezhitoye 2 (1910): 116-129. (R)

777 Mahler, Raphael. Hassidism - Haskalah in Galicia and the Congress Kingdom of Poland in the First Half of the 19th Century. Merhavya, Israel: 1961. 519p. (H)

778 Maimon, J. L., ed. Book on Besht. Jerusalem: Mosad Harav Kuk, 1960. 319p. (H)

779 Mandel, Arnold. Everyday Life of Hasidic Jews: From the 18th Century to Today. Paris: Hachette, 1974. 182p. (F)

780 Marek, P.S. "The Crisis of Jewish Autonomy and Hasidism." J.St. 12 (1928): 45-101. (R)

781 Marek, P.S. "Internal War Among Jews in the 18th Century." J.St. 12 (1928): 102-178. (R)

782 Nachman, Ben Sim Hah. From the World of Rabbi Nahman of Bratzlav. Jerusalem: Cultural Division, Dept. for Education and Culture in the Diaspora. 98p.

783 Nachman, Ben Sim Hah. A Voice Calls Out to God Based on the Works of Rabbi Nachman of Breslov and His Holy Disciples. Brooklyn, N.Y.: Mesivta Heichal Hakodesh, n.d.. 62p.

784 Nadav, M. "Rabbi Avigdor ben Haim's Struggle against Hasidism." Zion 36 (1971): 200-219. (H)

785 Newman, Louis Israel, compiler and translator in collaboration with Samuel Spitz. The Hasidic Anthology: Tales and Teachings of the Hasidim; the Parables, Folk Tales, Fables, Aphorisms, Epigrams, Sayings, Anectodes, Proverbs and Exegetical Interpretations of the Hasidic Masters and Disciples; Their Lore and Wisdom. New York and London: C. Scribner's Sons, 1934. xc, 720.

786 Perl, Joseph. Checking the Path of the Pious Zaddik. Prag: M.J. Landau, 1838. 120p. (H)

787 Perl, Joseph. Disclosure of the Mysteries. Lwów: M.J. Poremba, 1864. 70p. (H)

788 Piekarz, Mendel. "The Fathers of Hasidism in the Writings of a Lithuanian Preacher." Molad. 4 (1971), 298-303. (H)

789 Piekarz, Mendel. Studies in Braclaw Hassidism. Jerusalem: 1972. 244p. (H)

790 Prager, Moshe. "When Hasidim of Ger Became Newsman." In The Golden Tradition, edited by Lucy S. Dawidowicz, pp. 210-213.

791 Rabinowicz, Harry M. Guide to Hassidism. New York: T. Yoseloff, 1961. 163p.

792 Rabinowitsch, Wolf Zeev. Karlin Hasidism : Its History and Teaching. Tel-Aviv: Gebr. Hershbaum, 1935. 129p. illus. (G)

793 Rabinowitsch, Wolf Zeev. Lithuanian Hasidism. New York: Schocken Books, 1971. xiii, 263.

794 Raphael, Itzhak. Book of Hasidism. Tel-Aviv:1955. 564p.illus. (H)

795 Rubinstein, Aryeh, ed. Hasidism. Jerusalem: Keter Books, 1975. 120p. (H)

796 Rubinstein, Aryeh. "Notes to an Anti-Hasidic Tract." Tarbiz 39 (1962): 80-97. (H)

797 Rubinstein, Aryeh. "The Social Element in Hasidism." Gesher 22 (1960): 64-73. (H)

798 Rubinstein, Aryeh. "The Writings of R. Jacob Isaak Horovitz, the 'Seer of Lublin'." Kirjath Sepher 37 (1961): 123-126. (H)

799 Schatz (-Uffenheimer), Rivka. "Anti-Spiritualism in Hasidism: Studies in the Teachings of Schneur Zalman of Lida." Molad 20 (1962): 513-528. (H)

800 Schatz (-Uffenheimer), Rivka. "The Essence of the Hasidic Zaddik: Studies in the Teachings on the Zaddik in the Writings of Elimelech of Leżajsk." Molad 18 (1960): 365-378. (H)

801 Schatz (-Uffenheimer), Rivka. Hasidic Mysticism. Jerusalem: Magnes Press, 1968. vi, 192p. (H)

802 Schatz (-Uffenheimer), Rivka. "The Messianic Element in Hasidic Thought." Molad 1 (1967): 105-111. (H)

803 Schneersohn, Joseph Isaac. The 'Tzemach Zaddik' and the Haskala Movement, translated by Zalman I. Posner. Brooklyn, N.Y.: 'Kehot' Publication Society, 1962. 127p.

804 Scholem, Gershom Gerhard. "Besht Beyond His Legend." Evidences 12 (1960): 15-24. (F)

805 Scholem, Gershom Gerhard."Devekut, or Communion with God." The Review of Religion (January, 1950): 115-139.

806 Scholem, Gershom Gerhard. "Mysticism and Society." Diogenes (New York) 58 (1967): 1-24.

807 Scholem, Gershom Gerhard. "The Neutralization of the Messianic Element in Early Hasidism." Journal of Jewish Studies 20 (1969): 25-55.

808 Shazar, Zalman. "The Idea of Redemption in Hasidic Thought." In Time of Harvest: Essays in Honor of Abba Hillel Silver. New York: MacMillan (1963): 401-420.

809 Tishby, Israel. "The Messianic Idea and Messianic Aims in the Development of Hasidism." Zion 32 (1967): 1-45. (H)

810 Wander, N. "The First Prohibition of Publication of Hasidic Works." Tagim 1 (1969): 31-48. (H)

811 Weinryb, Bernard D. "Hassidim and Hassidism." In his The Jews of Poland. (Philadelphia, 1972): 262-303.

812 Weiss, J. "The Great Maggiod's Theory of Contemplative Magic." Hebrew Union College Manual. 31 (1960), 137-147.

813 Weiss, J. "R. Nahman of Bracław's Burnt Book." Kirjath Sefer.

45, (1970), 253-270. (H)

814 Weiss J. "R. Nahman of Bracław's Hidden Book on the Advent of the Messiah." Ibid. 44, (1969): 279-297. (H)

815 Weiss, J. "Via Passiva in Early Hasidism." Journal of Jewish Studies. 11(1960), 137-153.

816 Wiesel, Elie. Four Hasidic Masters and Their Struggle Against Melancholy. South Bend: University of Notre Dame Press, 1978. 131p.

817 Wilensky, Mordechai. Hasidim and Mitnaggedim: A Study of the Controversy between Them in the Years 1772-1815. 2 Vols. Jerusalem: Mosad Bialik, 1970. (H)

818 Wilensky, Mordechai. "Remarks Concerning the Controversy Between the Hasidim and the Mitnaggedim." Tarbiz, 30, (1961), 396-404. (H)

819 Ysander, Torsten, Bp. Studies of Besht's Hasidism in its History of Religions Special Field. Uppsala: Lundeguistska Bokahandeln. 1933. xxii, 430. (G)

820 Zinberg, Israel. Hasidism and the Enlightment, (1780-1820). Cincinnati: Hebrew Union College Press, 1976. xxi, 298.

14
Culture, Arts, Press and Folklore

821 Abramovitch, Raphael R., ed. The Vanished World. New York: Forward Association, 1947. 575p. illus. (Y)

822 Bałaban, Majer. "Fortified Synagogues in the Eastern Borderlands." Nowe Życie. Warsaw: 1 (1924): 197-203. (P)

823 Bałaban, Majer. Historical Monuments of Jews in Poland ... and the Report of the Institute of Judaic Studies in Warsaw for the Academic Years 1927/28 - 1928/29. Warsaw: Towarzystwo Krzewienia Nauk Judaistycznych, 1929. lxvi, 156p.illus. (P)

824 Bałaban, Majer. "Jewish Historical Antiquities in Poland." J.St. Petersburg: 1 (1909) 55-71. (R)

825 Bałaban, Majer. Jewish Learning and Institutions for Jewish Learning in Poland. Warsaw: 1927. 16p. (P)

826 Bałaban, Majer. "The March of Jewish Cultural Elements from the Rhine to the Vistula and the Dnieper." La Pologne 3 (Warsaw, 1933) 191-216. (G)

827 Bałaban, Majer. On the History and Art History of the Jews in Poland. Vienna: R. Löwit, 1927. 25p. (G)

828 Bałaban, Majer. "On the History of Hebrew Printshops in Poland." Soncino-Blätter. Berlin: 3 (1929), 1-51 et 65. (G)

829 Bałaban, Majer. "On the History of Jewish Printshops in Poland." Almanach Moment. Warsaw: (1921), 189-208. (Y)

830 Beregovskiy, Moisei Yakovlevich. Jewish Instrumental Folk-Music. Kiev: 1937. 28p. illus. (Y)

831 Borzemińska, Zofia. "Miesięcznik Żydowski (Jewish Monthly) -- On the Fiftieth Anniversary of the First Issue." BŻIH 3/119 (July-September 1981): 63-75. (P)

832 Breier, Alois, et al. Wooden Synagogues in Poland. Vienna: 1934. 68p. illus. (G)

833 Bystron, Jan Stanislaw. Notes on Ten Folksongs of the Polish

Jews. Warsaw: Książnica Polska Towarzystwa Nauczycieli Szkół Wyższych, 1923. 16p. (P)

834 Centnerszwerowa, R. "Culture and Education of Polish Jews: the Oldest Monuments of the Culture of Polish Jews." Izraelita 13-23 (Warsaw, 1905), 146-147; 158-160; 711-712; 182-183; 190-192; 202-204; 215-216; 227-228; 239-240; 249-252; 263-264. (P)

835 Czajkowski, P. "The Jewish Press in Poland." Przegląd Judaistyszny 3 (1922), 197-212. (P)

836 Dawidowicz, David. Polish Synagogues and Their Destruction. Jerusalem: 1960. 96p. illus. (H)

837 Dawidowicz, David. "Toward the Origins of the Use of Wood for Religious Building by the Jews of Poland." In Sefer Zeevi (Haifa, 1966): 94-103. (H)

838 Dawidowicz, Lucy S., ed. The Golden Tradition: Jewish Life and Thought in Eastern Europe. New York: Holt, Reinhart and Winston, 1967. 502p.

839 Dobroszycki, Lucjan and Kirschenblatt-Gimblatt, Barbara. Image Before My Eyes: A Photographic History of Jewish Life in Poland: 1864-1939. New York: Schocken Books, 1977. xviii, 269p. illus.

840 Drożdżynski, Aleksander, ed. and tr. Jewish Wise Sayings, illustrated by Szymon Kobylinski. Warsaw: 1961. 177p. illus. (P)

841 Eden, S. "The Institute of Higher Jewish Learning." In Samuel Kalman Mirsky, editor Mosdot Torah B'Eiropa B'Vinyanim Uve' hurbanam. New York: 1956, 561-584. (H)

842 Fater, Isaschar. Jewish Music in Poland Between the Two World Wars. Tel-Aviv: Velt-Federatsye Fun Poylishe Yidn., 1970. lxxviii, 424p. illus. (Y)

843 Fiszer, Artur. "Folklore and History of Jewish Customs." BŻIH 1/77 (January-March, 1971): 17-42. (P)

844 Flinker, David et al. The Old Jewish Press. Tel-Aviv: 1975. 688p. illus. (Y)

845 Friedberg, Bernhard. History of Hebrew Typography in Poland: from the Beginning of the Year 1534 to its Development Up to Our Days. Tel-Aviv: 1950. 195p. (H)

846 Fuks, Marian. From a Musical Diary: Profiles, Essays and Sketches. Warsaw: Żydowski Instytut Historyczny w Polsce, 2 vols. (vol.1, 1977.400p. and vol.2, 1983. 352p. illus.) (P)

847 Fuks, Marian. "The Jewish Press in Poland of the 19th and first Half of the 20th Century (to the end of World War II)." Rocznik Historii Czasopiśmiennictwa Polskiego 12, 1 (Warsaw, 1973): 27-56. (P)

848 Fuks, Marian, et al. eds. The Polish Jewry: History and Culture.

Warsaw: 1982. 196p. illus.

849 Gaster, Theodor Heryl. Festivals of The Jewish Year: A Modern Interpretation and Guide. New York: W. Sloane Assoc., 1964. xii, 308p.

850 Goldstein, Maksymiljan and Dresdner, K. R. Culture and Art of Jewish People in Polish Lands: Collections of Maksymiljan Goldstein. Lwów: M. Goldstein, 1935. xi, 208p. illus. (P)

851 Gomer, Abba. Contributions to Culture and Social History of the Lithuanian Jewry in 17th and 18th Centuries. Bochum: 1930. 67p. (G)

852 Grotte, Alfred. German, Czech and Polish Types of Synagogues From XI till the Beginning of XIX Century. Leipzig: Gesellschaft zur Erforschung jüdischer Kunstdenkmaler, 1915. vii, 104p. illus. (G)

853 Grotte, Alfred. "Synagogues" In his Kirchen in Silesien. Berlin: G. Hackebeil, 1930. pp. 3-12. (G)

854 Grotte, Alfred. Traces of the Synagogues in Silesian Churches. Wrocław: M. Marcus, 1937. 67p. (G)

855 Hafftka, Aleksander. "The Jewish Press in Poland to 1918." ŻPO 2 (Warsaw, 1935): 148-161. (P)

856 Heiman, H. "Cultural Political Life of Jews in Galicia." Haeszkol 1900. pp. 221-231. (H)

857 Hertz, Aleksander. Jews in Polish Culture. Paris: Instytut Literacki, 1961. 284p. (P)

858 Hertz, Aleksander. "Sabbath Lights are Extinghuished." Kultura, (1959), 5/139, 11-25; 6/140, 11-21. (P)

859 Herzog, Marvin I. The Yiddish Language in Northern Poland: Its Geography and History. Bloomington: Indiana University Press, 1965, xxix, 323p.

860 Heschel, Abraham Joshua. The Earth is the Lord's: The Inner World of the Jew in East Europe. New York: H. Schuman, 1950. 109p. illus.

861 History of Jewish Printing in Poland. Warsaw: 1949. 181p. illus. (Y)

862 Jamiński, Z. The Jewish Press in Poland. Lwow: 1936. 8p. (P)

863 Katz, J. "Jewish Civilization as Reflected in the Yeshivot, Jewish Centers of Higher Learning." Cahiers D'Histoire Mondiale 10 (Paris, 1967): 674-704.

864 Krajewska, Monika. The Time of the Stone. Warsaw: Interpress, 1982. 200p. illus. (G)

865 Kruszyński, Josef. Jewish Jargon. Włocławek: Księgarnia Powszechna, 1921. 49p. (P)

866 Kubiakowa, A.   "Jewish Monumental Architecture in Poland." BŻIH,(1953) Nr. 2-3 (6-7) et Nr. 4/8. (P)

867 Lebensohn, Micah Joseph. Jewish Songs. Wilno: 1887. (H)

868 Lewin, Izaak. From History and Tradition: Essays on History of Jewish Culture. Warsaw: Państwowy Instytut Wydawniczy, 1983. 241p.(P)

869 Lewin, Louis. "From the Jewish Cultural Struggle." Jahrbuch der jüdische literarischen Geselschaft. Frankfurt a/M. Xii, 1918. 165-197p. (G)

870 Levit, Tonja. Development of Jewish Folk Character in Poland. Wilno: J. Lewin, 1931. 119p. (G)

871 Lukomskii, Georgii. Jewish Art in European Synagogues: From the Middle Ages to the 18th Century. London and New York: Hutchinson, 1947. 182p. illus.

872 Majer, Dawid. "Jewish Libraries in Poland." Bicher-Welt (1922): 467-475. (Y)

873 Marstejn, Michal. Several Words on the Israelite Schools. Brody: Drukarnia J. Rosenheima, 1972. 19p. (P)

874 Mieses, Mateusz. "Participation of Polish Jews in Science and Learning: 19th Century and the Beginning of the 20th." ŻPO 2, 24-59. (P)

875 Miodunka, Władysław. "Names of Jewish Inns - Taverns in Poland." Językoznawca (1968): 86-93. (P)

876 Mirsky, Samuel Kalman. Jewish Institutions of Higher Learning in Europe; Their Developement and Destruction. New York: 1956. 730p. (H)

877 Mulkiewicz-Goldberg, O. "Changes in the Polish (Jewish) Village Wedding". Folklore Research Center Studies 4 (1974): 133-140.

878 Piechotka, Maria and Piechotka, Kazimierz. Wooden Synagogues. Warsaw: Arkady, 1959. 218p. illus.

879 Plantowski, Noah. History of Education Among Jews in Poland. Jerusalem: 1945/46. 46p. (H)

880 Plastic Arts by Jews in Poland. Warsaw: Yidish Bukh, 1964. 200p. illus. (Y)

881 Podhorizer-Sandel, Erna. "Dictionary of Jewish Artists." BŻIH 2/82 (April-June, 1972): 91-105. (P)

882 Podhorizer-Sandel, Erna. "The Exhibition of Works of Art in the Museum of the Jewish Historical Institute." BŻIH 4/80 (October-December, 1971): 65-73. (P)

883 Podhorizer-Sandel, Erna. "Jewish Society for Propagation of Fine

Arts." BŻIH 3/91 (July-September, 1974): 37-51. (P)

884 Rechtman, Abraham. Jewish Ethnography and Folklore. Buenos Aires: 1958. 352p. illus. (Y)

885 Rejduch-Samkowa, Izabella. "Polish Characteristics of Judaica in XIX century Artistic Craftsmanship." BŻIH Nr. 4/112. (November-December, 1979) pp. 87-100. (P)

886 Ringelblum, Emanuel. "On the History of Jewish Books and Printing in Poland in the Second Half of the 18th Century." BŻIH. 41, 1962. (P)

887 Rojchflajsz and Weiss L. Manual for Libraries. Warsaw:1929. 76p. (Y)

888 Roth, Leon. Jewish Thought as a Factor in Civilization. Paris: UNESCO, 1961. 64p.

889 Rozenfeld, Morris. Songs of the Ghetto. Translated from Yiddish. Warsaw: M.J. Rundo, 1906. 93p. (P)

890 Rszumot. Collection of Memoirs, Ethnogaphy and Jewish Folklore. Odessa - Tel-Aviv: Bialik and Rawnicki, 1920-1930. 6 vols. (Y)

891 Rubinstein, A. "The Pamphlet Collection of Popular Songs in Manuscript." Aresheth, Jerusalem, 3, 1961, 193-230. (H)

892 S-owa, M. "To the Question of Cultural and Economic Situation of Polish Jews." Jewrejskij Mir 2 (Petersburg, 1910): 222-229. (R)

893 Sandel, Józef. "On the Planned Historical Lexicon of Jewish Artists in Poland." BZIH 11 (1950): 19-20. (P)

894 Sandel, Józef. "Jewish Religious Art." In Straty Wojenne Zbiorów Polskich w Dziedzinie Rzemiosła Artystycznego. (Warsaw, 1953): 91 ff. (P)

895 Sandel, Jozef. Jewish Motifs in Polish Art. Warsaw: 1954. 301p. illus. (Y)

896 The Saved Culture: A Catalogue of an Exhibition of the Polish Jewry's Culture. Warsaw: Muzeum Narodowe, 1983. 140p. illus. (P)

897 Schiper, Ignacy. "Jewish Plastic Art in the Old Commonwealth." ŻPO 1, 308-336. (P)

898 Schiper, Ignacy. "Polish Jews and Fine Arts: (Music and Song - Theatre - Painting, Graphics, Sculpture - Artistic Industry) Until 1918." ŻPO 2, 114-147. (P)

899 Slutsky, Y. "Poland and Russia." Jewish Art and Civilization, edited by Geoffrey Widoger, pp.376-380. Vol.1. Fribourg: Office du Livre, 1972.

900 Stand, Adolf. "Jewish 'Moderna' in Galicia." Safrus (Warsaw, 1905): 30-40. (P)

901   Styczeń, Jan.   "Polish Inns."   Perspektywy 13 (1970): 28-31 illus.
(P)

902   Szyszko-Bohusz, A.   "Materials to the Architecture of Synagogues in Poland."   Kwartalnik Historii i Sztuki   (Kraków, 1927): 4,1.   11 ff.
(P)

903   Tartakower, Arieh.   "Jewish Culture in Poland Between the Two World Wars."   Gedank un Leben 4 (April-June 1946): 22-24.   (Y)

904   Vishniac, Roman.   Polish Jews: A Pictorial Record, with an Introductory Essay by Abraham Joshua Heschel.   New York: Schocken Books, 1947.   16p. 31 plates.

905   Vishniac, Roman.   A Vanished World, with a Foreword by Elie Wiesel.   New York: Farrar, Straus and Giraux, 1984.   192p. and 200 photographs.

906   Weissberg, M.   "Our Libraries and the Statistics of the Readers."   Literarisze Bleter (Warsaw, 1926): 2, 603-605.   (Y)

907   Werner, Alfred.   "Pioneers in Jewish Painting."   In Polish Jew, 11th Year Book, American Federation of Polish Jews (New York, 1944): 23-32.

908   Widoger, Geoffrey.   Jewish Art and Civilization.   Fribourg: Office du Livre, 1972.   2 vols. (1 vol. 376p. and 2 vol. 380p.)

909   Wischnitzer, Rachel.   The Architecture of the European Synagogue.   Philadelphia: Jewish Publication Society of America, 1964.   xxxii, 312p. illus.

910   Wischnitzer, Rachel.   "Synagogues in the Former Kingdom of Poland."   In Das Buch von der Polishen Juden,   edited by Agnon, S.J. and Eliasberg, Ahron, 85-105.   Berlin: 1916.   (G)

911   Yarmolinsky, A.   "On the Iconography of Eastern European Jews."   YIVO Bleter 28 (1946): 254-272 illus.   (Y)

912   Zajczyk, Szymon.   "Architecture of Baroque Stone Synagogues in Poland."   Biuletyn Naukowy Zwiazku Artystow Plastykow Polskich 4 (Warsaw, 1939):   (P)

15
Literature and Linguistics

913   Alejchem. (Rabinowitz) Szalom, <u>Deluge</u>. Warsaw: 1910. 458p. (H)

914   Altbauer, M. "More About Alleged 'Khazar' names of localities in Polish Lands." <u>Onomastica</u>. 13 (1968), 120-128. (P)

915   Altbauer, M. <u>Polish Language in the Jewish School</u>. Warsaw: 1934. 8p. (P)

916   <u>Anthology of Hebrew Poetry</u>. Transl. from Hebrew by Zew Szeps. London: Oficyna Poetów i Malarzy, 1974. 200p. (P)

917   Asch, Shalom. <u>Glory Be to the Name of the Lord: an Epic of 1648</u>, transl. from Yiddish by Rufus Learsi. New York: Arno Press, 1975.

918   Asch, Shalom. <u>Motke the Thief</u>. Warsaw: 1930. 347p. (Y)

919   Asch, Shalom. <u>Three Cities: a Trilogy (Petersburg, Warsaw, Moscow)</u>. New York: G.P. Putnam, 1933. 899p.

920   Bałaban, Majer. "Historical Basis of Opatoshu's." <u>Nowe Życie</u>. 2 (Warsaw, 1925): 334-348. (P)

921   Bałaban, Majer. "Historical Motifs in Opatoshu's Novel." <u>Bichervelt</u> (1922): 518-520. (Y)

922   Bałaban, Majer. "What Was the Spoken Laguage of Jews in Poland: In Response to the Book of Mrs. R. Centnerszwerowa." In his <u>Z Historii Żydów w Polsce</u>. (Warsaw, 1920): 22-31. (P)

923   Behr, Isachar F. <u>Poem of a Polish Jew</u>. Mietau und Leipzig: J. F. Hinz, 1772. 96p. (G)

924   Behr, Isachar F. <u>Supplement to the Poem of a Polish Jew</u>. Mietau und Leipzig: J. F. Hinz, 1772. 32p. (G)

925   Belmont, Leo. "The Servants of the Reborn Ghetto." <u>Zjednoczenie</u> 1 no.3 (Warsaw, November 13, 1951): 5-9. (P)

926   Bialik, Hayyim Nahman. <u>Two Languages - The Speech Problem of the</u>

Jews. Kaunas, Lithuania: Tarbut, 1930. 24p. (Y)

927   Bialik, Hayyim Nahman. Collected Works. Tel-Aviv: 1934. 282p.
(H)

928   Borochow, Ber. "How Old is the Yiddish-German Language with the Eastern Jews?." Pinkas (Wilno, 1913): 1-65. (Y)

929   Borochow, Ber. Selected Works. Warsaw: 1938. (P)

930   Borochow, Ber. "An Unpublished Letter (Borochow's Letter to the Editors of 'Der Frajnd' Regarding Reform of Jewish Grammar." Literarisze Bleter 51 (Warsaw, 1927): p.1001. (Y)

931   Brandstaetter, Roman. Jerusalem of Light and Darkness, a Poem. Warsaw: Nakładem Dwutygodnika "W Drodze," 1935. 13p. (P)

932   Brandys, Kazimierz. Samson. Warsaw: Czytelnik, 1948. 226p. (P)

933   Bursztyn, Michoel. By the Rivers of Mazovia. Moscow: 1941. 150p. (Y)

934   Centnerszwerowa, Róża. About the Language of Jews in Poland, Lithuania and Russia, Historical Essay. Warsaw: Księgarnia Powszechna, 1907. 43p. (P)

935   Cohn, Eduard. German, Polish or Yiddish? Considerations and Documents to the Question of Eastern Jews, by a Germano-Judaus (pseud.) Berlin: C.A. Schwetschke und Sohn, 1916. 34p. (G)

936   Cohn, J. "The Jargon Problem." 29 Izraelita, (Warsaw, 1887): (P)

937   Czynski, Jan. The Peasant King and the Jewess. Transl. from French by F. Funck. Prague: R. Brandeis, 1912. 287p. (G)

938   Dykman, S. "The Rebirth of Poland in Hebrew and Jewish Literature and Poetry." GGŻ 2, no.10-11 (1938): 299-302. (P)

939   Ehrenkranz, Benjamin Wolf. Makel-Noam: Folksongs in Polish-Jewish Dialect, with Hebraic Translation. Lwów: B. Lorje, 1869. 164p. (G)

940   Eliasberg, Alexander. Legends of Polish Jews: Collected and Transl. from Yiddish by Alexander Eliasberg. München: Georg Miller, 1916, 220p. (G)

941   Erter, Isaac, Watchman For The House of Israel: A Collection of Satirical Sketches. Edited by Meir Halevi Letteris. Warsaw: Alapin, 1908. 213p. (H)

942   Ettinger, Elzbieta. Kindergarten. Boston: Houghton Mifflin Co., 1970. 310p.

943   Fallek, Wilhelm, ed. Song Above Songs. Transl. from Hebrew by Z. Bromberg-Bytkowski. Łódź: 1924. (P)

944   Feldhorn, Juliusz. "For the Jewish Fairy-Tale and Legend in

Polish Language." M. Żyd. 1930/1931, 1, 266-268. (P)

945 Feldman, Wilhelm. Belittlers of the Giants: Literary Polemical Essays. Stanisławów: A. Stardacher, 1905. 132p. (P)

946 Fenster, A.H. "Twenty Years of Jewish Literature in Reborn Poland." GGŻ 2 no.10-11 (1938): 307-310. (P)

947 Frank, Bruno. THe Daughter: A Novel. Mexico, D.F.: El Libro Libre, 1943. 322p. (Y)

948 Frenkel, Jeremjasz. "New-Hebraic Literature in Poland." ŻPO 2 (1933): 60-73. (P)

949 Garfeinowa-Garska, Matylda Maria. The Story of the Polish Soul; The Fathers by Marja Zabojecka. Warsaw: Towarzystwo Wydawnicze, 1918. 234p. (P)

950 Glatstein, Jacob. The Selected Poems of Jacob Glatstein. Translated by Ruth Williams. New York: October House, 1972. 185p. illus.

951 Glicksman, William M. "The Halutz Ideology and Experience as Reflected in the Yiddish Novel in Poland, 1919-1939." YIVO Annual 14, (1969): 270-284.

952 Glicksman, William. In the Mirror of Literature: The Economic Life of the Jews in Poland as Reflected in Yiddish Literature, 1914-1939. New York: Living Books, 1966. 254p.

953 Gordon, Aaron David. Selected Essays. New York: Arno Press, 1973. xv, 303.

954 Hollaenderski, Leon. Meditations of a Prisoner: Poems. Paris: by the author, 1861. vii, 101p. (F)

955 Hollaenderski, Leon. Moschek: Polish Customs. Paris: Paulet Malkassis et De Broise, 1859. 268p. (F)

956 Howe, Irving and Greenberg, Eliezer, eds. A Treasury of Yiddish Stories. Drawings by Ben Sahn. New York: 1965. 620p. illus.

957 Howe, Irving and Greenberg Eliezer, eds. Voices from the Yiddish: Esays, Memoirs, Diaries. New York: Schocken Books, 1975. 332p.

958 Jaszuński, J, "Natural Sciences in Yiddish Literature." Bicher-Welt 7 (1928): 17-26. (Y)

959 Kacyzne, Alter. Collected Writings. Tel-Aviv: 1967, 1969. 2 vols. (Vol. I 320p; Vol. II 346p.) (Y)

960 Kapłun-Kogan, Wladimir Wolf. Jewish Language and Cultural Community in Poland: Statistical Study. Berlin -Vienna: R. Löwitt, 1917. 23p. (G)

961 Khayes, S. "Names of Galician Towns in Yiddish Sources." YIVO

bleter 7 (Wilno,1934): 229-242. (Y)

962   Kinderfreund, Aleksander. Bankrupts.   Warsaw: Gebethner i Wolff, 1892. 317p. (P)

963   Korczak, Janusz (pseud. of Goldszmit, Henryk). Selected Works of Janusz Korczak, translated from Polish by Jerzy Bachrach. Washington D.C.: National Science Foundation, 1967. lix, 742p.

964   Korczak, Janusz (pseud. of Goldszmit, Henryk). Selection of Works Introduced and Selected by Igor Newerly..Warsaw: Nasza Księgarnia, 1958. 4 vols. illus. (P)

965   Korczak, Janusz (pseud. of Goldszmit, Henryk).   Summer Camps. Warsaw: Książka: 1946. 151p. (P)

966   Kraushar, Aleksander. (pseud.Alkar) Strophes.   Kraków: Gebethner i Wolff, 1923. xii, 242. (P)

967   Kruszyński, Józef.   The Jewish Jargon.   Włocławek: Drukarnia Diecezjalna, 1921. 49p. (P)

968   Kupfer, Efraim F. and Strelcyn, Stefan.   Mickiewicz in Hebrew Translations. Wrocław: Zakład im. Ossolińskich, 1955. 34p. (P)

969   Lebensohn, Abraham Dob Baer.   Songs in the Sacred Hebrew Language. Wilno: 1861-1869.   3 vol. in 2.   (H)

970   Lebensohn, Micah Joseph.   Jewish Songs.   Wilno: 1869.   xii, 68p. (Y)

971   Lebensohn, Micah Joseph.   The Violin of Zion.   Wilno: 1870.   108p. (H)

972   Leftwich, Joseph, ed.   An Anthology of Modern Yiddish Literature. The Hague: Mouton and Co., 1974.   346p.

973   Lestchinsky, Jacob. "Jewish Language in Independent Poland." YIVO Bleter 22, no.2 (New York: November-December, 1943): 147-162. (Y)

974   Linetzki, Isaac Joel.   A Polish Youngster.   Lwów: 1896.   144p. (Y)

975   Liptzin, Solomon.   A History of Yiddish Literature.   Middle Village, New York: Yonathan David, 1972. x, 521p.

976   Łastik, Salomon and Słucki, A.   Anthology of Jewish Poetry. Warsaw: Państwowy Zakład Wydawniczy, 1983.   554p. (P)

977   Łastik, Salomon.   Jewish Literature Until the Classic Period Warsaw: 1950. 227p. illus.   (Y)

978   Madison, Charles A.   Yiddish Literature - Its Scope and Major Writers. New York: F. Ungar Publishing Co., 1968. xii, 540p.

979   Mapu, Abraham. Hypocritical Vulture.   Warsaw: 1925.   308p. (H)

980 Mapu, Abraham. <u>Lovers of Jerusalem</u>. Transl. from Hebrew by Bernard Chapira. Paris: L. Rodstein, 1946. 271p. (F)

981 Mapu, Abraham. <u>The Wine of Samaria</u>. Warsaw: 1911. 224p. (H)

982 Mark, Yudel. "The Yiddish Language: Its Cultural Impact." <u>American Jewish Historical Quarterly</u>. 59, no.11 (1969): 201-209.

983 Meltzer, Shimshon. <u>The Book of Ballads and Poems</u>. Tel-Aviv: 1949/1950. 314p. (H)

984 Meyersohn, Malwina. <u>David: A Glimpse from the Life of Contemporary Jews</u>. Warsaw: S. Silbersztejn, 1869. iv, 132p. (P)

985 Mieses, Mathias. <u>The Reason for the Origin of Jewish Dialect</u>. Vienna: R. Löwitt, 1915. 120p. (G)

986 Miron, D. <u>A Traveller Disguised: The Rise of Modern Yiddish Fiction in the Nineteenth Century</u>. New York: Schocken Books, 1973.

987 Nomberg-Przytyk, Sara. <u>Samson's Pillars</u>. Lublin: Wydawnictwa Lubelskie, 1966. 159p. illus. (P)

988 Nossig, Alfred. <u>Abarbanel: The Drama of a People</u>. Berlin: H. Steinitz, 1906. 64p. (G)

989 Nussbaum, Hilary. <u>Leon and Lajb: Social-Religious Study</u>. Warsaw: S. Orgelbrand's Sons, 1883. 136p. (P)

990 Olszewska, Maria. "King Maciuś the First - From a Novel to Film Scenario." In <u>Studia z Historii Literatury dla Dzieci i Młodzieży</u>. (Warsaw, 1971): 106-127. (P)

991 Opas, Tomasz. "Remarks Concerning the Influence of the Polish Language on Origins and Development of Family Names of Polish Jews in Earlier Ages (Second Half of the 16th to the end of the 18th Centuries)." <u>BŻIH</u> 89 (1974): 47-63. (P)

992 Opatoshu, Joseph. <u>In Polish Woods</u>, translated by Isaac Goldberg. Philadelphia: The Jewish Publication Society of America, 1938. 392p.

993 Pizem-Karczag, Ida. "The Jewish 'Trilogy' of Julian Stryjkowski." <u>Polish Review</u>. 28, (1983), 4, 89-97. (P)

994 Rappaport, Zenon. <u>Memoirs of a Vampire, or Vampire in the Artistic-Literary World: Glimpses, Sketches, Episodes, Biographies, Causeries, Customs' Outlines, Together With Minor Comedies, Smaller Works and Translations</u>. Warsaw: A. Lewiński, 1861. 2 vols in 1. illus. (P)

995 Rappoport, Solomon. (pseud. S. Ansky). <u>Collected Works</u>. Wilno, Warsaw and New York: 1922-1924. 6 vols. (Y)

996 Rappoport, Solomon. (pseud. S. Ansky). <u>The Dybbuk: Between Two Worlds</u>. (Transl. with a Biographical and Bibliographical Note and Introduction by S. Morris von Engel. Winnipeg, Manitoba:1953.xxviii,68p.

997 Roskies, David G. THe Genres of Yiddish Popular Literature, 1790-1860. New York: Max Weinreich Center for Advanced Jewish Studies, 1975. 30p.

998 Rudnicki, Adolf. The Rats. Warsaw: Towarzystwo Wydawnicze "Rój", 1932. 217p. (P)

999 Sadan, Dov. Yiddish Literature in Interwar Poland. Jerusalem: 1964. 160p. (H)

1000 Safrin, Horacy. By the Sabbatical Tallow Candles: Jewish Humour. Łódź: Wydawnictwo Łódzkie, 1966. 291p. (P)

1001 Sarnicki, Klemens. A Grammar of the Hebrew Language. Lwów: Nakładem Autora, 1899. viii, 354. (P)

1002 Schiper, Ignacy. "Colloquial Language of Polish Jews and Their Popular Literature in the Old Commonwealth." ŻPO. 1, 225-229. (P)

1003 Schiper, Ignacy. "Growth of Jewish Literature in Post-Partitioned Poland." ŻPO 2 (1933): 91-102. (P)

1004 Schultz, Bruno. The Street of Crocodiles. Transl. from Polish by Celina Wieniawska. New York: Penguin, 1977. 159p.

1005 Shulman, Abraham. The Old Country. New York: Charles Scribner's Sons, 1974. x, 210p. illus.

1006 Singer, Isaac Bashevis. The Collected Stories. New York: Farrar, Strauss, Giroux, 1982. viii, 610p.

1007 Singer, Isaac Bashevis. The Family Moskat, translated by A. H. Gross. New York: Farrar, Strauss and Giroux, 1965. 611p.

1008 Singer, Israel Joshua. The Brothers Ashkenazi. Transl. from Polish by Maurice Samuel. New York: Alfred A. Knopf, 1945. 642p.

1009 Stankiewicz, E. "Yiddish Place Names in Poland." In The Field of Yiddish, edited by Max Weinreich, pp.158-181. 1965.

1010 Stryjkowski, Julian. On the Willows our Fiddles. Warsaw: Czytelnik, 1974. 252p. (P)

1011 Stryjkowski, Julian. The Inn. Transl. from Polish by Celina Wieniawska. New York: Harcourt Brace Jovanovich, 1972. 205p.

1012 Szeps, Zew, ed. Anthology of Jewish Poetry (1868-1968). London: Oficyna Poetów i Malarzy, 1980. 368p. (P)

1013 Szulkin, Michał. "Articles of Janusz Korczak in the Columns of W Słońcu (In the Sun) Journal, 1919-1926." BŻIH 4/104 (1977): 49-53. (P)

1014 Teitelboim, Dora. "Shmulik - A Poem." Transl. from Yiddish by Aaron Kramer. The Polish Review xxiv, no.1 (1979): 62-63.

1015 Tilleman, O. "Hebrew Literature in Reborn Poland." GGZ 2, 10-11

(1938): 303-306. (P)

1016 Trunk, Jehiel Isaiah. Idealism and Naturalism in Jewish Literature. Warsaw: 1927. 234p. (Y)

1017 Weiner, Leo. The History of Yiddish Literature in the 19th Century. New York: C. Scribner's Sons, 1899. xv, 402p.

1018 Weinreich, Uriel. College Yiddish: An Introduction to the Yiddish Language and to the Jewish Life and Culture. N.Y. YIVO, 1953. 399p.ill.

1019 Weinreich, Uriel, ed. The Field of Yiddish: Studies in Language, Folklore and Literature. The Hague: Mouton, 1965. vii, 289.

1020 Weinreich, Uriel. History of the Yiddish Language: Concepts, Facts, Methods. New York: YIVO, 1973. 4 vols. (Y)

1021 Weinreich, Uriel and Weinreich, Beatrice. Yiddish Language and Folklore, a Selective Bibliography for Research. The Hague: Mouton, 1959. 66p.

1022 Weissberg, Max. "Literary Jewish Language in Galicia." KŻP. 2(1912), 1-16 et 3(1913), 101-132. (P)

1023 Weissberg, Max. "New-Hebraic Literature of Enlightment in Galicia." Monatsschrift für Geschichte und Wissenschaft des Judentums. 71 (1927), 54-62 et 100-109. (G)

1024 Wenig, N. "Myth of Yiddishism." M. Żyd. 26(1932), 566-568. (P)

1026 YIVO. Studies in Philology. 2 vols. Wilno: Vilner Farlag B. Kletskin, 1928. (vol.1, 428p; vol.2, xxviii, 515p.) (Y)

16
Jews in Polish Literature

1027 Bałaban, Majer. "The Polish Jews in the Memoires of Polish Noblemen." Menorah (Vienna, 1927): 382-383. (G)

1028 Bałucki, Michal. The Jewess: The Novel From the Last Years. Warsaw: Lewental, 1889. 266p. (P)

1029 Bartoszewicz, Włodzimierz. The Shanty in Powiśle. Warsaw: Państwowy Instytut Wydawniczy, 1966. 251p. (P)

1030 Begey, Atille. André Towiański and Israel: Documents (1842-1864) With a Letter of Władysław Mickiewicz to the Author. Rome: G. Romagna and Company, 1912. vii, 134p. (F)

1031 Belmont, Leo. "The Jews in the Mirror of Polish Literature: An Essay for the Monograph." Izraelita, (1907), pp. 39-40, 51-52, 74-76 et 111-112. (P)

1032 Bełza, Władysław. Jews in Polish Poetry: Poets' Comments About Jews. Lwów: H. Altenberg, 1906. xii, 104p. (P)

1033 Borowy, Wacław. "Emancipation of the Jews as Pictured in the Polish Novel." Pamiętnik Literacki 22-23 (1924): 394-403. (P)

1034 Brandstaetter, Roman. I'm a Jew from 'The Wedding'. Poznan: 1983. 60p. illus. (P)

1035 Brodowski, Feliks. Symcha's Child. Warsaw: E.Wende i Spółka, 1905. 27p.

1036 Bronikowski, Alexander. Moina. Dresden: Arnold, 1827. 208p. (G)

1037 Buczkowski, Leopold. Black Torrent. Translated from Polish by David Welsh. Cambridge, Mass.: MIT Press, 1970. 200p.

1038 Chciuk, Andrzej. The Story of Atlantis: The Great Duchy of Bałak. London: Polska Fundacja Kulturalna, 1969. 234p. (P)

1039 Czapska, Maria. Star of David: A History of One Family. London:

Oficyna Poetów i Malarzy, 1975. 135p. illus. (P)

1040 Daniłowski, Gustaw. Over the Ravine. Warsaw: E. Wende i Spółka, 1905. 25p. (P)

1041 Detko, Jan. "The National Aspect of the Jewish Question with Eliza Orzeszkowa." BŻIH 40 (October-December, 1961): 50-65. (P)

1042 Duker, Abraham G. "Adam Mickiewicz's Anti-Jewish Period: Studies in the Books of the Polish Nation and of the Polish Pilgrimage." In Salo W. Barron's Jubilee Volume. Jerusalem, American Academy for Jewish Research (1975): 311-343.

1043 Duker, Abraham G. "Mickiewicz and the Jewish Problem." In Adam Mickiewicz, Poet of Poland: A Symposium, edited by Manfred Kridl, pp.108-125. New York, Columbia Slavic Studies, 1951.

1044 Duker, Abraham G. "The Mystery of the Jews in Mickiewicz's Towianist Lectures on Slav Literature." Polish Review 7. no.3 (Summer, 1962): 40-66.

1045 Fajnhauz, Dawid. "From the Early Public Activity of Julian Klaczko." BŻIH no.43-44 (1962): 41-47. (P)

1046 Fallek, Wilhelm. "Jewish Creativity in Polish Literature, Until 1918." ŻPO vol.2 (1933): 74-90. (P)

1047 Fallek, Wilhelm. "Jewish Participation in the Literature of Reborn Poland." GGŻ 2, 10-11 (1938): 311-312. (P)

1048 Feldhorn, Julius. "Broken Monument: (Jewish Motifs in the Poetry of Cyprian Norwid)." Miesięcznik Żydowski (1928): 8-26. (P)

1049 Frank-Kapłanowa, B. "Jewish Participation in Polish Literature for National Freedom." GGŻ 2, 10-11 (1938): 297-298. (P)

1050 Fredro, Aleksander. Mr. Geldhab. Kraków: Przełom, 1945. 63p. (P)

1051 Gawroński, Franciszek. Jews in History and Folk Literature in Ruthenia. Warsaw: Gebethner i Wolf, 1924. xii, 266p. (P)

1052 Gołubiew, Antoni. Szaja Ajzenstok: The Three Menorahs. Kraków: Społeczny Instytut "Znak", 1985. (P)

1053 Gomulicki, Wiktor Teofil. Gabardine. Warsaw: E. Wende i Spolka, 1900. 36p. (P)

1054 Grubiński, Wacław. The Jewish Princess. Warsaw: F. Hesick, 1927. 107p. (P)

1055 Grynberg, Henryk. "The Jewish Theme in Polish Positivism." Polish Review 25 (3-4) (1980): 49-57.

1056 Hertz, Benedykt. Jewish Blood. Warsaw: Ludwik Fiszer, 1938. 48p. (P)

1057 Hollender, Tadeusz. Poland without Jews: A Satirical Novel. Lwów: Wydawnictwo "Wierch," 1937. 387p. (P)

1058 "Jednacz" (pseud.). "The Jewish Question in the Light of Polish Messianism ..." Pochodnia 1 (1919): 165-177. (P)

1059 Jeske-Choiński, Teodor. The Jew in the Polish Novel: A Study. Warsaw: Księgarnia Kroniki Rodzinnej, 1914. 105p. (P)

1060 Kasprowicz, Jan. "Szaja Ajzensztok." In Israel in Polish Poetry ed. by J. Winczakiewicz (Paris, 1958): 159-161. (P)

1061 Konopnicka, Maria. Mendel of Gdańsk. Warsaw: E. Wende i Spółka, 1905. 30p. (P)

1062 Korzeniowski, Jozef. The Jews: A Comedy in Four Acts. Złoczów: Wilhelm Zukerkandel, 1894. 104p. (P)

1063 Kościałkowska, Janina. "The Walking Willows." Wiadomości 34. no.21/1730 (Londyn, May 27, 1979): p.1. (P)

1064 Kot, Stanisław. "Poland: Paradise for the Jews, Hell for the Peasants, Heaven for the Nobility." Kultura i Nauka (Warsaw, 1937): 255-282. (P)

1065 Krasiński, Wincenty Korwin. Glance over Polish Jews by a Polish General. Warsaw: 1818. 54p. (F)

1066 Krasiński, Zygmunt. Undivine Comedy. Paris: A. Pinard, 1835. 164p. (P)

1067 Kraszewski, Józef Ignacy. Correspondence with Leopold Kronenberg, 1859-1876. Kraków: Gebethner i Wolff, 1925. xxxi, 466p. (P)

1068 Kraszewski, Józef Ignacy. Diseases of the Century: Pathological Study. Lwów: Księgarnia Gubrynowicza i Schmidta, 1874. 2 vol. in 1. (P)

1069 Kruszyński, Józef. Stanisław Staszic and the Jewish Question. Lublin: Lubelski Komitet Obchodu Setnej Rocznicy Zgonu Stanisława Staszica, 1926. 53p. (P)

1070 Kryński, Magnus J, "Politics and Poetry: The Case of Julian Tuwim." Pol. Rev. 18, (1973) 4, 3-33.

1071 Kusniewicz, Andrej. Zones. Warsaw: Państwowy Instytut Wydawniczy, 1971. 507p. (P)

1072 Levine, Madeline G. "Julian Tuwim: We, The Polish Jews." The Polish Review. 17, (1972), 4, 82-89.

1073 Loew, Chaim. " Jews- Romantics: A. Słonimski" M. Żyd., 2 (1933), 9/10. 153-161. (P)

1074 Loew, Chaim. " Wyspiański and the Jews: on the 25th Anniversary of His Death." Warsaw: Menorah, 1932. 19p. (P)

1075 Lukashevich, Olga. "Bruno Schulz's 'The Street of Crocodiles.'" The Polish Review 13, (1968), 2, 63-79.

1076 Lukaszewski, Witold. "The Unknown Letters of Maurycy Mochnacki to Antoni Ostrowski, 1833-1834." Kuznica 14/187 (Lodz, April 10, 1949): 5 ff. (P)

1077 Makuszyński, Kornel. The Fatal Pin: A Frightening but Deeply Moving Story. Warsaw: Wesoła Biblioteka, 1925. 165p. (P)

1078 Melcer, Wanda. The Black Continent. Warsaw: Dom Książki Polskiej, 1936. 175p. (P)

1079 Mickiewicz, Adam. "Concert Above All Concerts." In his Pan Tadeusz. Warsaw: Arkady, 1959. 351-356. (P)

1080 Mieses, Matthias. Jews in Poland and its Literature. Podgórze: S.H. Deutscher, 1905. vii, 64. (H)

1081 Niemcewicz, Julian Ursyn. Lejbe and Siora: or the Letters of Two Lovers-A Jewish Romance. Kraków: Gebethner i Wolff,1931. xi, 191. (P)

1082 Niemcewicz, Julian Ursyn. The Year 3333: or the Unheard of Dream. Warsaw: "Polak-Katolik", 1911, 31p. (P)

1083 Niemojewski, Andrzej. The Jewish Soul as Mirrored in the Talmud. Warsaw: 1920. 196p. (P)

1084 Norwid, Kamil Cyprian. "Polish Jews." In Israel in Polish Poetry ed. by J. Winczakiewicz, pp. 104-105. (P)

1085 Oberlaender, Ludwik. "Adam Mickiewicz's Jewish Complex." M. Żyd. 11, (May 1932) 1, 467-474. (P)

1086 Oppman, Artur. (pseud. Or-Ot) "Berek Jawor." In Israel in Polish Poetry, edited by J. Winczakiewicz, pp. 174- 177. Paris: 1958. (P)

1087 Orzeszkowa, Eliza. Eli Makower. Warsaw: Książka i Wiedza, 1950. 2 vols. in 1. (P)

1088 Orzeszkowa, Eliza. "Give Me a Flower." Translated from Polish by Szymon Deptuła. In Joseph L. Baron, editor, Candles in the Night: Jewish Tales by Gentile Authors. Philadelphia: The Jewish Publication Society of America, 1940. 209-239.

1089 Orzeszkowa, Eliza. Meir Ezofovitch: A Novel translated by Iza Young, with illustrations by Michael Elvivo Andriolli. New York: W.L. Allison Co., 1898. 359.

1090 Orzeszkowa, Eliza et. al. The Same Stream: Sixteen Short Stories by Ten Authors. Kraków: E. Wende i Syn, 1905. (P)

1091 Orzeszkowa, Eliza. The Strong Samson. Warsaw: Książka i Wiedza, 1950. 62p. (P)

1092 Ostrowski, Krystyan Józef. The Usurer: Comedy in Three Acts.

Paris: Księgarnia Luxemburska, 1868. 98p. (P)

1093 Pruszyński, Ksawery. "The Curvet from Meshed." In His Opowieści. Warsaw: Państwowy Instytut Wydawniczy, 1970. 191-231. (P)

1094 Radliński, Ignacy. Judeo-Christian Apocrypha: Introductory Book to Apocryphal Literature in Poland. Lwów: Ksiegarnia Narodowa, 1905. 219p. (P)

1095 Rey, Sydor. Kropiwniki: A Novel. Warsaw: Księgarnia F. Hoesicka, 1937. 393p. (P)

1096 Rostworowski, Karol Hubert. Judas from Karioth: Drama in Five Acts. Warsaw: Gebethner i Wolff 1913. 206p. illus. (P)

1097 Sandauer, Artur. On the Situation of 20th Century Polish Writers of Jewish Descent: A Book Which Should be Written Not by Me. Warsaw: Czytelnik, 1982. 100p. (P)

1098 Scheps, Samuel. Adam Mickiewicz: His Jewish Affinities. Paris: Nasel, 1964. 103p. illus. (F)

1099 Seailles, Gabriel. The Jewish Question in Poland: An Inquiry Paris: Fischbacher, 1915. 66p (F)

1100 Shatzky, Jacob. "Adam Mickiewicz and the Jews." Zukunft New York (1913), pp. 120-124. (Y)

1101 Słowacki, Juliusz. "Father Marek." Three Fragments In Israel in Polish Poetry (edited by J. Winczakiewicz), pp. 68-81. (P)

1102 Słowacki, Juliusz. Jan Bielecki (Edited by Henryk Bergelsen), Lwów: 1921. 55p. (P)

1103 Szaniawski, Franciszek. "About Jews", Pamiętnik Warszawski. 1 (1815): 438-441. (P)

1104 Szaniawski, Klemens (pseud. Klemens Junosza). The Citizen from Tamka Street and Other Stories Selected and Introduced by Józef Rurawski. Warsaw: Czytelnik, 1960. 309p. illus. (P)

1105 Szaniawski, Klemens. On the Life of Affairs of a Certain Mr. Symcha Boruch Kaltkugel in Five Parts. Warsaw: Nakładem Gazety Polskiej, 1899. 2 vols in 1. (P)

1106 Szaniawski, Klemens. Our Jews in Towns and Villages. Warsaw: Nakładem Niwy, 1889. 185p. (P)

1107 Szaniawski, Klemens (pseud. Klemens Junosza). The Patcher. Warsaw: E. Wende i Spółka, 1905. 28p. (P)

1108 Sztrem, Krystyna. Unbearable Foreigners. London: Polish Cultural Foundation, 1974. 199p. (P)

1109 Szymański, Adam. "Srul from Lubartów." In Joseph L. Baron, editor, Candles in the Night: Jewish Tales by Gentile Authors.

Philadelphia: Jewish Publication Society of America, 1940. 179-191.

1110 Świętochowski, Aleksander. Chawa Rubin. Warsaw: E. Wende i Spółka, 1905. 27p. (P)

1111 Tetmajer, Kazimierz Przerwa. Miss Mary: A Novel. Warsaw: Gebethner i Wolff, 1902. 258p. (P)

1112 Trznadel, Jacek. Concerning Mieczysław Jastrun's Poetry. Wrocław: Zakład im. Ossolińskich, 1954. 136p. illus. (P)

1113 Tuwim, Julian. The Dancing Socrates and Other Poems: Selected and Translated by Adam Gillon. New York: Twayne Publications, 1968. 63p.

1114 Ujejski, Jozef. King of New Israel: A Card from the History of Mysticim of the Enlightment Century. Warsaw: Kasa im. J. Mianowskiego, 1924. 177p. (P)

1115 Vincenz, Stanisław. The Jewish Themes. London: Oficyna Poetów i Malarzy, 1977. 219p. (P)

1116 Wilczyński, H. Jewish Characters in Polish Literature. Warsaw: 1928. 227p. (Y)

1117 Winczakiewicz, Jan. Israel in Polish Poetry: An Anthology. Paris: Instytut Literacki, 1958. 354p. (P)

1118 Wyka, Kazimierz. " Regarding 'Mr. Gelhab.'" Pamiętnik Literacki. (1951): 621-646. (P)

1119 Zabierowski, Stanisław. "Who actually is Juliusz (yes!) Paduch in 'Converting Judas'?" Ruch Literacki, Kraków 6 (1971): 356-364. (P)

1120 Zahorska, Stefania. "Smocza Street No. 13: Drama in Three Acts." Nowa Polska 9 (London,1944): 604-613 et 10, 654-668. (P)

1121 Zapolska, Gabriela. The Antisemitnik: A Novel. Lwów: Lektor, 1921. 139p. (P)

1122 Zapolska, Gabriela. "Malka Szwarcenkopf." In her Dramaty, edited by Anna Raszewska, pp.437-562. Vol.1. Wrocław: Zakład Narodowy im. Ossolińskich, 1960. (P)

1123 Zapolska, Gabriela. The Man (Ahaswer): Play in Three Acts. Krakow: D.C. Friedstein, 1902. 156p. (P)

1124 Życzynski, Henryk. "Aesthetic Analysis of A. Mickiewicz's Jankiel Concert." Miesięcznik Pedagogiczny 6/7 (1924): 168-185. (P)

17
Theatre

1125 Arnstein, Marc. <u>Noem: Drama in Three Acts.</u> Warsaw: Gebethner i Wolff, 1912., 89p. (P)

1126 Erckmann, Emille. <u>Polish Jew: Drama in Three Acts and Five Scenes.</u> Paris: J.Hetzel et Cie, 1867. 84p. (F)

1127 Erik, Max. "The Inventory for Yiddish Theatre Literature." <u>Cajtszrift.</u> 2-3 (Mińsk, 1928): 345-348. (Y)

1128 Ettinger, Solomon. <u>Serkele, or the Wrong Season: Comedy in Five Acts, Shown in Lwów.</u> Warsaw: 1875. 80p. (Y)

1129 Feldman, Wilhelm. <u>God's Trials: Drama in Four Acts From Jewish Life in Galicia.</u> Warsaw: J. Fiszer, 1899. 119p. (P)

1130 Feldman, Wilhelm. <u>Miracle Maker: Play in Four Acts.</u> Warsaw: Księgarnia J. Fiszera, 1901. 121p. (P)

1131 Glass, Montagu Mardsen. <u>Potash and Perlmutter: A Play in Three Acts.</u> London: S. French Ltd., 1935. 114p.

1132 Goldfaden, Abraham. <u>Goldfaden-Book</u> New York: Jewish Theatrical Museum, 1926. 100p. (Y)

1133 Goldfaden, Abraham. <u>Shulamit.</u> Warsaw: 1921. 70p. (Y)

1134 Gordin, Jacob. "Mirele Efros" In <u>Jüdisches Theater</u>, edited by A. Eliasberg, pp.197-326. München: 1919. (Y)

1135 Gorin, Bernard. <u>History of Yiddish Theater.</u> 2 vols in 1. New York: 1929. (Y)

1136 Kaminska, Ida. <u>My Life, My Theater.</u> Translated by Curt Leviant. New York: Macmillan, 1973. ix, 310p. illus.

1137 Kozłowski, Józef. "The Defeated Turned Victors - Polish Workmen's Drama Staged in Jewish Theater." <u>BŻIH</u> no.3/95 (1975): 53-60. (P)

1138 Kozłowski, Józef. "G. Hauptmann's 'Weavers' on Jewish Stage at the turn of the 19th Century." BŻIH 4/100 (1976): 95-101. (P)

1139 Lebensohn, Abraham Dob Ber. Faith and Truth. Wilno: 1870. x. 286p. (H)

1140 Levinsohn, Isaac. The Miraculous World. Warsaw: 1903. 75p. (Y)

1141 Mehnan, M. "Jewish Theatre in Poland: A Short Outline of Its Activity up to Day." Teatr no.5 (Warsaw 1950): (P)

1142 Młodożeniec, Stanisław. Herod: Tragedy in Three Acts Staged in Warsaw in 1934. (P)

1143 Rotbaum, Jakub. "Andrzej Pronaszko's Co-operation with Jewish Theatres: A Handful of Personal Reminiscences." BŻIH 3/79 (1971) 69-74. (P)

1144 Sandrow, Nahma. Vagabond Stars: A World History of Yiddish Theater. New York: Harper and Row, 1977. xi, 435p. illus.

1145 Schiper, Ignacy. History of Theater and Drama of the Jews. Warsaw: 3 vols. 1923-1928. (Y)

1146 Shatzky, Jacob, ed. Archives for the History of Jewish Theater and Drama. Vol. I. New York: 1930., 534p. (Y)

1147 Shatzky, Jacob. "A Model for a Theatrical Lexicon." Literarisze Bleter (Warsaw, 1928): 537-539. (Y)

1148 Szczepański, J.A. "An Excellent Theatre: Jewish State Theatre in Poland." Poland, Illustrated Magazine 4/20, pp.22-24. Warsaw: Polonia, 1956.

1149 Turkow-Grudberg, Isaac. Jewish Theatre in Poland. Warsaw: Yiddish Bukh, 1951. 199p. (Y)

1150 Turkow-Grudberg, Isaac. "Yiddish Theatre in Poland Between the Two World Wars." In Sefer Ha-Shanai Yorbukh 2 (1967): 325-358. (Y)

1151 Turkow-Grudberg, Isaac. Warsaw, the Cradle of Jewish Theatre. Warsaw: Yiddish Bukh, 1956. 74p. (Y)

1152 Zangwill, Israel. The Melting Pot: Drama in Four Acts. New York: Macmillan Co., 1939, ix. 215p.

1153 Zgliński, Daniel. Jakób Warka: Contemporary Drama in Four Acts. Warsaw: Gebethner i Wolff, 1893. 115p. (P)

18
Frankism and Neophytes

1154 Abraham of Szarogród. "The Terrible Deed in Podolia (A Story of Frank and Izrael from Miedzyborze)." In Majer Bałaban, editor, Quellen und Studien zur frankist Bewegung in Polen. Warsaw: 1927, 25-75. (P)

1155 Arnsberg, Paul. From Podolia to Offenbach: The Jewish Salvation Army of Jacob Frank, to the History of the Frankist Movement. Offenbach, Stadtarchiv: Geschichtsblätter no.14, 1965. 56p. (G)

1156 Bałaban, Majer. The History of the Frankist Movement. 2 vols. Tel-Aviv: 1934-1935. 320p. (H)

1157 Bałaban, Majer. "On the Frankist Movement." He' Atid (1913) 122-150. (H)

1158 Bałaban, Majer. "Studies and Sources to the History of the Frankist Movement in Poland." In Livre d'hommage a La Memoire du Dr. Samuel Poznański. (Warsaw, 1927): 25-75. (G)

1159 Berman, J. "Materials to the History of the Jews in Poland at the End of 18th Century: Resolution on the Neophites' (Frankists) for Right of Residents in Warsaw, 1775." Junger Historiker 1 (Warsaw, 1926): 102-106. (Y)

1160 Bosak, Meir. "Mickiewicz, Frank and the Conquest of Eretz - Israel." Molad 13 no.87 (October, 1955): 430-440.

1161 "Cathechism on Jews and Neophytes." MSC 6 (Warsaw, 1969): 466-480. (P)

1162 Didier, Stanisław. The Role of Neophites in Polish History. Warsaw: Mysl Narodowa, 1934. 130p. (P)

1163 Duker, Abraham Gordon. "Polish Frankism's Duration: From Cabbalistic Judaism to Roman Catholicism and from Jewishness to Polishness." JSS 25 (1963): 287-333.

1164 Duker, Abraham Gordon. "Some Cabbalistic and Frankist Elements in Adam Mickiewicz's Dziady." In Studies in Polish Civilization, edited by Damian Wandycz, pp.213-235. New York: Institute on East Central Europe and The Polish Institute of Arts and Sciences in America, (n.d.).

1165 "Frank's Court." MSC 6 (Warsaw, 1969): 176-182. (P)

1166 Gelber, Nathan Michael. "To the History of Frankist Propaganda in the Year 1800." In Aus Zwei Jahrhunderten, (Vienna, 1924): R. Löwitt, 265p. (G)

1167 Gershuni, Henry. "The Converted Nobleman." In Sketches of Jewish Life and History. (New York, 1873): 187-224.

1168 Graetz, Heinrich Hirsch. Frank and the Frankists: History of a Sect from the Last Half of the Previous Century. Wrocław: Jüdisch - Theologisches Seminar, Breslau. Jahresbericht, 1868. xxxv, 90p. (G)

1169 Jeske-Choiński, Teodor. Polish Neophytes: Historical Materials. Warsaw: Drukarnia P. Laskauera, 1904. 289p. (P)

1170 Katz, Jacob. Jews and Freemasons in Europe 1723-1939, translated by Leonard Oschry. Cambridge: Harvard University Press, 1970. viii, 293p.

1171 Kraushar, Alexander. Frank and His Community. Transl. from Polish by Nahum Sokołow. Warsaw: 1897. 287p. (H)

1172 "Letter to a Polish Friend." MSC 6 (Warsaw, 1969): 169-175. (P)

1173 Mandel, Arthur. The Militant Messiah or the Flight from the Ghetto: The Story of Jacob Frank and the Frankist Movement. Atlantic Highlands, New Jersey: Humanities Press, 1979. 185p. illus.

1174 Rabinowicz, O. "Jacob Frank at Brno." Jewish Quarterly Review, Seventy-Fifth Anniversary Volume. (Philadelphia, 1967): 429-445.

1175 "Response to One Envying Another's Posessions." MSC 6 (Warsaw, 1969): 182-187. (P)

1176 Schenk-Rink, A.G. The Poles in Offenbach. Frankfurt a/M.: 1866. (G)

1177 Scholem, Gershom. "The Career of a Frankist: Moses Dobruschka and his Metamorphoses." Zion 35 (1970): 127-181. (H)

1178 Shazar (Rubashov), Zalman. On the Ruins of Frankism. Berlin: 1922/1923. 23p. illus. (H)

1179 Skimborowicz, Hipolit. Life, Death and the Learning of Jakub, Jozef Frank. Warsaw: 1866. (P)

1180 Sulima, Zygmunt Lucjan (Przyborowski, Walery). History of Frank and the Frankists. Krakow: 1893. (P)

1181 Weinryb, Bernard. "Messianism's Aftereffect - Jacob Frank and Frankism." In his The Jews of Poland. (Philadelphia, 1972): 236-261.

1182 Wilhelm, K. "An English Echo of the Frankist Movement." Journal of Jewish Sociology, 16 (1965): 189-191.

19
Assimilation and Emancipation

1183 Aronson, Michael. "The Attitudes of Russian Officials in the 1880's Toward Jewish Assimilation and Emigration." Slavic Review, 31, no.1 (March, 1975): 1-18.

1184 Bartoszewicz, Kazimierz. The Jewish War in 1859: Origins of Assimilation and Antisemitism. Warsaw:1913. 92pp. (P)

1185 Belmont, Leo. "'No'- In Defence of a Jew Converted to the Christian Faith." Zjednoczenie 3 no.6-7 (Warsaw, June-July, 1933): 6-7. (P)

1186 Deutsch, Helene. Confrontations with Myself - An Epilogue. New York: W.W. Norton, 1973. 217p.

1187 Deutscher, Isaac. The Non-Jewish Jew and Other Essays; edited by Tamara Deutscher. London, New York: Oxford University Press, 1968. x, 164p.

1188 Eisenbach, Artur. "About Emancipation of Jews in the Kingdom of Poland." BŻIH 4/92 (1974): 71-89. (P)

1189 Eisenbach, Artur. "Emancipation of the Jews in Polish Lands in the 19th Century: With the European Comparative Background." Przegląd Historyczny 74, no,4 (Kraków, 1983): 615-629. (P)

1190 Feldman, Wilhelm. Assimilators, Zionists and the Poles. Kraków: 1893. (P)

1191 Frenk, Ezriel Nathan. Converted Jews in Poland in the 19th Century. Warsaw: 1923/24. 2 vols. 204p. (Y)

1192 Friedmann, Lazarus. Emancipation of Eastern Jews and Their Influence on the Western Jews: A Word to Justify the Time. Frankfurt: 1917. 54p. (G)

1193 Goldberg, Jakub. "Conversion and Marriage. "Kwartalnik Historyczny 91, no.1 (Warsaw, 1984): 137-144. (P)

1194 Hagani, Baruch. Emancipation of the Jews. Paris:1928. 270p. (F)

1195 Heller, C. S. "Assimilation; a Deviant Pattern Among the Jews of Interwar Poland." JJS 15 (1973) 221-237.

1196 Heller, C. S. "Poles of Jewish Background - The Case of Assimilation without Intergration in Interwar Poland." In Studies on Polish Jewry, 1919-1939, edited by Joshua A. Fishman, pp.242-276. (1974).

1197 Hemar, Marian. "Paraphrase." In Israel w Poezji Polskiej: Antologia, edited by Jan Winczakiewicz, pp.194-195. (Paris, 1958): (P)

1198 Hensel, J. "The Polish Nobles' Nation and the Jewish Middleman, 1815-1830: On the Vain Attempt for Jewish Emancipation in a Non-Emancipated Society." Forschubgen zur Osteuropaischen Geschichte vol.32 (Berlin, 1932): 114-115. (G)

1199 Katz, Jacob. Out of Ghetto: The Social Background of Jewish Emancipation, 1770-1870. Cambridge, Mass.: Harvard University Press, 1973. vi. 271p.

1200 Kirton, I. (Czaczkes). "To the History of Assimilation and Zionism in Galicia, 1880-1892." Moria (Kraków): 264-279 et 310-321. (P)

1201 Landsberger, J. "Promotion of Emancipation of South Prussian Jews by the Government." Historische Monatsblätter für die Provinz Posen. 6 (Poznan, 1903): 87-93. (G)

1202 Lewiński, A. "From Words to Deeds." Zjednoczenie. 2 no.2 (February 15, 1932): 1-2. (P)

1203 Lichten, Joseph. "About Assimilation of Jews in Poland: From the Outbreak of First World War until the End of the Second World War (1914-1945)." Zeszyty Historyczne 42 (1977): 96-134. (P)

1204 Loewenstein, Stanisław. "The Radiant Youth in Galicia." Niepodległość 10 (Warsaw,1934): 219-249. (P)

1205 Łastik, Salomon. "About the so-called Jewish War." Twórczość, 5 (Warsaw,1958): 40-43. (P)

1206 Marrus, R. "European Jewry and the Politics of Assimilation: Assessment and Reassessment." Journal of Modern History 46(1977): 88-109.

1207 Memorial Book of the First General Assembly of the Federation of Poles of Mosaic Religion from All Polish Lands. Warsaw: Zjednoczenie Polaków Wyznania Mojżeszowego Wszystkich Ziem Polskich, 1919. 100pp. (P)

1208 Mendelsohn, Ezra. "From Assimilation to Zionism in Lvov: The Case of Alfred Nossig." Slavonic and Eastern European Review 49 (London, 1971): 521-534.

1209 Mendelsohn, Ezra. "Jewish Assimilation in Lvov: The Case of Wilhelm Feldman." Slavic Review 28, 4(December, 1969):577-590.

1210 Mendelsohn, Ezra. "A Note on Jewish Assimilation in the Polish Lands." In Jewish Assimilation in Modern Times, edited by Bela Vago, 141-150. Boulder, Colorado, 1981.

1211 Mieses, Mathias. Poles - Christians of Jewish Origin. Warsaw: 1938. 2 vols. (P)

1212 The Project of By-Laws of the Federation of Poles of Mosaic Faith from All Polish Lands. Warsaw: S., Orgelbrand and Sons, 1919. 11pp. (P)

1213 Reicher, Aniela. Today's Mohicans. Melbourne: Nakładem Autorki, 1980 (P)

1214 S.H. "Types of Converted Jews." Zjednoczenie 3,5, (May, 1933) 7-10. (P)

1215 Shatzky, Jacob. "In the Drive for Total Assimilation." Yivo Bleter, 22,1 (New York: Septyember-October, 1943. (Y)

1216 Sterling, K. "The Past and Current Status of the Jewish Question in Poland." In Pamiętnik I Walnego Zjazdu Zjednoczenia Polaków Wyznania Mojżeszowego Wszystkich Ziem Polskich . Warsaw:1919. (P)

1217 Vago, Bela, ed. Jewish Assimilation in Modern Times. Boulder, Colorado: Westview Press, 1981. x. 220p.

1218 Warschauer, Jonathan. About Polonization of Galician Israelites. Kraków: Nakładem Autora, 1882. 42pp. (P)

1219 Weinryb, Bernard Dov. Jewish Emancipation under Attack, its Legal Recession until the Present War. New York: American Jewish Committee, 1942. 95pp.

20
Sociology and Social Welfare

1220 Alter, Wiktor. Man in Society. Warsaw: Swiatlo, 1938. (P)

1221 Bałaban, Majer. "Customs and Private Life of the Jews in the Old Commonwealth." ŻPO 1 (1932): 345-374. (P)

1222 Bałaban, Majer. "From one Ghetto to another, Roaming the large Polish Towns." Menorah (Vienna, 1927): 3477-354. (G)

1223 Bałaban, Majer. "Luxury Among the Polish Jews and the Fight Against It." Księga Jubileuszowa Gimnazjum im. Jana Długosza we Lwowie. Lwow:1928, pp.165-175. (P)

1224 Becker, Rafal. Nervousness Among Jews, its Varieties, Origins and its Therapy. Lwów: Snunit, 1923. 32p. (P)

1225 Becker, Rafal. The Problem of Jewish Race in Light of Theory. Warsaw: Księgarnia M.J. Freid, 1927. 53p. (P)

1226 Birnbaum, Nathan. To the Eastern Jews - Their Right. Vienna: 1915. 31pp. (G)

1227 Bischoff, Erich. Clarity in the Problem of Eastern Jews, Facts, Thoughts and Principles. Dresden: Globus, 1916. 60pp. (G)

1228 Bojarski, J.P. State of the Jews, Former and Present: Customs, Superstitions and the Future. Lwów 1891. 147pp. (P)

1229 Bornstein, I.L. "Pauperization Problems of the Jewish Population in Poland." ŻPO 2 (1933): 403-407. (P)

1230 Bornstein, I.L. "Professional and Social Structure of the Jewish Population in Poland." Sprawy Narodowościowe 13, no.1-2 (Warsaw, 1939): 1-37. (P)

1231 Bronsztejn, Szyja. "The Jewish Population of Poland in 1931." Jewish Journal of Sociology 6, no.1 (July 1964): 3-29.

1232 Buber, Martin. The Jewish Movement: Collected Essays and Addresses. Berlin: Jüdischer Ferlag, 1920. 2 vol. 222p. (G)

1233 Burszta, Jozef. The Village and the Inn: The Role of the Inn in the Life of the Villein Village. Warsaw: Ludowa Spółdzielnia Wydawnicza, 1950. 228p. illus. (P)

1234 Caro, Leopold. The Jewish Question: An Ethical Problem. Leipzig: F.W. Grünow, 1892. 66p. (G)

1235 Castellan, Georges. "Remarks on the Social Structure of the Jewish Community in Poland Between the Two World Wars." Revue Historique 249 (Paris, January-March, 1973): 77-90. (F)

1236 Circumcision from the Ritual, Surgical and Hygienic Standpoint. Warsaw: Drukarnia H.J. Rundo, 1883. 43p. (P)

1237 Czekanowski, Jan. "Anthropological Structure of the Jewish People in the Light of Polish Analysis." Jewish Journal of Sociology 2 (November, 1960) 236-243.

1238 Eisenbach, Artur. "The Health Condition of Jewish School Youth in Poland: Statistical Study Based on Official Data." Medycyna Społeczna nos.7-8 (Warsaw, 1938): 11-12. (P)

1239 Eitzen, D. Stanley. "Two Minorities - The Jews of Poland and the Chinese of the Philippines." Jewish Journal of Sociology 10, no.2 (December, 1968): 221-240.

1240 Ertel, Rachel. The Shtetl: The Jewish Townlet of Poland, from Tradition to Modernity. Paris: Payot, 1982. 321p. (F)

1241 Fishberg, Maurice. Racial Characteristics of the Jews: An Introduction to Their Anthropology with 42 Charts in Artistic Print. Münich: Ernst Reinhardt, 1913. 272p. (G)

1242 Frostig, M. Inkeeper's Problems in Galicia. Lwów: 1909. 23p. (Y)

1243 Glicksman, William M. Jewish Social Welfare Institutions in Poland: As Described in the Memorial (Yizkor) Books: Studies in Jewish Communal Activity. Philadelphia: M. Kalish Folkshul, 1976. xxii, 177p.

1244 Gliksman, Jerzy G. Polish Jews from the Occupational and Social Viewpoint: Historical Evolution, Present Situation and Future Perspective. Paris: Rieder, 1929. 196p. (F)

1245 Gliksman, Jerzy G. Occupational and Social Structure of the Jewish Population in Poland. Warsaw: Instytut Badań Spraw Narodowościowych, 1930. 55p.illus. (P)

1246 Goldman, Nachum. "Toward a Psychology of Eastern Jews." Süddeutsche Monatshefte (Münich, February 1916): 821-826. (G)

1247 Greeley, Andrew. "Ethnicity and Racial Attitudes - Case of Jews and Poles." American Journal of Sociology vol.80, no.4 (1975): 909-933.

1248 Gumplowicz, Ludwig. Race and State: Examination of the Law of the State Formation. Vienna: 1875. v.58p. (G)

1249 Gumplowicz, Ludwig. The Racial Struggle: Sociological Examinations. Innsbruck: Wagner'sche Univ. Buchhandlung, 1909. xv, 432p. (G)

1250 Halperin, I. "The Rush into Early Marriages among East European Jews." Zion 27 (1969): 36-58. (H)

1251 Heller, Celia S. "Deviation and Social Change in the Jewish Community of a Small Polish Town." American Journal of Sociology 60 (September, 1954): 177-181.

1252 Heller (Rosenthal), Celia S. "How the Polish Jew Saw His World." Commentary 18 (New York, July 1954): 70-76.

1253 Heller (Rosenthal), Celia S. "Social Stratification of a Jewish Community in a Small Polish Town." American Journal of Sociology 59 (July, 1953): 1-11.

1254 Hertz, Aleksander. "The Caste." Kultura 1/147-2/148 (Paris, 1960): 44-68. (P)

1255 Hertz, Aleksander. "Ours and the Strangers'." Kultura 9/143 (Paris, 1959): 17-25 et 10/144, pp.11-25. (P)

1256 Hertz, Jacob. The History of a Youth. New York: 1946, 589p. (Y)

1257 Hollaenderski, Leon. Philosophical and Popular Trilogy. Paris: Jaubert, 1850. 251p. (F)

1258 Hubmann, Franz, comp. The Jewish Family Album: The Life of a People in Photographs. Transl. by Miriam and Lionel Kochan, 317p. illus. Boston: Little Brown, 1975.

1259 Janecki, Marcelli. Did the Jews Obtain Nobility by Baptism in Poland? Berlin: J. Siffenfelt, 1888. (G)

1260 Jasiewicz, Krzysztof. "Elements of National Assimilation." Przegląd Socjologiczny 29 (1977): 349-391. (P)

1261 Katz, Jacob. Out of Ghetto: The Social Background of Jewish Emancipation, 1770-1870. Cambridge: Harvard University Press, 1973.

1262 Kaufmann, Fritz Mordechai. Collected Works, edited by L. Strauss, pp.264. Berlin: 1923. (G)

1263 Kligsberg, Moshe. "The Jewish Youth Movement in Interwar Poland (A Sociological Study)." In Studies On Polish Jewry, edited by Joshua A. Fishman, pp.137-278. (Y)

1264 Kowalska-Glikman, Stefania. "Mixed Marriages in the Polish Kingdom." Kwartalnik Historyczny 84, no.2 (Warsaw, 1977½. (P)

1265 Kowalska-Glikman, Stefania. "Once Again About Mixed Marriages in the Kingdom of Poland." Kwartalnik Historyczny 89, no.4 (Warsaw, 1982): 673-678. (P)

1266 Kroszczor, Henryk. "Jewish Social Organizations in the Years 1907-1915." BŻIH 3/99 (1976): 59-71. (P)

1267 Kroszczor, Henryk and Zabłotniak, Ryczard. "The Society for Protection of the Health of the Jewish Population." BŻIH 1/105 (1978): 53-68. (P)

1268 Landes, Ruth and Zborowski, Mark. "Hypotheses Concerning the Eastern European Jewish Family." In Herman D. Stein and Richard A. Cloward, eds. Social Perspectives on Behavior. (Glenview, Ill.: Free Press, 1958): 58-76.

1269 Landmann, Salcia. The Jewish Joke, Its Sociology and a Collection. Olten, Freiburg: Br. Walter-Verlag, 1968. 702p. (G)

1270 Lestchinsky, Jacob. "Aspects of the Sociology of Polish Jewry." JSS 28 no.4 (October, 1966): 195-211.

1271 Liebmann, Hersch. About Delinquency Among Jews in Poland. Warsaw: Księgarnia Powszechna, 1938. 119p. (P)

1272 Lilienthal, Regina. The Jewish Child. Kraków: 1927. 97p. (P)

1273 Mahler, Raphael. "Jews in Public Service and the Liberal Professions in Poland." JSS 6 (1944): 291-350.

1274 Nathan, Paul. The Problem of Eastern Jews: Past and Future. Berlin: Philo Verlag und Buchhandlung, 1926. 38p. (G)

1275 Opas, Tomasz. "Jews in Towns Owned by Nobles in the Lublin Region in the 18th Century." BŻIH (1968): 3-37. (P)

1276 Oppenheimer, Franz. National Autonomy for Eastern Jews: Central Organization for Lasting Peace. The Hague: 1917. 29p. (G)

1277 Osherowitch, Mendel. Towns and Townlets in the History of Jews in the Ukraine. New York: 1948. 2 vols. (Y)

1278 Roskies, David G. "Shtetl Society." Jewish Spectator 42 no.3 (Fall, 1977): 44-46.

1279 Roskies, Diane K. and Roskies, David G. The Shtetl Book. New York: KTAV Publishing House, 1975. xiii, 327p. illus.

1280 Samuel, Maurice. The World of Sholem Aleichem. New York: A.A. Knopf, 1943. vi, 331p.

1281 Sasson, Haim Hillel Ben and Ettinger, Samuel, editors. Jewish Society Through the Ages. London: Valentine, Mitchell, 1971. 352p.

1282 Schiper, Ignacy. "Sociological Basis of Jewish Religion: Critical Review of Max Weber's Work." Nowe Życie 1 (Warsaw,1924): . 39-47 et 204-210. (P)

1283 Szacki, Jerzy. "Sociological Problems of the National Question." Nowe Drogi (Warsaw, May 1970): pp. 135-143. (P)

1284 Szczepaniak, Marian. The Inn, The Village and the Manor: Propination's Role in the Great Poland Village from the middle of XVII till the end of the XVIII Century. Warsaw: Ludowa Spółdzielnia Wydawnicza, 1977, 186p. (P)

1285 Szmeruk, Chone. "The Hassidic Movement and the Arendars." Zion, 35 (1970) 182-192. (H)

1286 Szpidbaum, Henryk. "Racial Structure of Polish Jews." ZPO 2 (1933): 165-184. (P)

1287 Tartakower, Arieh and Grossman Kurt R. The Jewish Refugee New York: Institute of Jewish Affairs of the American Jewish Congress and World Jewish Congress, 1944. xiii, 676p, illus.

1288 Tartakower, Arieh. "The Jewish Refugees: A Sociological Survey." JSS 4 no.4 (1942): 311-348.

1289 Tomaszewski, Jerzy. " The Consequences of the Multi-National Structure of Poland's Population in the 1918-1939 Period for Integration Processes of Society." in Drogi Integracji Społeczeństwa w Polsce IX-XX Wieku. edited by Henryk Zieliński. Wrocław: !976. pp. 109-138. (P)

1290 Weinreich, Max. Study of Jewish Youth: Program and Research of Jewish Youth Method by the Jewish Institute of Learning. Poznań: Katolicka Spółka Akcyjna, 1935. 55p. (P)

1291 Zborowski, Mark and Herzog, Elizabeth. Life is with People: The Jewish Little Town of Eastern Europe. New York: International Universities Press, 1952. 456p.

1292 Zivier, Ezechiel. To the Question of Race and Eastern Jews. Poznan: J. Jolowicz, 1916. 41p. (G)

1293 Zlotnik, Jehuda Leib. Studies of Internal Life of Old Jewiush Communities. Montreal: 1927, 78p. (Y)

21
The Labor Movement and Class Struggle

1294 Abramsky, Chimen. "The Jewish Labor Movement: Some Historiographical Problems." Soviet Jewish Affairs 1 (London, 1971): 45-51.

1295 Auerbach, Julian. "The All-Jewish Labor Party." BZIH 50 (April-June 1964) 37-58. (P)

1296 Bross, Jacob. "The Beginnings of the Jewish Labor Movement in Galicia." YIVO, Annual of Jewish Social Science 5, 1950.

1297 Buchbinder, Naum Abramovich. History of the Jewish Workers' Movement in Russia. Wilno: 1931. 440p. (Y)

1298 Cherykower, A. "The Beginning of the Jewish Socialist Movement." Historysze Szryftn 1 (Warsaw, 1929): 469-582. (Y)

1299 Fleischer, Ziegfried. "Workers of the Austrian-Jewish Union and of the Galician Assistance Associations." Enquete über die Lage d. jüd. Bevölkerung Galiziens. Vienna: 1910. pp. 209-231. (G)

1300 Gabara, Edward and Gejler, Lazarz. "The Chronicle of the Jewish Worker and Unionist Movement in the Years 1918-1935." BŻIH 67 (1968), 133-161. (P)

1301 Garncarska-Kadari, Bina. "The Layers of Jewish Workers in Interwar Poland." Gal-ed. 3, (Tel-Aviv: 1976): 141-189. (H)

1302 Gorni, Yosef. The Union of Labor, 1919-1930: The Ideological Foundations and the Political System. Tel-Aviv: 1973. 459p. (H)

1303 Grinberg, Maria. "Struggle for the 'Right to Work' (from the History of Jewish Labor Unions in Poland)." BŻIH 3/119 (1981): 3-19. (P)

1304 Hertz, Jacob Sholem. Fifty Years in the Jewish Labor Organization. New York: 1950. 422p. (Y)

1305 Kirznic, A.D. The Jewish Labor Movement in 1905. Moscow: 1928. xi, 407p. (R)

1306 Landau, Saul Rafael. Under the Jewish Proletariat: Travel Descrtiptions from East Galicia and Russia. Vienna: L. Rosner, 1898. 80p. (G)

1307 Laskowski, Kazimierz. Jews in Work. Warsaw: Drukarnia S. Chmielewskiego "Wiek XX", 1912. 110p. (P)

1308 Marek, L. "The Beginning of the Unionist Movement Among Jewish Salesmen in Warsaw." BŻIH 58 (1966): 81-105. (P)

1309 Mark, Bernard. "Jewish Proletariat during the January-February 1905 Struggles." BŻIH 17/18 (1965): 34ff. (P)

1310 Mark, Bernard. "Jewish Workers on the Eve of 1905." BŻIH 13/14 (1955): 12ff. (P)

1311 Mendelsohn, Ezra. Class Struggle in the Pale: The Formative Years of the Jewish Workers' Movement in Tsarist Russia. Cambridge, England: Cambridge University Press, 1970. 180p.

1312 Mendelsohn, Ezra. "Jewish and Christian Workers in the Russian Pale of Settlement." JSS 30 no.4, (October, 1968): 243-251.

1313 Meyer, David. "The Present Situation of the Labor Movement in Poland." Der Wecker 3 (New York: August 16, 1924): 12-14. (Y)

1314 Mill, Josif. "The Pioneering Period of the Jewish Labor Movement." Historishe Szriftn 3, (Warsaw-Paris: YIVO, 1939) pp. 388ff. (Y)

1315 Mishkinski, Moshe. "Regional Factors in the Formation of the Jewish Labor Movement in Czarist Russia." YIVO Annual of Jewish Social Science 14 (New York,1969): 27-53.

1316 Moszkowicz, Bronislaw et al. "The Chronicle of the Jewish Worker and Unionist Movement in July-December 1923." BŻIH 75 (1970): 97-118. (P)

1317 Moszkowicz, Bronisław et al. "The Chronicle of the Jewish Worker and Unionist Movement in January-June 1924." BŻIH 1/77 (71): 79-112. (P)

1318 Moszkowicz, Bronisław et al. "The Chronicle of the Jewish Worker and Unionist Movement in July-December 1924." BŻIH 3/79 (1971): 91-119. (P)

1319 Patkin, Abraham L. The Origin of the Russian Jewish Labor Movement. Melbourne: F.W. Cheshire Pty, Ltd., 1947. 275p. illus.

1320 Piasecki, Henryk. "The Jewish Working Class in the 1905 Revolution." BŻIH 2/98 (1976): 39-52. (P)

1321 Polak, A. "The Struggle of Jewish Workers for the Equal Right to Work." Robotniczy Przegląd Gospodarczy 4 (1927): 12-15. (P)

1322 Rojter, Pinkas. Collective Book for History of Jewish Workers'

Movement. Warsaw:1921. 206p. (Y)

1323 Rywes, M. On Problems of the Jewish Proletarian Movement in Poland. Warsaw: Nasz Przegląd, 1931. 34p. (P)

1324 Soloveichik, Leontii Albertovich. The Unknown Proletariat: Study of the Social and Economic Situation of Jewish Workers. Bruxelles: H. Lamertin, 1898. 128p. (F)

1325 Szajkowski, Zosa. "Paul Nathan, Lucien Wolf, Jacob H. Schiff and the Jewish Revolutionary Movement in Eastern Europe, 1903-1917." JSS 29 (1967): 3-26.

1326 Tartakower, Arieh. "The Jewish Proletariat's Movement in the Prewar Era." ŻPO 1 (1932): 531-541. (P)

1327 Tartakower, Arieh. "The Jewish Proletariat in Poland." ŻPO 2 (1933): 570-589. (P)

1328 Żarnowska, Anna. "Ethnic Composition of the Working Class in the Kingdom of Poland at the Turn of the 19th-20th Centuries." Kwartalnik Historyczny, 80, no.4, (Warsaw: 1973): 787-816. (P)

22
Bund and Jewish Socialism

1329 Abramovitch, Raphael R. "The Jewish Socialist Movement in Russia and Poland, 1897-1919." In The Jewish People: Past and Present. New York: Jewish Encyclopedic Handbooks - Central Yiddish Cultural Organization, 1946. 2, pp. 369-398.

1330 Aronson, Gregor et al., eds. The History of Bund. New York: 1960. 4 vols. (Y)

1331 Bund in the 1905-1906 Revolution. Warsaw: 1930. 119p. (Y)

1332 The Case of Henryk Ehrlich and Victor Alter. London: Liberty Publications, 1943. 26p.

1333 Chmurner (Lestchinsky) Joseph. "The Change." Unzer Cajt 3 (Warsaw, January 1922): 5-7. (Y)

1334 Ciołkosz, Adam. "Bund in Poland in the Years 1917-1943." Unzer Cajt (New York: October-December, 1972): 65-67. (Y)

1335 Dworak, Stanisław. "Reminiscences About Jewish Worker Activists." BŻIH 47-48 (1963): 93-112. (P)

1336 Erlich Henryk and Victor Alter: Memorial Book. Buenos Aires: Agrupacion Socialista Israelita "Bund", 1943. illus. (Y)

1337 Erlich, Henryk. "A Change?" Unzer Cajt 3 (January 1929), pp.9-10. (Y)

1338 Erlich, Henryk. The Basis of Bundism. Warsaw: Algemajner Jidiszer Arbeiter Bund, 1934. (Y)

1339 Erlich, Henryk. "In the Struggle Against Revisionist Illusions." Unzer Cajt 3 (Warsaw: March-April, 1929): 1-3. (Y)

1340 Erlich, Henryk. The Struggle for Revolutionary Socialism. Transl. by Haim Kantorovitch and Anna Bercowitz. New York: The Bund Club of N.Y., 1934. 64p.

1341 Frenkel, Jonathan. Prophecy and Politics, Socialism, Nationalism and The Russian Jews, 1862-1917. New York and Cambridge: 1985. xxii. 686p. illus.

1342 Fuks, Marian. "Materials for the Bibliography of Jewish Labor and the Socialist Press in Poland in the Years 1918-1939." BŻIH 2/106 (1978): 59-89. (P)

1343 Hertz, Jacob Sholem. "The Bund in Independent Poland, 1918-1925." In Die Geshikhte fun Bund. 6 (New York: 1972). Edited by Gregor Aronson et al. pp. 219-287. (Y)

1344 Hertz, Jacob Sholem. "The Bund's Nationality Program and its Critics in the Russian, Polish and Austrian Movements." YIVO Annual of Jewish Social Science, 14, (1969): 53-67.

1345 Hertz, Jacob Sholem. Henryk Erlich and Wiktor Alter. New York:1943. 96p. illus. (Y)

1346 Hertz, Jacob Sholem. The Jewish Labor Bund. New York: Unser Tsait, 1958. 188p. illus.

1347 Hertz, Jacob Sholem and Aaronson, Gregor. The History of Bund. New York: 2 vols. illus. (Y)

1348 Hertz, S. "Several Factors Regarding the Jewish Labor Movement." Socialistyisze Bleter 1, (June 1931): 41-43. (Y)

1349 Johnpoll, Bernard K. The Politics of Futility: The General Jewish Workers' Bund of Poland, 1917-1943. Ithaca: Cornell University Press, 1967. xx, 298.

1350 Katz, Alfred. "Bund: The Jewish Socialist Labor Party." The Polish Review 10 no.3 (Summer 1965): 67-74.

1351 Kazhdan, Chaim Szlama. From Cheder and School till Tsisko: the Russian Jewry's Struggle for School, Language and Culture. Mexico City: Imprenta Moderna, 1956. (Y)

1352 Kazhdan, Chaim Szlama. "There is a Desire and a Drive." Socialistisze Bleter. 1 (June 1931): 24 ff. (Y)

1353 Kossofsky, Vladimir. "Why and How the Bund was Split?" Zukunft, 24 (1921): 38- 39. et no.26 (1921): 40-42. (Y)

1354 Kozłowski, Jozef. " The Oath of Jewish Workers." BZIH 62, (1967): 59-62. (P)

1355 Lenin, Vladimir I. "The Bund's Situation in the Party." Sochineniia 5th Edition, 8 (Moscow, 1959): 65-76. (R)

1356 Levin, Nora. While Messiah Tarried: Jewish Socialist Movements, 1871-1917. New York: Schocken Books, 1977. xi,554. illus.

1357 Medem, Vladimir. "Why I Oppose Zionism." Naye Velt 10, (New York: July 2, 1920) , p.12 ff. (Y)

1358 Medem, Vladimir. "Why the Polish Bund Did Not Break Down."
Zukunft 26 (1921): 160ff. (Y)

1359 Medem, Vladimir. "The Youth of a Bundist." GT (1967): 426-434.

1360 Menes, Abraham. "The Jewish Socialist Movement in Russia and
Poland, 1870's - 1897." In The Jewish People: Past and Present, edited
by Raphael R. Abramovitch. 2, pp. 355-368.

1361 Mus, E. "Bund and Sejm Elections." Unzer Cajt 2, (Warsaw: March-
April 1928): p.2 ff. (Y)

1362 Novogrodsky, Emanuel. "The Bund in Independent Poland Between the
Two World Wars." Unser Tsait. 17, (New York: November-December 1957)
pp. 23ff. (Y)

1363 Ohler, Leon. "The Left Wing of Bund in Poland." In Churner Bukh.
New York: Ferlag Unser Tsait, 1958, 30-31. (Y)

1364 Ozher, Mauritzi. "Our Daily Order: Socialism." Socialistisze
Bleter. 1, (June 1931): 24-25. (Y)

1365 Pizyc, H. "We and the P.P.S." Socialistisze Bleter 1 (June
1931): 11-12. (Y)

1366 Rabinowicz, Sz. "Twenty Years Back." In Socialistisze Bawegung
Byz der Grunding fun "Bund". Forschungen, Zychrojns, Materialn. Editors
E. Czerikower et al. Wilno-Paris: 1939. pp. 314-347. (Y)

1367 Rafes, Moisei Grigorevich. Sketches on the History of the "Bund."
Moscow: 1923. vii, 440. (R)

1368 Ratman, A. (pseud. of Gershom Ziebert). "The Bund in Poland." Di
Naye Velt 7, (Warsaw: September 3, 1920) : 9-19. (Y)

1369 Rowe, Leonard. "Jewish Self-Defense: A Response to Violence." In
Studies on Polish Jewry, 1919-1939. Edited by Joshua A. Fishman (New
York: 1974), 105-149.

1370 Shulman, Victor. "Medem in Poland." In Vladimir Medem Tsum
Tsvantsikstn Yortsayt. (New York: Amerikaner Representants fun
Algemajner Idishn Arbeiter Bund in Poyln, 1943. pp. 108ff. (Y)

1371 Szerer, Emanuel. Socialism and Zionism. Warsaw: Komitet Centralny
"Bundu" w Polsce, 1929. 64p. (P)

1372 "Third Conference of the General Jewish Labor Bund in Poland."
Arbeter Luach 6, (Warsaw, 1925): 243 ff. (Y)

1373 Tobias, Henry Jack. The Jewish Bund in Russia: From its Origins
to 1905. Stanford: Stanford University Press, 1972. xvii, 409.

1374 Trunk, Isaiah. "The Beginning of the Jewish Labor Movement." In
Di Geshikhte fum Bund. 1, (New York: 1959): 46-66. (Y)

1375 Wajsbrot, Jakub. "The Jewish Socialist Youth Organization

'Cukunft' in Poland." Pokolenia. 1, 3, (Warsaw: Komisja Historyczna Komitetu Centralnego Związku Młodzieży Socjalistycznej, 1963) : 43-49. (P)

1376 Wasserman, Abraham, ed. Before the Congress: Special Issue. Kraków: Żydowska Partia Socjal-Demokratyczna, June 1905. 12p.

1377 Zhabotinskii, Vladimir. The Bund and Zionism. Odessa: Kadima, 1906. (H)

1378 Zineman, Jacob. Socialism and the Jews. Warsaw: 1927. 32p. (P)

1379 Zylberfarb, M. " Several Critical Remarks About the Bund's Electoral Campaign." Unzer Cajt 2 (Warsaw, March-April, 1928) (Y)

23
Zionism and Revisionism in Poland

1380 Adler, Max. The National Idea in Light of Revolutionary Socialism and Some Remarks About Poalej-Zionism. Warsaw: Z.S.P.R. "Poalej-Sjon", 1939. 19p. (P)

1381 Asaf, Michael. "Be Bold!" Hazak ve emats 4-5 (July-August, 1919): 13-17. (H)

1382 Askenazy, Szymon. "The First Polish Zionist." Biblioteka Warszawska 12 (1908): 78-94. (P)

1383 Bardichevski, Aharon. "Chapters from History of the Pioneers' Movement in Poland." Measef le-truat he haluts. Warsaw: 1930, pp. 119-127. (H)

1384 Ben-Yeruham, H. The Book of Betar: A History and Sources. Jerusalem-Tel Aviv: 1969. 2 vols. (H)

1385 Birnbaum, Nathan. (pseud. Mathias Acher). The Stepchild of Social Democracy. Vienna: W. Fischer's Buchdruckerei, 1905. 31p. (G)

1386 Bohm, Adolf. The Zionist Movement: A Short Presentation of Its Growth. Berlin: Welt-Verlag, 1921. 2 vols in 1. (G)

1387 Czas (Special Jewish Issue of Time Daily), Krakow: Sepmber 9, 1936. (P)

1388 Droujanoff, Abraham Alter. Zionism in Poland. Tel Aviv: 1932. 125p. (H)

1389 Dubnov, Semen Markovich. "Origins of Jewish Nationalism." Jewrejskaiia Zizn. 8 (1906): 23-51. (R)

1390 Eliasberg, Ya'akov. In the Universe of Revolts and Storms. Jerusalem: 1965. 329p. illus. (H)

1391 Elmer, Aleksander. Jewish National Thought. Tarnopol: Ludowe Stowarzyszenie Sjon, 1933. 34p. (P)

1392 Endres, Franz Carl. Zionism and World Politics. Munchen, Leipzig:

Duncker und Humblot, 1918. 112p. (G)

1393 Fritz, Georg. The Question of Eastern Jews: Zionism and Frontier Closing. Munchen: I.F. Lehmann, 1915. 48p. (G)

1394 Gelber, Nathan Michael. History of the Zionist Movement in Galicia, 1875-1918. Jerusalem: 1958. 2 vols (918p) (H)

1395 Gelber, Nathan. To the Prehistory of Zionism: Jewish State Projects in the Years 1695-1845. Vienna: Phaidon Verlag, 1927. 318p. (G)

1396 Gordon, David. Zionism and Religion. Odessa: E. Sherman. 1900. (P)

1397 Grunbaum, Isaac. ed. Zionist Collection. Petersburg:1917. 79p. (Y)

1398 Hertzberg, Arthur. ed. The Zionist Idea: A Historical Analysis and Reader. Garden City, N.Y.: Doubleday, 1959. 638p.

1399 Herzl, Theodor. The Jewish State. Transl. by Jakob Appenszlak. Warsaw: M.J. Freid, 1929. (P)

1400 Horowitz, David. "Our Stand with Regard to The Youth Movement." Haszomer 9 (June-July 1918): 182ff. (P)

1401 Horowitz, David. "The Szomer-Pioneers Colony." Haszomer 1 (Łódź: September 1919): 7-10. (P)

1402 Horowitz, David. "Theses of a Report Concerning Objective Foundations of the Szomer Movement." Haszomer (Łódź: April 1, 1920): 15-16. (P)

1403 Jidiszer Arbeiter Pinkas. "From History of the Jewish Labor Movement 'Poale Cijon': Reminiscences, Materials, Documents." Warsaw: 1927. pp. 648. (P)

1404 Kantorowicz, N. "The Zionist Workers' Movement in Poland." Yearbook 1. New York: American Federation of Polish Jews, 1964. pp. 110-157. (Y)

1405 Kazenelson L. "Remembrances On the First Hacefira." Książka Jubileuszowa Hacefiry. Warsaw: 1912. 70-76. (Y)

1406 Klausner. Israel. The Awakening of the People. Jerusalem, 1962. 558p. (H)

1407 Klausner, Israel. Opposition to Herzl. Jerusalem, 1960. 259p. (H)

1408 Klejnman, Moses. "In Time of Storm." Hasziloach 42, pp. 278-282, 367-373, 465-470, 516-518. (H)

1409 Kohn, Hans. Chapters From the History of Zionist Thought. Warsaw: Biblioteka Jesodth, 1929/1930. 2 vols. (H)

1410 Lewin, Epstein A. "Scouting for the Youth." Hozak ve-emats 2 (February-March, 1919): 5-7. (Y)

1411 Lewinson, Abraham. "Fifty-Two Years of Hapoel Hacaira." M. Żyd. (April, 1933): 356-363. (P)

1412 Lipsky, Louis. A Gallery of Zionist Profiles. New York: Farrar, Strauss and Cudahy, 1956. 226p. illus.

1413 Margalit, Elkana. "Hashomer Hatzair": From Its Origin to Revolutionary Marxism, 1913-1936. Tel Aviv: 1971. 359p. (H)

1414 Margalit, Elkana. "Social and Intellectual Origins of the Hashomer Hatzair Youth Movement, 1913-1920." Journal of Contemporary History 4 no.2, (April 1969): 25-46.

1415 Measef I'tnuas he Chaluc. (Collecive Book to Celebrate the Tenth Anniversary of the Chaluc Organization) Warsaw: 1930. 336p. (H)

1416 Mendelsohn, Ezra. "Polish Zionism between the Two Wars." Dispersion and Unity 17/18 (Jerusalem, 1973): pp. 81-87.

1417 Mendelsohn, Ezra. Zionism in Poland: The Formative Years, 1915-1926. New Haven and London: Yale University Press, 1981. xi, 373p.

1418 Nossig, Alfred. Zionism and Jewishness: The Crisis and its Solution. Berlin: Interterritorialen Verlag "Renaissance", 1922. 76p. (G)

1419 Oppenheim, Israel. "Chapters in the History of the Halutz Hakshara in Poland between the Two World Wars." In Studies on Polish Jewry, 1919-1939. Edited by Joshua A. Fishman. (New York: 1974): 229-335. (Y)

1420 Otiker, Yisrael. The Hehalutz Movement in Poland, 1932-1935. Tel Aviv: 1972, 226p. (H)

1421 Pasmanik, Daniil Samoilovich. Three Lectures on Poale-Syon. Tarnopol: Verlag des Zionistischen Komitees, 1907. 48p. (G)

1422 Perelman, Jakob. Revisionism in Poland: 1922-1936. Warsaw: Wydawnictwo "Europa", 1937. xii, 370p. (P)

1423 Program of the Jewish Social-Democratic Workers' Party "Poale Syon". Warsaw: Młot, 1918. 19p. (P)

1424 Rakowski, Puah. "A Mind of My Own." In The Golden Tradition Edited by Lucy S. Dawidowicz (New York: 1967): 388-393.

1425 Report of the Executive Committee to the 20th Regional Conference for the Period of March 27, 1938 to March 26, 1939. Kraków: Zionist Organization of Galicia and Silesia, 1939. 56p. (P)

1426 "Report of the Israeli Office." In Report from Activities of the Central Council of the Zionist Organization in Poland. Warsaw: 1921. pp. 1-11. (H)

1427 Schechtman, Joseph B. and Benari, Yehuda. History of the Revisionist Movement: vol. 1, 1925-1930. Tel-Aviv: Hadar Publishing House, Ltd., 1970.

1428 Schiper, Ignacy. "History of Zionism on Polish Lands (till 1918)." ŻPO 1 (1932): 518-530. (P)

1429 Schiper, Ignacy. Polish-Lithuanian Jews and Palestine: Historical Contribution to the Romantic Era of Zionism. Vienna: "Moriah", 1917. 32p. (P)

1430 Shazar, Zalman. The Dawn. Tel Aviv:, 1951. 298p. (H)

1431 Sokołow, Nahum. The Tasks of Jewish Intelligentsia: Draft of a Program. (Reprint from Izraelita). Warsaw: Drukarnia J. Filipowicza, 1890. 110p. (P)

1432 Sokołow, Nahum. History of Zionism, 1600-1918. London: Longman's Green and Co., 1919. 2 vols. illus.

1433 Stand, Adolf et al. Herzl Thodor: Memorial Book. Lwow: 1914. 85p. (P)

1434 Sterner, Henryk. "About the Pre-war Haszomer Organization." Haszomer. 9 (Lodz: June-July, 1918): 193-198. (P)

1435 Sztajnberg, Chaim, ed. Free Publications on Jewish Socialist Thought: A Collection. Warsaw: 1930, 192p. (Y)

1436 Taylor, Alan. "Zionism and Jewish History." Journal of Palestine Studies 1 (Winter 1972): 35-51.

1437 Thon, Ozjasz. Essays for Zionist Ideology. Berlin-Charlottenberg: Buchhandlung "Kedem", 1930. xv, 430p. (G)

1438 Vital, David. The Origins of Zionism. Oxford: Clarendon Press, 1975. xvi, 396p.

1439 Vital, David. Zionism: the Formative Years. New York: Oxford University Press, 1982. xviii. 514p.

1440 Weinberg, Joseph. Zionism: Perpetuity of the Jewish People. Paris: Editions Dialogues, 1975. 36p. (F)

1441 Weinreich, Max. The Way to Our Youth: Elements, Methods and Problems of Research on Jewish Youth. Wilno: 1935. viii, 309p. (Y)

1442 Yaari, Meir. " We and Palestine." Haszomer (Lodz, April 1, 1920): 18-19. (P)

1443 Zhabotinskii, Vladimir Evgen'evich. The Betar Ideology: Outline of the Betar World View. Łuck: A. Kaulbar, 1935. 31p. (G)

1444 Zhabotinskii, Vladimir. Evgen'evich. The Jewish State. Warsaw: Rennaissance, 1934. 179p. (P)

1445 Zhabotinskii, Vladimir Evgen'evich.   The Jewish War Front.
London: G. Allen and Unwin Ltd., 1940. 255p.

1446 Zhitlowski, Chaim. From Assimilation to Poale-Zionism. New York:
1919. 56p. (Y)

1447 Zineman, Jacob.   History of Zionism.   Paris: Richard, 1950.   1
252p. illus. (F)

1448 The Zionist Organization in the Polish Kingdom in the Matter of
Political and National Legal Rights of the Jew.   Warsaw: Drukarnia
Współczesna, 1918. 16p. (P)

24
Emigration

1449 Alpersohn, Marcos. <u>Maurizio Colony - Thirty Years of I.C.A. Colonization in Argentina</u>. Buenos Aires: 1922, 381p. (Y)

1450 Alter, L. "Jewish Emigration." <u>Kwartalnik Instytutu Naukowego do Badan Emigracji i Kolonizacji</u>. 1, no.1 (Warsaw, December 1926): 80-91. (P)

1451 Bałaban, Majer. "Jewish Learning in Reborn Poland and Polish Jews Abroad." <u>GGŻ</u> 2, no.10-11 (1938): 279-282. (P)

1452 Baron, Salo W. "On the Eastern Jewish Immigration to Prussia, 1803-1817." <u>Aktenstücke</u> (Berlin, 1931): 193-204. (G)

1453 Beer, M. "The Russian and Polish Jews in London." <u>Neue Zeit</u> 2, no.12 (1894): 730-734. (G)

1454 Benari, Yehuda. "Zhabotinskii's Evacuation Program and his Predictions on the Fate of Polish Jews." <u>Geszer</u> 4 (1936): 44-54. (H)

1455 Breslauer, Bernhard. <u>Emigration of Jews from the Poznań Province</u>. Berlin: B. Levy, 1909. 13p. (G)

1456 Eliaszew (pseud. of Baal Machszowis). "The Jewish Youth from Poland and Russia in the 1890's Abroad." <u>Zukunft</u> (New York, 1914): 67-70, et 163-167. (Y)

1457 Fermi, Laura. <u>Illustrious Immigrants: The Intellectual Migration from Europe, 1930-1941</u>. Chicago: University of Chicago Press, 1968. xi, 440p.

1458 Fine, David M. "Attitudes Toward Acculturation in the English Fiction of the Jewish Immigrant, 1900-1917." <u>American Jewish Historical Quarterly</u> 63, no.1 (September, 1973) 45-56.

1459 Gainer, Bernard. <u>The Alien Invasion: The Origins of the Aliens, Act of 1905</u>. London: Heinemann Educational Books, 1972. 305p.

1460 Glanz, Rudolf. "The 'Bayer' and the 'Pollack' in America." <u>JSS</u> 17 (1955), 27-ff.

1461 Grossmann, Kurt R. and Tartakower, Arieh. The Jewish Refugee. New York: Institut of Jewish Affairs of The American Jewish Congress and World Jewish Congress, 1944. 676p.

1462 Hass, Ludwik. "The Jewish Refugees From the Former Nobles' Republic in the Freemasonic Lodges of Western Europe (19th Century)." BŻIH 1/109 (1979): 41-62. (P)

1463 Henish, M. "Galician Jews in Vienna." In The Jews of Austria Edited by J. Fraenkel. London: 1967. pp.361-373.

1464 Horain, Juljan. "Polish Jews in America: Based on Recent Memories." Tygodnik Powszechny 6 (Kraków, 1882): 811-826. (P)

1465 Hourwitz, Zalkind. "Apology from the Jews in Response to a Question: Is it Possible to Make the Jews More Content and Useful in France?" Paris: 1789. 90p. (F)

1466 Joseph, Samuel. Jewish Immigration to the United States from 1881 to 1910. New York: Columbia University Press, 1914. 209p.

1467 Kallen, Horace Meyer. Frontiers of Hope. New York: H. Liveright, 1929. viii, 452.

1468 Kapiszewski, Andrzej. "The Analysis of Polish-Jewish Relations in the United States of America." Przegląd Polonijny. 4, No. 4. (Kraków, 1978): 5-24. (P)

1469 Kruk, Abraham. "The Holy Blessing." In Pamietnik Wzniesienia i Odsłonięcia Pomników Tadeusza Kosciuszki i Kazimierza Pulaskiego Tudzież Połączonego z tą Uroczystoscia Pierwszego Komitetu Narodowego Polskiego w Waszyngtonie, D.C. Edited by Romuald Piątkowski. 1911. pp. 611-612. (P)

1470 Lestchinsky, Jacob. "National Groups in Polish Emigration." JSS. 5, no. 2. (April 1943): 99-114.

1471 Lestchinsky, Jacob. "Professional Composition of the Jewish Immigration in the United States." Weltwirtschaftliches Archiv, 97, Jena, 1928. (G)

1472 Lewitz, L. The Problem of Jewish Immigration to Palestine in Light of the Economic Situation of the Country: Lecture Delivered on November 29, 1934 in the Institute of Nationalities' Affairs. Warsaw: Polsko-Palestyńska Izba Handlowa, 1935. 19p. (P)

1473 Lichten, Joseph L. "Polish Americans and American Jews: Some Issues which Unite and Divide." The Polish Review 18, No.4. (1973): 52-62.

1474 Liebman, Hersch. The Vagrant Jew of Today: Study of Jewish Emigration from Eastern Europe to United States of America. Paris: Girard, 1913. 325p. (F)

1475 Linder, Menachem. "Jewish Emigration from Poland in the Times of Crisis, 1929-1933." M. Żyd. 5, no. 3/4 (1935): 142-172. (P)

1476 Linder, Menachem. "Occupational Structure of Jewish Emigration from Poland to Palestine." Palestyna i Bliski Wschód 5, (1936), 555-557. (P)

1477 Linder, Menachem. "The Problem of Jewish Emigration in Reborn Poland," GGŻ 2, no. 10-11. (Warsaw: October-November 1938) : 274-276. (P)

1478 Mahler, Raphael. "The Economic Background of the Jewish Emigration from Galicia to the United States." YIVO Annual of Jewish Social Science 7 (New York, 1952): 255-267.

1479 Metzer, Emmanuel. "Polish Diplomacy and Jewish Emigration During the 1935-1939 Period." Gal Ed. 1 (1973): 211-249. (H)

1480 Neubach, Helmut. Expulsions of Poles and Jews from Prussia, 1885-1886: A Contribution to Bismarck's Polish Politics and to the History of German Polish Relations. Wiesbaden 1967. x, 293. (G)

1481 Neuman, I.M. "Letters from Abroad: A People All but Lost." Menorah Journal 18, no.3 (Jerusalem, March 1930): 243-252.

1482 Neumann, Salomon. The Fable About Jewish Mass Immigration: A Chapter from Prussian Statistics with a Postscript Contained in Answer to Messers Adolf Wagner and Heinrich Treitschke and Their Jewish Mass Immigration. Berlin: Königliche Preussischen Statistischen Bureau, 1881. 66p. (G)

1483 Ormicki, W. "Conditions and Possibilities of Jewish Emigration." Sprawy Narodowościowe 11 (Warsaw, 1937): 280ff. (P)

1484 Pollner, Majer J. Emigration and Regroupment of Polish Jews. Warsaw: Drukarnia M. Nomberga, 1939. 126p. (P)

1485 Rochaway, Robert A. "The East European Jewish Community in Detroit, 1881-1914." YIVO Annual of Jewish Social Sciences 15 (New York, 1974).

1486 Rostanski, Karol. American Polonia's Affair with the Jews in the Era of Restoration of the Polish State. Warsaw: Spółka Wydawnicza "Rozwój", 1925. 86p. (P)

1487 Rosenberg, Henryk. "Emigration of Polish Jews to the United States in the Period of 1925-1929." M. Żyd. 3 (1933): 526-546. (P)

1488 Segal, Benjamin Wolf. The World War and the Fate of the Jews: The Voice of a Galcian Jew and His Co-religionists in the Neutral Countries, especially in America. Berlin: 1916. 144p. (G)

1489 Shulvass, Moses Avigdor. From East to West: The Westward Migration of Jews from Eastern Europe during the 17th and 18th Centuries. Detroit: Wayne State University Press, 1971. 161p.

1490 Stern, Norton B. "The Major Role of Polish Jews in the Pioneer West." Western States Jewish Historical Quarterly 8, no.4 (Los Angeles: July, 1976): 326-344.

1491 Szajkowski, Zosa. "The European Attitude to East European Jewish Immigration (1881-1893)." Publications of the American Jewish Immigrations 40 (1951): 127-162.

1492 Szerer, Emanuel. "The Essence of the Emigration Problem." Myśl Socjalistyczna 20 (February, 1939): 1-8. (P)

1493 Tartakower, Arieh. "Jewish Emigration from Poland in Post-War Years." Jewish Social Service Quarterly. 16, No.3. (1940) : 273- 279.

1494 Tartakower, Arieh. "Jewish Migratory Movements in Recent Generations." In The Jews of Austria. Edited by J. Fraenkel. (London : 1967) : 286-289.

1495 Tartakower, Arieh. Jewish Wanderings in the World. Jerusalem: 1941. 156p. (H)

1496 Tartakower, Arieh. The Problem of Jewish Emigration. Parios: World Jewish Congress, 1936. 46p. (Y)

1497 Tenzer, Morton. "The Jews." In The Immigrants' Influence on Wilson's Peace Policies. Edited by Joseph P. O'Grady. Lexington, Ky.: Universioty of Kentucky Press, 1967. pp. 287-317.

1498 Tomaszewski, Jerzy. "Diplomatic Report on the Situation of Polish Jews in Germany at the Beginning of 1936." BŻIH 2/106 (1978) : 101-109. (P)

1499 Traub, Michael. Jewish Migrations Before and After the World War. Berlin: Jüdischer Verlag, 1930. 115p. (G)

1500 Vereta, Meir. "Polish Suggestions for a Territorial Solution to the Jewish Problem." Zion 6 (1940-1941): 148-155 et 203-213. (H)

1501 Wischnitzer, Mark. To Dwell in Safety: The Story of Jewish Migration Since 1800. Philadelphia: The Jewish Publication Society of America, 1948. xxv, 368p. illus.

1502 Wróblewski, Wacław. "From the Realm of Emigration: Based on the Report of the Warsaw Information Bureau for the Jewish Emigrants." Społeczeństwo 24, (Warsaw, 1910): pp. 273 ff. (P)

1503 Wróblewski, Wacław. "Jewish Emigration." Społeczeństwo 9, (1909): pp. 101 ff. (P)

1504 Yahil, Lewi. " Madagascar: Phantom of a Solution for the Jewish Question." In Jews and Non-Jews in East-Central Europe. Edited by Vago Bella and George Mosse. (New York, 1974) : 315-334.

1505 Ziemiński, Jan (pseud. of Jan Wagner). The Problem of Jewish Emigration. Warsaw: Związek Pisarzy i Publicystów Emigracyjnych, 1937. 74p. (P)

25
Foreign Relief and Philanthropy

1506 Adler, Cyrus and Margalith, Aaron M. "Poland: American Intercession on Behalf of Jews in the Diplomatic Correspondence of the United States, 1840-1938." American Jewish Historical Quarterly. 36, (1943), pp. 140ff.

1507 American Jewish Joint Distribution Committee. Minutes of the Conference in the Matter of Reconstruction of Homes Destroyed by the War Operations in Polish Republic, May 9-10, 1923. Warsaw, 1923: 97p. (P)

1508 Bauer, Yehuda. My Brother's Keeper: A History of the American Jewish Joint Distribution Committee, 1929-1939. Philadelphia: Jewish Publication Society of America, 1974. xi, 350p.

1509 Berkovich, Sh. "Poll Taking in the Question of Jewish Easter Assistance in 1934." Dos virtshafgtlekhe lebn 4-5. (Warsaw, 1934): 6ff. (Y)

1510 Davies, Norman. "Great Britain and the Polish Jews." Journal of Contemporary History. 8 (London, April, 1973) : 119-142.

1511 Diner, Sz. "Relief Committee and No-Interest Provident Fund Institutions." Hajnt-Jubilee Issue 1918-1928. pp. 17-18. (Y)

1512 Handlin, Oscar. A Continuing Task: The American Jewish Joint Distribution Committee, 1914-1964. New York: Random House, 1965. vi,118p.

1513 Kroszczor, Henryk and Zabłotniak Ryszard. "Jewish Organizations for Help to Victims of the First World War." BŻIH 4/92 (1974): 15-29. (P)

1514 Lestchinsky, Jacob. "Towards a Constructive Plan of Help for Polish Jews." Jidisze Ekonomik. 7-9, (1938): 311-312. (Y)

1515 Mayzel, Maurycy. " On Activities of Jewish Communities in the Sphere of Social Welfare." Głos Gminy Żydowskiej. 2, No.4. (April 1938): 75-76. (P)

1516 Merzan, Ida. "Janusz Korczak and The Society 'Help for Orphans.'" BŻIH 2/90 (1974) : 91-93. (P)

1517 Merzan, Ida. "Janusz Korczak's Home for the Orphans." BŻIH 2/78. (1971): 31-54. (P)

1518 Merzan, Ida. "The Society 'Help for Orphans'." BŻIH 3/99 (1976): 73-84. (P)

1519 Szajkowski, Zosa. "The Alliance Israelite Universelle and East European Jewry in the 1860's." JSS. 4 (1942): 139-160.

1520 Szajkowski, Zosa. "American Jewish Relief in Poland and Politics, 1918-1923." Zion 34 (1970): 225ff.

1521 Szajkowski, Zosa. "Concord and Disconcord in American Jewish Overseas Relief, 1916-1925." YIVO Annual 14 (1969): 99-158.

1522 Szajkowski, Zosa. "Disunity in the Distribution of American Jewish Overseas Relief, 1919-1939." American Jewish Historical Review 58 (1969): 376-407.

1523 Szajkowski, Zosa. "Reconstruction versus 'Palliative Relief' in American Jewish Overseas Work, 1919-1939." JSS 32 (1970) : 14-43.

1524 Szajkowski, Zosa. "Western Aid and Intercession for Polish Jewry, 1919-1939." In Studies on Polish Jewry, 1919-1939. Edited by Joshua A. Fishman. (New York: 1974): 150-241.

1525 Tygel, Zelig, ed. The Jews in Poland: Their History, Their Tragedy, Their Future. A Program for Relief and Reconstruction. New York: American Committee for the Relief of Jews in Poland Inc., 1936. 46p. illus.

1526 Yishay, Bar and Web, Marek. "Care of Orphans and Child Welfare in Poland, 1919-1939." In Studies on Polish Jewry, 1919-1939, edited by Josha A Fishman. (New York, 1974): 99-136. (Y)

26
Jews in the Polish Socialist Party (PPS)

1527 Aubac, Stéphane. The Unknown Part of a Compaign: The Jewish Question in Poland and the Socialist Opinions on the "Pogroms". Paris: J. Matot, 1919. 94p.

1528 Baumgarten, Leon. "Feliks Kon in Prison and Before Court Martial." BŻIH 57 (1966): 39-61. (P)

1529 Borski, Jan M. The Jewish Question and Socialism: Polemics with the Bund. Warsaw: Robotnik, 1937. 25p. (P)

1530 Głowacka-Maksymiuk, Urszula. "PPS and Bund During the Revolution Years in Siedlce Region: In the Light of Police Documents." Rocznik Mazowiecki 6 (Warsaw, 1976): 205ff. (P)

1531 Kaufman, Mojżesz (pseud. Mezryczer, Mojsie). "Beginnigs of PPS's Jewish Activity." Niepodległość 7, no.3 (Warsaw, 1933): 335-350. (P)

1532 Kaufman, Mojzesz (pseud. Mezryczer, Mojsie). "Contributions to the History of the PPS's Jewish Organization." Niepodległość 12, no.1 (Warsaw, 1935): 22-52. (P)

1533 Król, Michał. "The Jewish Organization of PPS, 1893-1903." In Żydzi Bojownicy o Niepodległość Polski: Historyczna Monografia. Edited by N. Getter et al. Lwów, 1939: 22-31. (P)

1534 Kwiatek, Józef. The Conference of Jewish Comrades in Lwów, May 9 and 10, 1903. Przedświt 6, Krakow, 1903: 252-257. (P)

1535 "Letter of the Jewish Members of PPS to the Central Workers' Committee of December 1895." In Materiały do Historii PPS, edited by Władysław Pobóg-Malinowski 1 (1934): 161-163. (P)

1536 Luxemburg, Rosa. "The PPS on the Jewish Workers' Movement." Przegląd Socjalistyczny 4, No.4. (1904): 159-162. (P)

1537 Piasecki, Henryk. The Jewish Section of the Polish Social-Democratic Party in 1892-1919/20 Period. Warsaw, Ossolineum - Żydowski Instytut Historyczny, 1982: 350p. illus. (P)

1538 Piasecki, Henryk. "Jewish Workers and the Polish-Jewish Intelligentsia of the Polish Socialist Party Left Against the Background of Scissions and Secessions in the Years 1907-1919." BŻIH. 1-2/129-130 (January-June 1984), pp. 15-23. (P)

1539 Piasecki, Henryk. "Józef Kwiatek, Organizer of the Armed Demonstration in 1904." BŻIH. 90 (1974½: 47-61. (P)

1540 Piasecki, Henryk. "The Origin and First Years of the Polish Socialist Party's Jewish Organization, 1893-1900." BŻIH 4/96 (1975): 37-66. (P)

1541 Piasecki, Henryk. The Polish Socialist Party's Jewish Organization: 1893-1907. Wrocław: Zakład Narodowy im. Ossolińskich, 1978. 273p. illus. (P)

1542 Piasecki, Henryk. "Postęp (Progress) of Herman Lieberman." BŻIH 4/120 (1981): 5-15. (P)

1543 Pietkiewicz, Kazimierz. "Mojżesz Lurje and the 'Raboczeje Znamia.'" Niepodległość 6, 1/12, (Warsaw, 1932): 26-40. (P)

1544 Piłsudski, Józef. "An Appeal to the Socialist Jewish Comrades in Polish Annexed Territories." Przedświt 5 (London, May 1983): 8-10. (P)

1545 Próchnik, Adam. "Participation of the Jews in Fighting Operations Under the Banner of PPS." Glos Gminy Żydowskiej 2 No.10-11 (October-November 1938): 242-244. (P)

1546 Tryman, Maurycy. "Jewish Workers' Groups of the PPS-Left and the SDKPiL in Warsaw: Memoirs." BŻIH 38 (1961): 128-145. (P)

1547 Wajner, M. "To the History of PPS in Lithuania: Reminiscences About Jewish Organization of PPS in Grodno." Niepodległość 9, No.2/22 Warsaw, 1934: 223-224. (P)

27
Philo-Semitism

1548 "Appeal to Polish Brothers of Mosaic Faith (1863)." In Manfred Kridl, et al., eds. Za waszą wolność i naszą. New York: 1942, 96-98. (P)

1549 Banasiak, A. et al. Poles About Jews: Seventeen Responses to Antisemites. Warsaw: Polska Unia Zgody Narodów,1937. 115p. (P)

1550 Bernstein, Herman. "The Polish-Jewish Pact to End Anti-Semitism." Current History (Philadelphia, October 1925): 77-78.

1551 Centnerszwerowa, Róża. Lelewel's Position with Regard to the History and Problems of Polish Jews. Warsaw: Izraelita, 1911: 24p. (P)

1552 Chajn, Leon, ed. Materials to the History of Democratic Clubs and the Democratic Party in the Years 1937-1939. Warsaw: Wydawnictwo Epoka, 1964. 2 vol. 1, 603p.; 2, 563p. illus. (P)

1553 Chołoniewski, Antoni. Us, Jews and the Congress. Kraków: Towarzystwo im. Stefana Buszczyńskiego, 1919: 58p. (P)

1554 Chołoniewski, Antoni. What to Think About Anti-Jewish Disturbances: A Word to Our People. Kraków: Nakładem Autora, 1919: 16p. (P)

1555 Czacki, Tadeusz. Treatise on the Jews and Karaites. Wilno: J. Zawadzki, 1807. 242p. (P)

1556 De Courtenay, Jan Baudoin. The Jewish Question in the Polish State. Warsaw, 1923. (P)

1557 "Defense of the Jews." Pamiętnik Warszawski 5 (Warsaw, 1816): 199-205. (P)

1558 Dembiński, Henryk. "The Jewish Benches." Po Prostu. 4 (Wilno, January 26, 1936) (P)

1559 Eisenbach, Artur. "Polish Fraternization of All Religious Creeds." Kwartalnik Historyczny 86, No.1. (Warsaw,1979): 43-66. (P)

1560 Freytag, Lucjan. Sacrifice of Brotherly Blood: Poland and Russia and the Jews. Warsaw: W. Piekarniak i S-ka, 1920. 23p. (P)

1561 Ganszyniec, Ryszard. "The Question of the 'Numerus Clausus' (1925): For the Jewish Population's Rights to Education." In For Your Freedom and Ours: Polish Progressive Spirit From the 14th Century to the Present. Frederick Unger Publishing Co., 1981: 229-233.

1562 Gelber, Nathan Michael. "Reverend Father Piattoli and the Jewish Question at the Great Diet." Nowe Życie. 6, Warsaw, 1924: 321-324. (P)

1563 Grinberg, Maria. The Workers' Congress' Struggle Against Antisemitism." BŻIH 1-2/129-130 (January-June 1984): 39-60. (P)

1564 Gronowicz, Antoni. Antisemitism Ruins my Country: Remarks About Contemporary Reality Delivered December 17, 1937 on Invitation of the Society of the Workers' University (TUR). Lwów, 1938: 39p. (P)

1565 Grydzewski, Mieczysław. " Polish Literature - Philosemitic Literature." Wiadomości 376 (1760/1761) (London, December 1979): p.9. (P)

1566 Hass, Ludwik. "Jews and the Jewish Question in Old Polish Freemasonry, up to the 1820's." BŻIH 4/104 (1977): 3-26. (P)

1567 Hertz, Alexander. "A Case of Polish Gentile-Jewish Empathy." The Polish Review 18, No 4, (1978): 79-82.

1568 Kelles-Krauz, Kazimierz, "In Question of Jewish Nationality." Krytyka 1, no.6. (1904): 52-61 et 120-130. (P)

1569 Korboński, Stefan. "Poles and Jews: A Common Bond." ACEN News. 143, New York, December 1969.

1570 Kotarbiński, Tadeusz. "After the Storm of November 22, 1931." Racjonalista. 12, Warsaw, 1932: 177-184. (P)

1571 Kotarbiński, Tadeusz. "Religious Bars." Racjonalista. 6, Warsaw, 1931: 81-84. (P)

1572 Kridl, Manfred et al., eds. For Your Freedom and Ours: Polish Democratic Thought Through the Centuries; Anthology. New York: Polish Labor Group, 1945. 423p. (P)

1573 Kulczyński, Stanisław. "From an Open Letter in Defence of the Freedom of Learning, 1938." In For Your Freedom and Ours: Polish Progressive Spirit edited by Krystyna M. Olszer. New York, 1981: 234-235.

1574 Lange, Antoni. On Contradictions of the Jewish Question. Warsaw: 1911. 77p. (P)

1575 Le Moal, Francoise. "Tolerance in Poland: Political Choice and Tradition." In The Tradition of Polish Ideals: Essays in History and Literature edited by W.J. Stankiewicz. pp. 52-84. London: Orbis Books Ltd., 1981.

1576 Lelewel, Joachim. The Jewish Question in 1859: From the Letter to Ludwik Merzbach. Poznań: Nakładem L. Merzbacha, 1860. 29p. (P)

1577 Lerski George J. "Social-Democratic Youth of Lwow, 1937-1939." Zeszyty Historyczne 47 (Paris, 1939): 149-182. (P)

1578 Lipski, Jan Józef. "Polish Jews." Kultura 6/429 (Paris,1983): 3-8. (P)

1579 Łukasinski, Walerian. Remarks by a Certain Officer Concerning the Need for Proper Arrangement of Jewish Life in Our Country, and with Regard to Some Recent Publications in that Matter. Warsaw: 1818. 26p. (P)

1580 Moszczeńska, Izabella. Progress at the Crossroads. Warsaw, 1911: 101p. (P)

1581 Nowak, Jan et al. "The Problem of Jewish-Polish Realtions." Kultura 9/432 (Paris,1983): 92-94. (P)

1582 Orzeszkowa, Eliza. On the Jews and the Jewish Question. Warsaw: Gebethner i Wolff, 1913. 234p. (P)

1583 Orzeszkowa, Eliza. "Thirteen Letters from Grodno to Attorney Adolf Kohn in Warsaw." Transl. into Russian. J.St. (1914):42-61. (R)

1584 Prus, Bolesław (pseud. of Aleksander Głowacki). "The Jewish 'Little' Question." In Za Waszą Wolność i Naszą edited by M. Kridl et al. New York, 1944: 146-149. (P)

1585 Pruszyński, Ksawery. "In Greatest Abbreviation." Wiadomości Literackie. 21, Warsaw, May 16, 1937. (P)

1586 Pruszyński, Ksawery. "In Light of Logic and Documents." Wiadomości Literackie. 22, Warsaw, May 23, 1937. (P)

1587 Scholars and the 'Ghetto' Voices from Poland and Abroad. Warsaw: Wydawnictwo Polskiej Unii Zgody Narodów, 1938: 68p. (P)

1588 Sempołowska, Stefania. Jews in Poland. Warsaw: Księgarnia Naukowa, 1906: 56p. (P)

1589 Smolka, Franciszek. Speeches of Deputy Franciszek Smolka Delivered in Jewish Question at the Galician Diet Meetings of September the 30th and October the 8th, 1868. Lwów: Przełożenstwo Zboru Izraelickiego we Lwowie, 1899. (P)

1590 Stojowski, Andrzej. "Apotheosis." Podróż do Nieczujny. Warsaw: Czytelnik, 1968: 210-221. (P)

1591 Teslar, Tadeusz. Jews on the Soviet Volcano: Antisemitism in Soviet Union. Warsaw: Towarzystwo Wydawnicze Strzelczyk i Rosinowski, 1928. 126p. illus. (P)

1592 Turowski, Stanisław. "Poland: Jewish Paradise." KŻP 3 (Warsaw, 1913): 73-100. (P)

1593 Turowicz, Jerzy. "Church and Synagogue." Tygodnik Powszechny. Kraków, February 2, 1975. (P)

1594 Wardziński, Mieczysław. "Antisemitism - the State's Colour-Blindness." Wiadomości Literackie. Warsaw, August 4, 1937. (P)

1595 Wasilewska, Wanda. I seek out Antisemitism. Lwów: Wydawnictwo Wiedza. 16p. (P)

1596 When Hate Rages . . . Opinions of Christian Priests. Warsaw: Hoesick, 1936. 99p. (P)

1597 Wielopolska, M.J. The Bejlis Case and its Conclusions: Lecture Given under the Auspices of 'Życie' in the Little Theatre in Lwów on November 27, 1913. Stanisławów, 1914. (P)

1598 Wyszomirski, Jerzy. "Letter from Wilno." Wiadomości Literackie. 3, Warsaw, January 17, 1937. (P)

1599 Zaborowski, Jacek. "Jewish Affairs or Antisemitism." Spotkania: Niezależne Pismo Młodych Katolików. 1-2 (Lublin, 1977): 20-35. (P)

1600 Zabłotniak, Ryszard. "The Association of Physicians of the Polish Republic." BŻIH 73 (1970): 87-89. (P)

1601 Zaderecki, Tadeusz. The Mysterious Jews' Science. Warsaw: Żydowskie Towarzystwo Wydawnicze "Cofim," 1937. 173p. (P)

1602 Zadarecki, Tadeusz. The Talmud in the Fire of Centuries. Warsaw: F. Hoesick, 1936. vii, 112p. (P)

1603 Zaremba, Zygmunt, at al. About Jews and Antisemitism. Warsaw: 1936. 61p. (P)

28
Jews in Polish Public Life

1604 Apenaszlak, Jacob. "Jewish Political Thought in Poland." In Polish Jew, 11th Yearbook. New York: American Federation of Polish Jews, 1944: 5-14.

1605 Bloch, J.S. Selection of his Letters' Collection edited by Grunwald. Vienna, 1930: 24p. (G)

1606 Byk, Emil. The Speech of Deputy Dr. Emil Byk in the Session of the Austrian Parliament. Lwów: 1898: 16p. (G)

1607 Byk, Emil. Three Speeches. Lwów, 1903: 24p. (P)

1608 Cang, Joel. "The Opposition Parties in Poland and Their Attitude towards the Jews and the Jewish Question." JSS 1, No.2. (1939): 241-256.

1609 Chajn, Leon. "The Polish Chapter of 'B'nei B'rith'." BŻIH 1/83 (1973): 7-42. (P)

1610 Diamand, Herman. Speeches in the Diet of the.Polish Republic, 1919-1930. Warsaw: Księgarnia Robotnicza, 1933. 556p. (P)

1611 Eisenbach, Artur. "Central Representation of the Jews in the Duchy of Warsaw." Bleter far Geshikhte 1938, 2 (Warsaw, 1938): 33-88. (Y)

1612 Farbstein, Joshua Heshel. Diet-Speeches. Warsaw, 1923. 83p. (Y)

1613 Feldman, Wilhelm. "Jewish Parties and their Political Programs." In his Stronnictwa i Programy Polityczne w Galicji, 1846-1906. vol. 2. (Kraków:1907): 265-314. (P)

1614 Gabel, Henryk. The Jewish Parliamentary Club. Buczacz: 1909. 164p. (Y)

1615 Glatman, Ludwik. Historical Essays. Kraków: Spółka Wydawnicza Polska, 1906. 303p. (P)

1616 Groth, Alexander J. "The Legacy of Three Crises: the Parliament and Ethnic Issues in Prewar Poland." Slavic Review. 27, no.4 (December, 1968): 564-580.

1617 Grünbaum, I. Speeches in the Polish Diet. Warsaw: 1922. 230p. (Y)

1618 Hafftka, Aleksander. "Jewish Political Parties in Reborn Poland." ŻPO 2 (1933): 249-285. (P)

1619 Hafftka, Aleksander. "Parliamentary and Political Activity of Jewish Deputies and Senators in Reborn Poland." ZPO. 2 (1933): 313-359. (P)

1620 Hafftka, Aleksander. "Parliamentary Life of the Jews in Reborn Poland." ŻPO. 2, pp. 286-311. (P)

1621 Halpern, L. "Jewish Politics in the Sejm and Senate of the Republic." Sprawy Narodowościowe 1 (1933): 14ff. (P)

1622 Hanecki, Michał. "Participation of Physicians and Naturalists of Jewish Origin in the Development of Medical Sciences in the Poland of the 19th Century." BŻIH 3/75 (1970): 85-96; 1/77 (1971): 43-64; 1/81 (1972): 99-115. (P)

1623 Hartglas, Apolinary Maksymilian. The Diet Speeches, 1919-1922. Warsaw: Verlag Yidishe Nationalrat in Poyln, 1923. 156p. (Y)

1624 Indelman, M. "Jewish Political Parties in Poland." Hajnt, 1908-1928: Księga Jubileuszowa. Warsaw, 1928: 99-100. (P)

1625 Kaffe, Ph. Pact of the Jewish Clubs with Poland: A Warning for Security Politics. Berlin: A. Stein, 1925. 8p. (G)

1626 Kaufman, Michal. A Critique of Jewish Politics. Warsaw: Nakładem Autora, 1937. 55p. (P)

1627 Kiel, Mark. " The ideology of the Folks-Party." Soviet Jewish Affairs 5, no.2. (London, 1975): 75-89.

1628 Korzec, Paweł. "The Agreement Between the Grabski Cabinet and the Jewish Parliamentary Representation." Jahrbücher für Geschichte Osteuropas. 20, no.3 (September, 1972): 331-366. (G)

1629 Kruszyński, Józef. Politics of the Jews. Włocławek: Księgarnia Powszechna, 1921. 65p. (P)

1630 Landau, Moshe. "The Coup d'État of May 1926: Expectation of Polish Jews for Political Change and the Dissolution of the Diet." Gal-ed. 2 (1975): 237-286. (H)

1631 Landau, Moshe. "The 1925 'Ugoda' Agreement: Its Place in Mutual Polish-Jewish Relations." Zion 47, (1972): 66-110. (H)

1632 Landau, Saul Raphael. The Polish Club and Its Chamber-Jews: Forward with the 'Hausjuden'! . . . Basic Lines for Jewish Popular Politics. Vienna: C.W. Stern, 1907. 42p. (G)

1633 Lewin, Aron. The Diet Speeches. Lwow: 1926. 73p. (P)

1634 Lewin, Isaac. "Political Orientations." In Tsu der Geschikhte fun Agudas Isroel. New York: Orthodox Library, 1964. pp. 29-30. (Y)

1635 Litman, A. "Jewish Participation in Legislative Bodies of the Polish Republic." Glos Gminy Żydowskiej 2, no. 10-11 (Warsaw: October-November, 1938): 313-317. (P)

1636 Mahler, Raphael. "Jews in Public Service and the Liberal Professions in Poland." JSS 6(1944): 291-350.

1637 Mendelsohn, Ezra. "The Dilemma of Jewish Politics in Poland." In Jews and Non-Jews in Eastern Europe, edioted by Bela Vago and George Mosse (New York): 203-220.

1638 Mendelsohn, Ezra. "The Politics of Agudas Yisrael in Interwar Poland." Soviet Jewish Affairs 2, no.2. (1972): 47-60.

1639 Mintsin, Y. "Jewish Participation in Elections to the Polish Diet, 1919-1922." Bleter far Yidishe demografie, statistik, un ekonomik 2, (1923): 86-90. (Y)

1640 Pryłucki,Nojach. Speeches. Warsaw, 1920: 174p. (P)

1641 Ringel, Michal. The Jewish Question in Poland: Speech Delivered on the Plenary Session of the Senate . . . During the Discussion for the 1925 Budget. Warsaw: F.Hoesick, 1925. 29p. (P)

1642 Rothschild, Joseph. "Ethnic Peripheries Versus Ethnic Cores: Jewish Political Strategies in Interwar Poland." Political Science Quarterly. 96, no. 4. (Winter 1981-1982): 591-1982.

1643 Stand, Adolf. Jewish Situation in Galicia: Parliamentary Speech Lwów, 1911. 30p. (P)

1644 The Situation of Polish Jewry in Light of Speeches in the Budgetary Debate for 1930-1931. Warsaw: Biuletyn no.5. Klubu Posłów i Senatorów żydowskich, 1930. 165p. (P)

1645 Szretter, A. "Jewish Participation in the Work of the Codification Committee of the Polish Republic." Glos Gminy Żydowskiej 2, (Warsaw, October-November, 1938): 329-330. (P)

1646 "Text of the Government's Agreement with the Jewish Club signed on July 7, 1925 and Proclaimed on May 6, 1926 by the Jewish Club." Gal-ed 1, (1973): 203-207. (H)

1647 Thon, Ozjasz. Diet Speeches, 1919-1922. Warsaw: Yidisher Nationalrat in Poyln, 1923. 72p. (Y)

1648 Tomaszewski, Jerzy. "Political Struggle within Jewish Communities in the Thirties in the Light of Parliamentary Questions." BŻIH 1/85, (1973): 85-110. (P)

1649 Tomaszewski, Jerzy. "Questions Concerning Jewish Communities asked by Diet Members." BŻIH 2/90, (April-June, 1974): 63-67. (P)

1650 Weinstejn, L. "The Jewish Role in the Towns' Administration in Galicia." Woschod. 28, (1911): 21-26. (R)

29
Reform Projects

1651 Anski, S.A. "The Jewish Delegation in the Wilno Committee of 1869." J.St. 5, (1912): 187-201. (R)

1652 "Arranging the Life of the Jewish People in the Entire Polish Nation." MSC 6 (1969): 491-515. (P)

1653 Butrymowicz, Mateusz Topór. "The Method of Adjustment for Polish Jews." In MSC 6, (Warsaw, 1969): 78-93. (P)

1654 Butrymowicz, Mateusz Topór. "The Method of Adjustment for Polish Jews." In MSC 6, (1969): 118-128. (P)

1655 Chaimowicz, Pejsak. "A Proposal in Relation to the Arrangement of the Jewish Court." Ibid., pp. 272-276. (P)

1656 Chołoniewski, Ignacy. "A Project Concerning Jews and Debts of Jewish Communities-Consistories." Ibid., pp. 269-271. (P)

1657 Czacki, Michał. "Reflections on Reform of the Jews." Ibid., pp.206-212. (P)

1658 Eisenbach, Artur. "The Problems of Polish Jews in 1861 and Reform Projects of Margrave Aleksander Wielopolski." Acta Poloniae Historica 20, (Warsaw, 1969): 138-162. (F)

1659 "From the Correspondence of King Stanisław August, Piattoli and Kołłątaj." In MSC 6 (1969): 295-343. (P)

1660 Gadon, Lubomir. A Collection of Enactments and Rites that Demand the Speediest Reform of the Israelites Settled in the Provinces Belonging to Poland. Paris: 1835. (P)

1661 Gelber, Nathan Michael. "The Jews and the Jewish Reform at the Polish Four-Years Diet." In Dubnow-Festschrift (1930): 136-153.

1662 Gelber, Nathan Michael. "Mendel Lepin-Stanower and his Suggestions for the Reform of the Life of the Jews before the Great Sejm of 1788-1792." Abraham Weiss Jubilee Volume. New York: 1964, 271-305. (H)

1663 Goldstein, M. "Project of K.F. Voyda in 1815 Concerning Organization of the Jews in Poland." J.St. (1928): 301-314. (R)

1664 Gołuchowski, Jozef. "About the Reform of the Jews: Project Submitted in 1841." Poznań, 1845. (P)

1665 Gumplowicz, Ludwig. Stanisław August's Reform Project for the Polish Jewry. Kraków: Księgarnia Adolfa Dygasińskiego, 1875. 61p. (P)

1666 Hekker, Helena. "Projects to Reform Jewish Life in Poland at the End of the XVIII century." J. St. (1914): 206-218 et 328-340. (R)

1667 Hiliewski, Krzysztof. "A Project or the New Light." MSC 6, (Warsaw, 1969): 46-78. (P)

1668 Hirszowicz, Abraham. "Project for Reform and Improvement of Morals." Ibid., pp.519-524. (P)

1669 Hryniewiecki, Kajetan. "Comments on the Project of Reform of the Jews." Ibid., pp.153-168. (P)

1670 Jankielewicz, Mowsza (pseud. Jan Kamieński). About the Means to Make Reform of the Jews in Poland Effective. (Warsaw, Drukarnia Pilarskiego, 1819. 46p. (P)

1671 "Jewish Demands." In MSC 6 (1969): 276-283. (P)

1672 The Jews: Or the Dire Need to Reform the Jews in the Lands of Polish Commonwealth, by an Anonymous Citizen. Warsaw: Michał Groll, 1785. 40p. (P)

1673 Józefowicz, Herszel. "The Thoughts Proper to the Way of Formation of Polish Jews." MSC 6 (Warsaw:1969): 98-105. (P)

1674 Karpinski, Franciszek. "Project Concerning the Jews." Ibid., pp.484-491. (P)

1675 Lypacewicz, Waclaw. A Solution of the Jewish Question in Poland. Warsaw: Gebethner i Wolff, 1939. 44p. (P)

1676 "Memorandum to Serve the Project of Reform of the Jews." MSC 6 (Warsaw, 1969): 358-378. (F)

1677 Nossig, Alfred. An Attempt to Solve the Jewish Question. Lwów: Drukarnia Polska, 1887. ii, 89p. (P)

1678 Nossig, Alfred. Poles and Jews: Polish-Jewish Understanding of Arrangement of the Jewish Question in Poland. Vienna: Interterritorialen Verlag "Renaissance", 1930 72p. (G)

1679 "Observations of Justice Prima Instantiae" MSC 6, (Warsaw, 1969): 344-346. (L)

1680 Ostrowski, Antoni Jan. Ideas for Needed Societal Reform in General and Especially with Regard to Israelites by the Founder of

Tomaszów Mazowiecki Municipality. Paris: Drukarnia Gisserni a Pinard, 1834. iv, 372p. (P)

1681 Piattoli, Scipione. "Plan for the Jews." MSC 6. (Warsaw, 1969): 350-355. (F)

1682 "Points for Consideration of the Most Honorable Committee for Reform of the Jews of 1790." MSC 6, (Warsaw, 1969): 228-235. (P)

1683 Polonus, Salomon. "Project for Reform of the Jews." Ibid., pp. 421-433. (P)

1684 Radomiński, Jan. What Delays Jewish Reform in the Our Country and What Should Precipitate it? Warsaw: 1820. 88p. (P)

1685 "Reform of the Jews." In MSC 6 (1969): 486-491. (P)

1686 "Reform of the Jews: Project of the Committee to Which it was Assigned." MSC 6 (Warsaw, 1969): 215-228. (P

1687 Ringelblum, Emanuel. "Projects and Attempts of Regroupment of Jews in the Era of King Stanislaw." Sprawy Narodowościowe. (Warsaw: 1934): pp. 189-225. (P)

1688 Satanower, Mendel. "Draft of a Plan." MSC 6 (Warsaw, 1969): 409-421. (F)

1689 "Thoughts About Jewish Arrangement Drawn from Practiced Regulations and Adjusted if Possible to the Circumstances of Republic's Interests." Ibid., pp. 433-450. (P)

1690 "To H.E. Małachowski, Speaker of the Diet." Ibid., pp. 93-98. (P)

1691 Świtkowski, Piotr. "Remarks Concerning Jewish Reform Proposed by M. Butrymowicz." Pamiętnik Historyczno-Polityczno-Ekonomiczny. 8 12 (Warsaw, December 1789): 1151-1170. (P)

1692 Werses, S. "Isaac Satanow and His 'Mishley Asef'." Tarbiz 32 (1963): 370-392. (H)

1693 Wischnitzer, Mark. "Reforms of Jewish Life in the Duchy of Warsaw and Kingdom of Poland." (based on unpublished materials) Perezhytoe: Sbornik posviashchennii obshestvennoi i kulturnoi Istorii Evreev v Rossii. 1 (Petersburg, 1908): 165-221. (R)

1694 Witkowski, Marek (pseud "Niedowiarek"). A Solution for the Jewish Question in Poland: Talks with Politicians. Warsaw:1938. 82p. (P)

1695 Wolfowicz, Szymel. "Prisoner in Nieswiez to Estates Debating the Need for Jewish Reform." MSC 6 (Warsaw, 1969): 141-153. (P)

30
Communism

1696 Alef, Gustaw (pseud. Bolkowiak). Three Fighters for a Free Socialist Poland. Warsaw: Yidish Bukh, 1953. 17p. illus. (Y)

1697 Auerbach, Julian. "Some Problems Concerning the Activity of the Communist Party of Poland (KPP) Among Jews in the Depression Years, 1929-1933." BŻIH 55 (1965): 33-56. (P)

1698 Baumgarten, Leon. "A Valuable Document from the History of the 'Proletariat' and the 'People's Will'." BŻIH 24 (1957): 21-41. (P)

1699 Baumgarten, Leon. "Feliks Kon in Jail and Before the Military Court." BZIH 57 (1966):36-61. (P)

1700 Baumgarten, Leon. "Revolutionaries of Jewish Origin in the First Polish Socialist Circles and in the 'Great Proletariat'." BŻIH 47/48 (1963): 3-28. (P)

1701 Brustin-Berenstein, Tatiana. KPP (Communist Party of Poland) in the Struggle against Antisemitism. Warsaw: Yidish Bukh, 1956. 132p. (Y)

1702 Brustin-Berenstein, Tatiana. "KPP (Communist Party of Poland) in the Struggle Against the Pogroms, 1935-1937." BŻIH 15/16 (1955): 3-74. (P)

1703 Fuks, Marian. "Materials to the Bibliography of the Jewish Labor and Socialist Press Published in Poland, 1918-1939: Part One, Communist Press." BŻIH 3/103 (1977). (P)

1704 Gamska, Larysa. "The Attitude of the Left of Jewish Socialist Parties Towards the Third International and the Communist Workers' Party of Poland, 1918-1923." BZIH 1/97 (1976): 61-75. (P)

1705 Halicki, Waclaw. Christianity, Communism and Judaism. Lwów: 1933. 39p. (P)

1706 Iwański, G. "Jewish Communist Workers' Union 'Kombund' in Poland, 1921-1923." Z Pola Walki 4/66 (Warsaw,1947): 43-76. (P)

1707   Kolat, Yisrael.   "Poale Tsiyon Between Zionism and Communism." Asufot 2, no. 15. (November, 1971): 30-52. (H)

1708   Korsch, Rudolf (pseud of Kazimierz Krippendorf).   Jewish Subversive Groups in Poland. Warsaw: Drukarnia P.K.O., 1925. 215p. (P)

1709   Marek, Lucjan.   " From Reminiscences of a Member of the Communist Party in Poland." BŻIH 2/78 (1971): 73-105. (P)

1710   Margalit, Elkana.   From a Community of Youths to Revolutionary Marxism, 1913-1936. Tel Aviv: 1971. 399p. (H)

1711   Młot, Jan (pseud of Szymon Dickstein).   Who Lives from What? Geneva: Wydawnictwo Walki Klas, 1885. iv, 46p. (P)

1712   Poland Behind Bars.   New York: Verlag "Tsu-Hilf", 1938. 29p. (Y)

1713   Prajs-Brystygier, Julia.   Sign H.   Warsaw: Czytelnik, 1962. (P)

1714   Rosenthal-Schneiderman, A.   "Jews in the Polish Communist Movement: Jewish Majority - An Obstacle." Molad 3, no.13. (January-February, 1970): 81-96. (H)

1715   Rybak, P.   "Memories of the Communist Party of Poland's Struggle Against Anti-Semitic Pogroms." BŻIH 13/14 (1955): 68-273. (P)

1716   Sedecki, Wacław (pseud. of Julian Unszlicht).   On the Program for Polish People: The Role of the Social-Litwaks During the Recent Revolution.   Kraków: 1912. 374p. (P)

1717   Szajkowski, Zosa. "Paul Nathan, Lucien Wolf, Jacob H.Sciff and the Jewish Revolutionary Movement in Eastern Europe, 1903-1917." JSS 29, (1967)

1718   Szerer, Barbara, ed.   From the Recent Past: Recollections of the KPP (Communist Party of Poland) Members.   Wrocław: Zakład Narodowy im. Ossolińskich, 1959. 354p. (P)

1719   Unszlicht, Julian (pseud. Waclaw Sedecki).   Socialists - Litwaks in Poland: from the Theory and Practice of "Social Democracy of the Polish Kingdom and Lithuania." Kraków: by the author, n.d. 167p. (P)

1720   Zachariasz, Szymon.   The Communist Movement Among the Working Jewish Class in Poland. Warsaw: Yidish Bukh, 1954. 187p. illus. (Y)

31
Anti-Semitism

1721 Adus, Maurice. "Remarks on Witos' Memoirs: On the Fiftieth Anniversary of Jablonna." <u>Zeszyty Historyczne</u> 20 (1971): 173-177. (P)

1722 Alter, Wiktor. <u>Economic Antisemitism in Light of Statistics</u>. Warsaw: Wydawnictwo Myśli Socjalistycznej, 1937. 64p. (P)

1723 Andreski, Stanisław. "An Economic Interpretation of Anti-Semitism in Eastern Europe." In <u>The Uses of Comparative Sociology</u>, Berkeley University of California Press, 1965: 291-307.

1724 Andrzejewski, Jerzy. "Problems of Polish Antisemitism." In <u>Martwa Fala: Zbiór Artykułów o Antysemityźmie</u>, edited by L. Szenwald. (Warsaw, 1947): 28 ff. (P)

1725 Anonymous. <u>The International Jew; A Most Important Universal Problem: Jewish Activity in the United States; Jews and Poland</u>. Reprint from a Series of Articles printed in <u>The Dearborn Independent</u> from October 1920 to March 1921. Transl. from English by Anna Szottowa. Poznań: Księgarnia Społeczna, 1923. 251p. (P)

1726 Anonymous. <u>Protocols of the Meetings of the Wise Elders of Zion</u>, translated from Russian in 1905 by Sergiusz Nilus. Warsaw: 1920. 62p. (P)

1727 "Anti-Jewish Riots." <u>Robotnik</u> 57 (November 28, 1904): 3-4. (P)

1728 <u>Antisemitism</u>. Warsaw: PPS (Polish Socialist Party). (September, 1906): 13p. (P)

1729 <u>Appeal to Polish Public Opinion</u>. Paris: Éditions "Pour la Dignité Humaine, 1937. 16p. (F)

1730 Bałaban, Majer. "Antisemitic Literature in Poland." <u>Hatkufa</u> 12 (Warsaw, 1922): 501-942. (H)

1731 Batault, Georges. <u>The Jewish Question</u>. Transl. from French by M.L. Warsaw: Perzyński i Niklewicz, 1923. 164p. (P)

1732 "<u>Bench Ghetto</u>" in Polish Universities: An Appeal to Polish

Scholars. Paris: ICC, 1938. 23p. (F)

1733 "Bench Ghetto in Institutes of Higher Learning." Myśl Socjalistyczna. (Warsaw, October 15, 1937): 1 ff. (P)

1734 Bernstein, Herman. "The Polish-Jewish Pact to End Antisemitism." Current History 22 (October, 1925): 77-81.

1735 Blit, Lucjan. The Eastern Pretender. London: Hutchinson, 1965. 223p.

1736 Bojomir-Mileski, Waclaw. Decree to the Jews of the Entire World. Poznań: Drukarnia Handlu i Przemysłu, 1924. 8p. (P)

1737 Borwicz, Michal. "Comments Concerning the Camp of Jabłonna: in Connection with Witold Babiński's Article in Kultura 12/83." Zeszyty Historyczne 67 (Paris, 1984): 226-229. (P)

1738 Chasanowicz, Leon. Anti-Jewish Pogroms in Poland and in Galicia in November and December, 1918: Facts and Documents. Stockholm: Bokforlaget Judaea, 1919. 150p. (F)

1739 Chołoniewski, Antoni. On the Jewish Question: Three Polemical Letters. Kraków: Organizacya Jedności Narodowej, 1914. 91p. (P)

1740 Cohen, Israel. Report on the Pogroms in Poland. London: Central Office of the Zionist Organizations, 1919. 35p.

1741 Cohn, Norman Rufus Collin. Warrant for Genocide: The Myth of the Jewish World Conspiracy and the Protocols of the Elders of Zion. New York: Penguin, 1969. 336p.

1742 Czajkowski, R. The Abnormal Factor - The Jews. Warsaw: "Pro Patria", 1927. 14p. (P)

1743 Dmowski, Roman. "The Jewish Question." In his Świat Powojenny i Polska . Warsaw: M. Niklewicz i J. Zaluska, 1932. pp. 319-356. (P)

1744 Dmowski, Roman. "Jews and the War." In his Polityka Polska i Odbudowanie Państwa. Warsaw: Perzyński, Niklewicz i Ska., 1925. pp.352-367. (P)

1745 Dmowski, Roman. Separatism of the Jews and its Sources. Warsaw: Gazeta Warszawska, 1909. 29p. (P)

1746 Doumont, Eduard. Jews Against France: The New Poland. Paris: Librairie antisemite, 1899. 106p. (F)

1747 Drohojowski, Jan. Brief Outline of the Jewish Problem in Poland. Brooklyn, N.Y.: Polish National Alliance, 1937. 28p.

1748 Duker, Abraham G. "The Fight Against Ghetto Benches in Polish Universities." School and Society. 46 (New York, 1937): 502 ff.

1749 Eger, Feliksa. Jews and Freemasons in Common Work. Warsaw: 1908. 256p (P)

1750 Evidence of Pogroms in Poland and the Ukraine. New York: The Information Bureaus of the Committee for tghe Defense of Jews in Poland and other East European Countries, 1929. 190p.

1751 Fishman, Joshua A. "Minority Resistance: Some Comparisons Between Interwar Poland and Postwar U.S.A." SPJ (New York, 1974): 3-11.

1752 "From Kishineff to Białystok: A Table of Pogroms from 1903 to 1906." American Jewish Yearbook, 5667 Philadelphia, 1906: 38-89.

1753 Gajewski, Kazimierz. Here Come the Jews. Poznan: "Samoobrona Narodu", 1937. 32p. (P)

1754 Gajewski, Kazimierz. Let's Save Poland. Poznań: Drukarnia Lotnicza, 1935. 31p. (P)

1755 Giertych, Jedrzej. "The Jews in Poland." In his In Defense of My Country. London: The Roman Dmowski Society, 1981. pp. 243-316.

1756 Giertych, Andrzej. The Tragic Nature of Poland's Vicissitudes. Pelplin: Księgarnia Pielgrzyma, 1937. 343p. (P)

1757 Glock, Charles Y. and Stark, Rodney. Christian Beliefs and Anti-Semitism. New York: Harper and Row, 1966. xxi, 266p.

1758 Golczewski, Frank. Polish-Jewish Relations, 1881-1922: A Study on History of Antisemitism in East Europe. Wiesbaden: Steiner, 1981. ix, 391p. (G)

1759 Grabowski, Ignacy. For Jews: Palestine! Warsaw: P.S.W. "Placówka", 1919. 171p. (P)

1760 Grabowski, Ignacy. On the Jewish Question: Ungrateful Guests. Warsaw: Drukarnia Piotra Laskauera, 1912. 50p. (P)

1761 Grynberg, Henryk. "Is Polish Anti-Semitism Special?" Midstream (New York, August-September, 1983): 19-23.

1762 Gurland, Jonas. History of Anti-Jewish Legislation: Contribution to the History of Antisemitism. 7 vols. Przemyśl: 1887-1892. (H)

1763 Haupt, G. and Korzec, Paweł. "The Socialists and the Antisemitic Campaign in Poland in 1910: and Unpublished Episode." Revue du Nord 57, no.225 (Paris, 1975): 189ff. (F)

1764 Hauptmann, Zygmunt. Vows of Częstochowa or "Death to the Jews!". Jerusalem: 1946. 32p. (P)

1765 Healy, Ann E. "Tsarist Anti-Semitism and Russian - American Relations." Slavic Review 42, no.3 (Fall, 1983): 408-425.

1766 Hekker, Helena. "Hatred of Jews in 18th Century Poland." J.St. (1913): 439-454. (R)

1767 Hollaenderski, Leon. Eighteen Centuries of Christian Prejudices, Presided by the Letter of Approval of A. Cremieux. Paris: M. Lévy

Freres, 1869. xx, 192p. (F)

1768 How to Get Rid of the Jews? Plock: Odbitka z Mazura, 1912. 76p. (P)

1769 Hrabyk, Klaudiusz. The Jewish Question. Lwów: Związek Młodych Narodowców, Odbitka z Akcji Narodowej, no.8/9, 1934. 46p. (P)

1770 Jeleński, Jan. Jews, Germans and Us. Warsaw: 1880. 190p. (P)

1771 Jeske-Choiński, Teodor. About Jews: What Outstanding Men and Scholars of Various Nations Thought and Think up to now. Warsaw: 1919. 40p. (P)

1772 Jeske-Choiński, Teodor. What did the Jews do in Poland? Warsaw: 1918. 20p. (P)

1773 Jeske-Choiński, Teodor. Where are the Jews Leading? Warsaw: Drukarnia Społeczna Stowarzyszenia Robotników Chrzescijańskich, 1927. 23p. (P)

1774 "Jews are Fettering Poland Using the Peace Conference." In Międzynarodowy Żyd, by anonymous autor. Poznań: Księgarnia Społeczna (1923): 227-239. (P)

1775 Jonicz, Stefan. Fighting Judea. Poznan:1918. 24p. (P)

1776 Katz, Jacob. From Prejudice to Destruction: Anti-Semitism, 1700-1933. Cambridge, Mass.: Harvard University Press, 1980. viii, 392p.

1777 Klatzkin, Jakob. Persecutions of Jews in Galicia and Rumania: Speech at the Mass Demonstration of the Action Committee of Eastern Jewish Organizations in the Zurich Peoples' House. Lausanne: Verlag der Loge Al Hamischmar, 1918. 16p. (G)

1778 Kołakowski, Leszek. "Antisemites: Five Not Entirely New Theses and a Warning." Po Prostu 22 (Warsaw, May 27, 1956): 1-7. (P)

1779 Koneczny, Feliks. Jewish Civilization. London: Towarzystwo im. Romana Dmowskiego, 1974. 439p. (P)

1780 Koniuszyński, Eugeniusz. "Evolution of National Democrats in the Years 1925-1928." Więź 12 (Warsaw, December, 1976): 128-138. (P)

1781 Konopczyński, Władysław. "About Pogroms in Poland: Response to Jerzy Brandes." In his Umarli Mowią Poznań, Wielkopolska Księgarnia Nakładowa K. Rzepeckiego. (1929): pp.87-97. (P)

1782 Konopczyński, Władysław. "Struggle for numerus clausus." Ibid., 98-119. (P)

1783 Korzec, Paweł. "Antisemitism in Poland as an Intellectual, Social and Political Movement." SPJ (New York, 1974): 12-104.

1784 Korzec, Paweł. "The Steiger Affair." Soviet Jewish Affairs 3 (London, 1973): 28-57.

1785 Kościesza, Zbigniew. How to Counteract Jewish Influence: Guide for All Poles. Warsaw: Wydawnictwo "Swój do Swego", 1913. 15p. (P)

1786 Kościesza, Zbigniew. Who are the Jews and Where are They Leading? Warsaw: Tłocznia "Polaka-Katolika" i Posiewu, 1912. 32p. (P)

1787 Kovalsky, S. Polish Antisemitism. Lausanne: Éditions de la Loge Sioniste Al Hamishemar, 1919. 51p. (F)

1788 Krasnowski, Zbigniew. Jewry's World Policy. Warsaw: "Patria", 1934. 181p. (P)

1789 Kruszyński, Józef. Antisemitism, Antijudaism, Antigoism. Włocławek: Wydawnictwo Księgarni Powszechnej i Drukarni Diecezjalnej, 1924. 28p. (P)

1790 Kruszyński, Józef. The Jewish Danger. Włocławek: Księgarnia Powszechna, 1923. 93p. (P)

1791 Kruszyński, Jozef. Jews and the Jewish Question. Włocławek: Wydawnictwo Księgarni Powszechnej i Drukarni Diecezjalnej, 1920. 158p. (P)

1792 Kruszyński, Józef. Jews and Poland. Poznań: Drukarnia Robotników Chrześcijańskich T.A., 1921. 27p. (P)

1793 Kruszyński, Józef. Present Tendencies of the Jews. Włocławek: Wydawnictwo Drukarni Diecezjalnej, 1921. 36p. (P)

1794 Kruszyński, Józef. Stanisław Staszic and the Jewish Question. Lublin: Komitet Obchodu Setnej Rocznicy Zgonu Stanisława Staszica, 1926. 53p. (P)

1795 Kruszyński, Józef. World Role of Jewry. Włocławek: Księgarnia Powszechna, 1923. 227p. (P)

1796 Laudyn, Stephanie. America and Poland Facing the Jewish Question. Gniezno: "Lech", 1925. 51p. (P)

1797 Laudyn, Stephanie. A World Problem: Jews - Poland - Humanity, translated by A.J. Zielinski and W.K.. Chicago: American Catalogue Printing Company, 1920. 365p.

1798 Lengyel, Emil. "Europe's Anti-Semitic Twins: Part II, Poland." Current History 48, (1938): 44-45.

1799 Lestchinsky, Jacob. "The Anti-Jewish Program: Tsarist Russia, The Third Reich and Independent Poland." JSS 3, no.2. (April 1941): 141-158.

1800 Lestchinsky, Jacob. "Anti-Jewish Rioting in Poland." Dipim leheker ha-shoa be-ha-mered. 2 (Februray 1952): 37-92. (H)

1801 Lew, Aba. "Pogroms of Galician Jews During the Bloody Years of the War." Jewreiskaia Letopis 3, (Leningrad-Moscow, 1924): 169-176. (R)

1802 Lewitter, I.R. "Dmowski, Namier and Mr. Aszkenazy." Wiadomości 34, no. 2 (London, January 14, 1979 et no. 3 (January 21, 1979). (P)

1803 Liev, Ziskind. Poland: The Slaughterhouse for Men. New York: 1933. 71p. illus. (Y)

1804 Mahler, Raphael. "Antisemitism in Poland." In Koppel S. Pinson ed. Essays on Antisemitism. (New York: Conference on Jewish Relations, 1946. pp. 203-219.

1805 Marchlewski, Julian. Antisemitism and the Workers. Warsaw: Drukarnia R. Olesiński i W.Markel, 1920. 99p. (P)

1806 Mazowiecki, Tadeusz. "Antisemitism of the Gentle and Good People." Więź 5 (Warsaaw, 1960): 21-40. (P)

1807 Miedziński, Bogusław. Remarks On the Jewish Problem Together with Resolutions of the Supreme Council of O.Z.N. ("Camp of National Unity") Voted on May 21, 1938. Warsaw: Obóz Zjednoczenia Narodowego, Oddzial Propagandy, 1938. 38p. (P)

1808 Milwicz, Edmund. Polish-Jewish War. Poznań: Drukarnia Polska T.A., 1921. 31p. (P)

1809 Morawski, Kazimierz Marian. The Source of Poland's Partitions: Studies and Sketches from the Era of the Saxons and Stanisławs. Poznań: Księgarnia Sw. Wojciecha, 1935. 367p. illus. (P)

1810 Moskowitz, Moses. "Polish Public Opinion on the 'Ghetto Benches.'" Menorah Journal 26, (January-March, 1938): 94-102.

1811 Moskowitz, Moses. "Totalitarianism and Anti-Semitism in Poland." Contemporary Jewish Record 2 (January, 1939): 16-35

1812 Motzkin, Leo. The Antisemitic Campaign in Poland: Troubles at the Universities - Numerus Clausus Question - Economic Boycott - Attitude of the Courts. Paris: Rousseau, 1932. 186p. (F)

1813 Mroczkowski, Stanislaw. "Antisemitism." Kultura 7/225 -8/226, (Paris, July/August 1966): 136-148. (P)

1814 Niebudek, Stefan. Przytyk: The Great Trial of the Poles and Jews. Warsaw: Sprawa Narodowa, 1936. 64p. (P)

1815 Niemojewski, Andrzej. Jewish Law Concerning non-Jews. Warsaw: Nakładem Autora, 1918. 16p. (P)

1816 Niemojewski, Andrzej. The Jewish Soul Mirrored in the Talmud. Warsaw: 1920. 196p. (P)

1817 Nowaczyński, Adolf. Anonymous Power: Inquiry into the Jewish Question. Warsaw: Perzyński, Niklewicz i S-ka, 1921. 415p. (P)

1818 Nowakowski, Marian Antoni. Beware of Jews and Bolsheviks. Czestochowa:1918. 20p. (P)

1819 Nowicki, Stefan. A Great Misunderstanding. Sydney, Australia: Nakładem Autora, 1970. 167p. (P)

1820 Ordyński, A.P. (pseud. of Antoni Potocki). "A Jew in the Village." Głos 41, (1889): 42-54.

1821 Ostrowski, Wiktor. Anti-Semitism in Byelorussia and its Origin: Material for Historical Research and Study of the Subject. London: Byelorussian Central Council, 1960. 76p.

1822 Parkes, James William. Antisemitism. Chicago: Quadruple Books, 1963. xiii,192p.

1823 Penzik, Abraham. Antisemitism and Necrophilia: Remarks on the Jewish Question in Poland. New York: 1944. 31p. (P)

1824 Pinson, Koppel Shub. (ed) Essays on Antisemitism. New York: Conference on Jewish Social Studies, 1946. xi,269p.

1825 The Pogroms in Poland and Lithuania. Special no. of the Jewish Labour Correspondence 1, no.9. London: Jewish Socialist Labour Confederation Poale-Zion, 1919. 46p.

1826 "Pogroms in Poland Must be Stopped!" Jewish Life. (Jewish Bureau of the Central Committee, Communist Party, USA) 1, no.3. (October 1937): 12-14.

1827 "Polish Mirror for the Public." MSC 6, (1969): 235-268. (P)

1828 Ponisz, Piotr. The Jewish Question in Poland from the National and Catholic Viewpoint. Częstochowa: A. Gmachowski, 1938. 93p. (P)

1829 Poradowski, Michał. The Church Menaced from Within. London: Veritas, 1983. (P)

1830 Pranaitis, Iustin Bonaventura. The Talmud Unmasked: The Secret of Rabbinical Teachings Concerning Christians. Transl. of author's Latin Text. New York: 1939. 94p.

1831 "Problem of Antisemitism: Kultura's Inquiry." Kultura 1/111-2/112 (Paris, January-February, 1957): 56-79. (P)

1832 Pulzer, Peter G. The Rise of Political Anti-Semitism in Germany and Austria, 1867-1918. New York: John Wiley and Sons Inc., 1964. xiv,364p. illus.

1833 R.J. ("Farmer from Vistula Lands"). The City of Warsaw's Sewage System as an Instrument of Judaism and Charlatanry in Order to Destroy Polish Agriculture and to Exterminate the Slavic Population Along the Vistula River. Kraków: Skład w Księgarni G. Gebethnera i Spółki, 1900. (P)

1834 Radliński, Ignacy. Jehowa, Medieval Darkness and Wilhelm II, King of Prussia. Warsaw: Księga Pomocy i Przezorności Pomocnikow Księgarskich, 1919. 203p. (P)

1835 Ringel, Michal. Antisemitism in Poland. Warsaw: Wende i S-ka, 1924. 49p. (P)

1836 Rohling, August. Pernicious Principles of Talmudism: For Sincere Consideration of Jews and Christians of All Classes. Lwów: Gazeta Wiejska, 1875. 113p. (P)

1837 Rolicki, Henryk, (pseud. of Tadeusz Gluziński) The Twilight of Israel. Warsaw: Myśl Narodowa, 1932. 420p (P)

1838 Rowe, Leonard. "Jewish Self-Defense: A Response to Violence." SPJ (1974): 105-149.

1839 Rowe, Leonard. "Politics Under Stress: The Jewish Response in Poland." The Bennington Review 4, (Spring 1968): p.45ff.

1840 Skierko, Adam. Jews and the Polish Question. Paris: Imprimerie Carlos-Courmont,1919. 37p. (F)

1841 Smolar, Boris. "What Polish Jews are Facing." The Nation. 124, (New York, January 17, 1932): 99-100.

1842 Sokołowski, Jan Optat. The Jewish Question in the Legal Profession. Warsaw: Narodowe Zrzeszenie Adwokatów, 1934. 35p. (P)

1843 Staszic, Stanisław. "Concerning the Causes of Jews Being Harmful and On the Means to Make them Useful to Society." Appendix to August Rohling's Pernicious Principles of Talmudism (Lwów, 1875): 91-113. (P)

1844 Szenwald, L., ed. THe Dead Wave: Collection of Articles on Antisemitism. Warsaw: 1947.

1845 Tomaszewski, Jerzy. "Two Documents on the Pogrom in Brześć in 1937." BŻIH 49 (1964): 58-67. (P)

1846 Trunk, Isaiah. "Economic Antisemitism in Poland between the Two World Wars." SPJ (New York, 1974): 3-98. (Y)

1847 Trunk, Isaiah. "Polish Democracy and Native Antisemitism: Response to Adam Ciołkosz." Tsukunft (New York, May-June 1973): 226-230. (Y)

1848 Trzeciak, Stanisław. Dejudaize the Production and Sale of Devotional Objects! Warsaw: 1937. 30p. (P)

1849 Trzeciak, Stanisław. Facing the Horror. Warsaw: Offprint from the Young Catholics' Monthly Pro Christo, 1937. 8p. (P)

1850 Trzeciak,Stanisław. The Jewish Question and Us Christians. Paris: O.P.N., 1937. 15p. (P)

1851 Trzeciak, Stanisław. Messianism and Jewish Question. Warsaw: Księgarnia Przeglądu Katolickiego, 1934. 377p. (P))

1852 Trzeciak, Stanisław. The Talmud On the Goys and the Jewish Question in Poland. Warsaw: Księgarnia A. Prabuckiego, 1939. 379p. (P)

1853 Trzeciak, Stanisław. The World Program of Jewish Policy: Conspiracy and its Unmasking. Warsaw: Gebethner i Wolff, 1936. 147p. (P)

1854 Valentin, Hugo. Antisemitism Historically and Critically Examined, transl. from Swedish. New York: The Viking Press, 1936. 324p.

1855 Vishniac, M. "Antisemitism in Tsarist Russia: A Study in Government-Fostered Antisemitism." In Essays on Antisemitism, edited by K.S. Pinson, pp.79-110. New York: 1946.

1856 Walichnowski, Tadeusz. Zionist Organizations and Activists. Katowice: Wydawnictwo Śląsk, 1968. 82p. (P)

1857 Werytus, Antoni. The Motherland without Jews: Images of the Future. Warsaw: 1914. 32p. (P)

1858 "Why the Jews are not Pleased with Morgenthau's Report." Chapter XX In Miedzynarodowy Żyd (International Jew), transl. from English by Anna Szottowa, pp.215-226. Poznań: Księgarnia Społeczna, 1923.

1859 Wierczak, K. The Most Important Matter. Warsaw: Stronnictwo Narodowe, n.d. 15p. (P)

1860 Wildecki, H. In Jewish Captivity. Poznan:Gryf, 1937. 74p. (P)

1861 Wildecki, H. The Jewish Menace. Poznań: Nakładem Autora, 1934. 95p. (P)

1862 Wynot, Edward. "A Necessary Cruelty: The Emergence of Official Antisemitism in Poland, 1936-1939." American Historical Review. 76, no.4. (October, 1971): 1035-1058.

32
Autobiographies, Memoirs and Correspondence

1863 Ansky, S. (pseud. of Solomon Zaynal Rapaport). "I Enlighten a Shtetl." GT (New York, 1984): 306-311.

1864 Ansky S. Memoirs. 2 vols. Warsaw, 1922: 198p et 245p. (Y)

1865 Aron, Izaks. Autobiography. Translated by Stif. Berlin, 1922: 118p. (G)

1866 Axer, Erwin. Exercises of Memory. Warsaw: Państwowy Instytut Wydawniczy, 1984. 265p. (P)

1867 Bader, Gershom. My Memoirs: from Kraków to Kraków. Buenos Aires: 1953. 410p. (Y)

1868 Ber of Bolechów (Birkenthal). The Memoirs of Ber of Bolechów. Transl. from Hebrew by Mark Vischnitzer. London: Oxford University Press, 1922. ix, 188p.

1869 Berenson, Leon. From the Condemned Cell: Memoirs of a Defense Counsel in Political Cases. Warsaw: 1929. 34p. (P)

1870 Berliber, Abraham. "From My Boyhood." Jahrbuch für Jüdische Geschichte und Literatur. (Berlin, 1913): 165-190. (G)

1871 Berman, Adolf Abraham. At the Place Assigned to Me by Fate. Tel-Aviv, 1977. 290p. (H)

1872 Bernfeld, Simon. "Memoirs." Rszumot 4, (Odessa, 1926): 145-193. (Y)

1873 Bierman, Jacob. The Penalty of Innocence: From the Diary of Yakoiv Zeir Weiler. New York: Vantage Press, 1973. vii, 123p.

1874 Blaustein, Miriam Umstadter. Memoirs of David Blaustein Educator and Communal Worker. New York: Arno Press, 1975. 308p. illus.

1875 Blum, Hillel. Memoirs of a Bundist. New York: 1940. 188p. (Y)

1876 Bloch, Joseph Samuel. My Reminiscences. Transl. by the Author.

New York: Arno Press, 1973. 576p.

1877 Brainin, Reuben. From the Book of My Life. New York: YKUF, 1946. 383p. illus. (Y)

1878 Brainin, Reuben. "I Become a Hebrew Writer." GT (1984): 281-286.

1879 Bunimowicz, J. Memoirs. Edited by Ch.Lewin. Wilno: 1928. 367p. (Y)

1880 Byk, Emil. Today and Forty Years Ago. Lwow: Jednosc, 1908. 41p. (P)

1881 Cahan, Abraham. The Education of Abraham Cahan. Translated from Yiddish by Leon Stein, et al. Philadelphia: Jewish Publication Society of America, 1969. xviii. 450p. illus.

1882 Cohen, Israel. Travels in Jewry. New York: E.P. Dutton & Co. 372p. illus.

1883 Czarny, D. Chronicle and Memoirs of the 1888-1901 Period. Wilno, 1927. 64p. (Y)

1884 Czarny, J.J. "The Story of My Life: Memoirs of A Jewish Traveller and Writer." Rszumot 6 (1930): 125-166. (H)

1885 David, Janina. A Square of Sky: Recollections of My Childhood New York: Norton, 1966. 221p.

1886 Dawison, Bogumił. "Letters of Bogumił Dawison." Edited by Tymon Terlecki. Scena Polska 1/4 (Warsaw, 1937), 268-305. (P)

1887 Diamand, Herman. Memoirs of Herman Diamand Based on Excerpts from Letters Written to His Wife. Kraków: Towarzystwo Uniwersytetu Robotniczego "TUR", Oddział im. Adama Mickiewicza, 1932. 317p. (P)

1888 Drobner, Bolesław. A Ceaseless Battle: Memoirs, 1883-1935. Warsaw: Państwowy Instytut Wydawniczy, 1962. 2 vols. (P)

1889 Elenbogen, Herman. My Journey Through Poland and Lithuania. Chicago, 1920. 80p. (Y)

1890 Elimelech of Lezajsk. No'am Elimelekh. Lwów: M.F. Poremba, 1856. 60p. (H)

1891 Epstein Baruch Ha-Levi. Baruch's Memoirs. Wilno: 1920. 3 vols. 2038p. combined. (H)

1892 Epstein, Melech. Pages from a Stormy Life: An Autobiographical Sketch. Miami Beach, Florida: I. Bloch Publisher, 1971. 168p.

1893 Ettinger, Solomon. Collected Works. Wilno: E. Karman, 1925. 2 vols in i. lxiv. 616p. illus. (H)

1894 Fajersztejn, J. Through All Sufferings: Memoirs. Warsaw: 1928. 335p. (Y)

1895 Flugjan, Cwajfel, Fin. "Letters to J.L. Gordon." Rszumot 6 (1930): 492-498. (H)

1896 Fuszkof, P. Inages and Recollections from the Old Country and My Own Life. New York: 1928. 224p. (Y)

1897 Gawze, Aaron. "Memoirs of a Long-time Co-Worker of Hajnt." Hajnt, Księga Jubileuszowa. Warsaw: 1928. pp.4-5. (Y)

1898 Ginzberg, Asher (pseud. Achad, Haam). Fragments of Memoirs and Letters. Tel-Aviv: 1930. 192p. (H)

1899 Goldman, Pierre. Dim Memoirs of a Polish Jew Born in France. Transl. by Joan Pinkham. New York: Viking Press, 1977.

1900 Goldmmann, Nahum. The Autobiography of Nahum Goldmann: Sixty Years of Jewish Life. Tranl. by Helen Sebba. New York: Holt, Rinehart and Winston, 1969. viii, 358p. illus.

1901 Goldmann, Nahum. Statesman Without a State: Autobiography. Cologne und Berlin: Kiepenheuer und Witsch, 1970. 474p. illus. (G)

1902 Gordon, Jakub. Dim Images of Tsarism: Memoirs. Leipzig: 1863. xvi, 222p. (P)

1903 Gordon, Judah Leib. "An Entry in My Diary." GT (New York: 1984): 133-135.

1904 Gordon, Judah Leib. Letters. (ed. by Jacob Isaac Weissberg). Warsaw: 1894. 2 vols in 1. ((H)

1905 Gordon, Judah Leib. "Memoirs." Rszumot 1 (Odessa:1921): 69-96 et Rszumot 5 pp. 61-85. (H)

1906 Gottesfeld, Chone. My Journey Across Galicia. New York: Faraynigte Galitsyaner Yiden in Amerike, 1937. 199p. (Y)

1907 Graubart, Judah Leib. Book of Memoirs. Lodz: 1925/1926. vii, 333p. (H)

1908 Grines, M. When Life Was Blooming. Buenos Aires: 1934. 471p. (Y)

1909 Grosser, Bronisław. "From Pole to Jew." GT (New York: 1967): 435-441.

1910 Gruber, Henryk. Memoirs and Comments. London: Gryf Publications, 1968. vii, 574p. (P)

1911 Grynberg, Henryk. Child of the Shadows. London: Vallentine, Mitchell, 1969. 127p.

1912 Grynzburg, Isaac. About My Generation. Tel-Aviv: Ferlag Mokor, 1959. 380p. (Y)

1913 Gunzburg, Mordecai Aaron. Autobiography. Wilno: 1861. xix,

170p. (H)

1914 Harkavy, W.O. "Excerpts of Memoirs." Pierezitoie, 4, (1913): 270-287. (R)

1915 Hertz, Jacob Sholem. Story of a Youth. New York: 1946. 580p. (Y)

1916 Hirszfeld, Ludwik. The Story of One Life. Warsaw: Czytelnik, 1946. 369p. (P)

1917 Horowitz, David. My Yesterday. Jerusalem and Tel- Aviv, 1970. (H)

1918 Infeld, Leopold. "Neither Pole nor Jew." In GT (New York, 1984): 360-363.

1919 Infeld, Leopold. Quest: The Evolution of a Scientist. London: Victor Gollancz, 1941. 312p.

1920 Infeld, Leopold. Sketches from the Past: Memoirs. Warsaw: Państwowy Instytut Wydawniczy, 1964. 298p. (P)

1921 Iwenicki, Abraham. When the Roads Cross. Wilno: 1924. 77p. (Y)

1922 Isbitzki, Joseph (pseud. Beinish Michalewicz). Memoirs of a Jewish Socialist. Warsaw: 1921-1923) 3 vols. (Y)

1923 Jolles, Zachariah Isaiah. Dissertations and Letters. (ed. by his son Zusman). Wilno: 1912/1913. 2 vols. (H)

1924 Kamińska, Ida. My Life: My Theater. Edited and transl. by Curt Levant.) New York: Macmillan Publishing Co., 1973. 135p.

1925 Kandel, David. "From the Correspondence of Rabbi Meizels." In KZP 1 (1912): 114-115 et 3, 183-188. (P)

1926 Kapelow, I. It was Sometimes. New York: 1926. 379p. (Y)

1927 Klausner, Israel. From Katowice to Basel. Jerusalem: 1964. 2 vols. (H)

1928 Kopff, Wiktor. Memoirs from the Last Years of the Kraków Republic. Kraków: Drukarnia Czasu, 1906. xxl, 158p. (P)

1929 Kotik, Abraham. The Life of a Jewish Intellectual: Zabłudower Pinkas. (New York: 1925). 259p. (Y)

1930 Kotik, Jezechiel. My Memoirs. Berlin: 1922. 2 vols. (347p. et 266p). (Y)

1931 Kraushar, Aleksander (pseud. Alkar). Leaves from the Memoirs of Alkar. Kraków: vol.1. 187p. et vol.2. 183p. (P)

1932 Kronenberg, Leopold. Letters of Leopold Kronenberg to Mieczysław Waligórski Written in 1863. Edited by Stefan Kieniewicz and transl.

from German by Zofia Dąbrowska. Wrocław: Zakład im. Ossolinskich, 1955. xxxiv, 151p. (P)

1933 Leszczyński, Józef (pseud. Chmurner). Chmurner Book. New York: 1958. 231p. illus. (Y)

1934 Lin, Joseph. "From My Memoirs." Achiasaf. (1902): 341-353. (Y)

1935 Lipschitz, Jacob Lipman. Ya'akov's Memoirs. Kovno: 1924-1930. 3 vols. (H)

1936 Locker, Berl. From Kitow to Jerusalem. Jerusalem: 1970. 367p. (H)

1937 Maimon, Salomon. Autobiography: With an Essay on Maimon's Philosophy by Hugo Bergman. Transl. from German, with Additions and Notes by J. Clark Murray. London: East and West Library, 1950. 207p. illus.

1938 Maimon, Salomon. "My Near-Conversion." In GT (New York: 1967): 145-147.

1939 Maimon, Salomon. Solomon Maimon's Life-Story: Written by Himself. Weimar: G. Kiepenhauer, 1960. 2 vols. (G)

1940 Majerowicz, M.L. "Collection of First Seeds." Rszumot 1, (Odessa, 1925): 136-147. (H)

1941 Majzel, N. Letters and Speeches of Perec. Wilno: 1929. 293p. (Y)

1942 Mantel, Feliks. A Fan of Recollections. Paris: Ksiegarnia Polska, 1980. 255p. (P)

1943 Margoshes, Joseph. Memories of My Life. New York, 1936. 335p. (Y)

1944 Medem, Vladimir Davidovich. From My Life. New York: 1923. 2 vols. (Y)

1945 Meisel, Nachman. A Good Life that Once Was. Buenos Aires: 1951. 399p. (Y)

1946 Meizel, Eliahu Chaim. Rabbi Eliahu Chaim's Remembrances:Part I. Lodz: 1927. 299p. (Y)

1947 Mill, Joseph Solomon. Pioneers and Builders. New Yor: 1943-1946. 2 vols. (Y)

1948 Newerly, Igor. Live Bonds. Warsaw: Czytelnik, 1966. 410p. illus. (P)

1949 Nissenbaum, Isaac. My Life. Warsaw: 1928-1929. xii, 355p. (H)

1950 Nordon, Haskell. The Education of A Polish Jew: A Physician's War Memoir. New York: D. Grossman Press, 1982. 314p.

1951 Nussbaum, Hilary. "From the Notebook of a Veteran Member of the Jewish Kehilla." Izraelita. 49, (Warsawa, 1875): 51-56. (P)

1952 Peczenik, M.L. "Letter of I.L. Peretz to Szolem Alejchem."YIVO Fil. Szriftn. 3 (Wilno, 1929): 379-410.

1953 Pennell, Joseph. A Jew at Home: Impressions of a Summer and Autumn. New York: D. Appleton, Co., 1892. 105p. illus.

1954 Peretz, Isaac Loeb. My Memoirs. Wilno: 1927. 151p. illus. (Y)

1955 Peretz, Isaac Loeb. "Letters in Polish to Wife and Son." IWO Bleter. 12 (Wilno, 1937): 3-144. (P)

1956 Plakser, Menachem. From the Recent Past. New York: 1957. 3 vols. (Y)

1957 Pragier, Adam. Past Tense Executed. London: B. Świderski, 1966. 943p. (P)

1958 Prawin, Jakub. Memoirs. Warsaw: Książka i Wiedza, 1959. 164p. illus. (P)

1959 Rabinowicz, Alexander Siskind. Book of Memoirs. Tel Aviv: 1924. xxiii. 128p. (H)

1960 Rabinowitz, Alejchem (pseud. Szolem, Alejchem). "Seven Letters of Szolem Alejchem to I.D. Friszman, Sz. Czernowic, I. Ch. Rawnicki and Ch. N. Bialik." Rszumot 5 (Odessa, 1927): 426-430. (Y)

1961 Rabinowitz, Alejchem. From the Market Place. Transl. by Adam Chajej. New York: 1916-1917. 3 vols. (H)

1962 Rabinowitz, Alejchem. Notes of a Traveller. Translated by Jakób Apenszlak. Warsaw: Państwowy Instytut Wydowniczy, 1958. 199p. (P)

1963 Rabinowitz, Alejchem. "Thirty Unpublished Letters of Szolem Alejchem." YIWO, Filolog. Szriftn 3 (1929): 1531-172. (Y)

1964 Rak, Elimelech. Memoirs of a Jewish Craftsman. Buenos Aires: 1958. 234p. illus. (Y)

1965 Rakowski, Puah. "A Mind of My Own." GT (New York, 1967): 388-393.

1966 Rappaport, Charles. "The Life of a Revolutionary Emigre: Reminiscences." YIVO Annual 6 (New York, 1951): 206-236.

1967 Rapoport, Solomon Judah. "Letters to Rafael Kirchheim edited by B. Dinaburg." Kiriat Sefer 3 (Jerusalem, 1926): 222-236 et 306-319. (H)

1968 Rappoport, Salomo Leib. "From the Correspondence of S.L. Rappoport." Jewish Studies in Memory of George A. Kohut. New York,1935: 47-71. (G)

1969 Rozenbaum, M.M. Recollections of a Revolutionary Socialist.

Warsaw: 1924. 2 vols. viii, 279+377p. (Y)

1970 Rubinstein, Arthur. My Young Years. New York: Alfred A. Knopf, 1973. xiii, 478p. illus.

1971 Rubinstein, Helena. My Life for Beauty. New York: Simon and Schuster, 1966. 251p. illus.

1972 Safrin, Horacy. Amusing Stories from My own Life. Łódź: Wydawnictwo Łódzkie, 1970. 240p. (P)

1973 Sandauer, Artur. Notes from the Dead City: Autobiographies and Para-Biographies. Warsaw: Czytelnik, 1963. 130p. (P)

1974 Schneersohn, Joseph Isaac. Lubavitcher Rabbi's Memoirs. Edited by Nissan Mindel. Brooklyn: Otzar Hachassidim, 1966. 2 vols.

1975 Schulz, Bruno. Book of Letters: Collected and Edited by Jerzy Ficowski. Kraków: Wydawnictwo Literackie, 1975. 190p. illus. (P)

1976 Schwarzbard, Isaac Ignacy. Between the Two World Wars. Buenos Aires: 1958. 385p. (Y)

1977 Segel, Benjamin Wolf. The World War and the Fate of the Jewish People: Voice of a Galician Jew and His Coreligionists in Neutral Countries, Particularly in America. Berlin: G. Stilke, 1915: 144p. (G)

1978 Shatzky, Jacob. In the Shade of the Past. Buenos Aires: Tsentral-Farband Fun Poylishe Yidn in Argentine, 1947. 239p. (Y)

1979 Shtift, Nokhum. "Autobiography." YIVO-bleter. 5 (Wilno, 1933): 195-225. (Y)

1980 Singer, Bernard (pseud. Regnis). My Nalewki Street. Warsaw: Czytelnik, 1959. 171p. (P)

1981 Steiger, Stanislaw. "Between Death and Freedom." Moment. 4, (Warsaw,1926): 1-28. (Y)

1982 Szechter, Szymon. A Stolen Biography. Transltors F. Carroll and N. Karsov. London: Nina Karsov, 1985. 172p.

1983 Torres, Tereska. The Converts. New York: Alfred A. Knopf, 1970. 308p. 1987 Turkow, Zygmunt. Theatre Memoirs of a Stormy Period. Buenos Aires, 1956. 374p.

1984 Ulam, Stanisław M. Adventures of a Mathematician. New York: Scribner, 1976. xi, 317p.

1985 Wachstein, Bernhard. "Letters of Wolwel Ehrenkranz from Zbaraz." YIVO Filog. Szriftn 2 (Wilno, 1928): 1-42.

1986 Wat, Aleksander. My Century: Oral Memoirs. London: Polonia Book Fund Ltd., 1977. 373p. (P)

1987 Weinlos L. "From J. Perl's Archives: Letters." Historisze Szriftn IVO. 1 (Warsaw, 1929): 809-814. (P)

1988 Weizmann, Chaim. "My Early Days." GT (New York: 1967): 375-383.

1989 Weizmann, Chaim. Trial and Error: The Autobiography. Westport, Conn.: Greenwood Press, 1972. vii, 408p.

1990 Wieviorka, Annette and Niborski, Itzok. Books of Recollections: Memoirs of Polish Jews. Paris: Éditions Gallimard/Julliard, 1983., 184p. (F)

1991 Wolf, Zeew. Collection of Letters, Articles and Memoirs of Rabbi Zeew Wolf from Strykow. Łódź: 1925. 48p. (H)

1992 Wudzki, Leon. Diary of a Student. Warsaw: Państwowy Instytut Wydawniczy, 1961. 336p. (P)

1993 Zelmanowich, Ephraim L. Episodes from My Life. Mexico City: Gezelshaft far Kultur un hilf, 1956. 286p.

1994 Zunser, Miriam Shomer. Yesterday. New York: Stackpole Sons, 1939. 271p.

33
Biographies and Biographical Materials

Aaron of Starosielce

1995 Jacobs, L. Seeker of Unity: The Life and Works of Aaron of Starosielce. London: Vallentine, Mitchell, 1966. 168p.

Adler, Jankel

1996 Themerson, Stefan. "Jankel Adler, an Artist Seen from One of Many Angles." Nowa Polska. 11 (London, 1944): 762-767. (P)

Ahad, Ha-Am, (pseud.of Asher Ginzberg)

1997 Simon, Sir Leon. Ahad Ha-am, Asher Ginzberg: A Biography. Philadelphia: Jewish Publication Society of America, 1960. 348p. illus.

Alter, Abraham, Mordecai

1998 Prager, Moshe. "When Hasidim of Ger became Newsmen." GT (New York, 1984): 210-213.

Ansky S. (pseud. of Solomon Zaynvl Rapoport)

1999 Lunsky, Haykel. "A Half Year with Ansky." GT (New York, 1984): 311-313.

Askenazy, Szymon

2000 Dutkiewicz, Józef. Szymon Askenazy and His School. Warsaw: Państwowe Wydawnictwo Naukowe, 1958. 249p. (P)

2001 Kukiel, Marian. Szymon Askenazy. Warsaw: Dom Książki Polskiej, 1935. 24p. (P)

2002 Szulkin, Michał. "Szymon Askenazy and His Contribution to Historical Science." BŻIH 2/82 (1972): 3-13. (P)

2003 Woliński, Janusz. "The Warsaw University Years of Szymon Askenazy, 1883-1887." Rocznik Warszawski (Warsaw, 1971): 143-158. (P)

Babel, Izaak E.

2004 Satajczyk, J. "Polish Episode in Izaak E. Babel' Biography." Zeszyty Naukowe WSP w Opolu 9, (Opole: September 1973): 103-106. (P)

Balaban, Majer

2005 Horn, Maurycy. "Majer Bałaban the Outstanding Historian of Polish Jews and Pedagogue, 1877-1942: On the Fortieth Anniversary of His Death." BŻIH 3-4/123-124, (1982): 3-15. (P)

2006 Kroszcor, Henryk. "Majer Bałaban's Publicism in the Columns of Nasz Kurier and Nasz Przegląd." BZIH 3/103 (1977): 49-73. (P)

2007 Szulkin, Michał. "Professor Dr. Majer Bałaban: On the Hundredth Anniversary of His Birth." BŻIH 1/101 (1977): 3-16. (P)

Begin, Menachem

2008 Korboński, Stefan. "An Unknown Chapter in the Life of Menachem Begin and Irgun Zvai Leumi." East European Quarterly 13, no.3. (1977): 373-379.

Beniowski, Bartłomiej

2009 Stocki, E. "Bartłomiej Beniowski: Forgotten Physician, Political Activist and Journalist." BŻIH 21, (1957): 115-117. (P)

Ben-Ya'akov, Issac

2010 Haberman, A.M. "Yitshak Aiosik Ben-Ya'akov Creator of 'The Treasury of Books'." YIVO Bleter 1, (October, 1951): 1-6. (H)

Bernstein, Aryeh Leib

2011 Gelber, Nathan Michael. "Aryeh Leib Bernstein, Chief Rabbi of Galicia." Jewish Quarterly Review 14 (1923/1924) : 303-327.

Bloch, Jan

2012 Sokołow, Nahum. "Jan Bloch: The Loyal Convert." GT (New York: 19667): 344-349.

Bluth, Rafal

2013 Weintraub, Wiktor. "Rafał Bluth." In Straty Kultury Polskiej, 1939-1944. Edited by Adam Ordęga (pseud. of Witold Hulewicz) and Tymon Terlecki. (Glasgow: Książnica Polska, 1945) 2, pp.273-283. (P)

Brummer, Wiktor

2014 Terlecki, Tymon. "Wiktor Brummer." In Straty Kultury Polskiej. 2 (Glasgow, 1945): 284-290. (P)

Budko, Joseph

2015 Friedeberger, Hans. <u>Joseph Budko, 1888-1940</u>. Berlin: F, Gurlitt, 1920. 22p. illus. (G)

Czyński, Jan

2016 Ciołkosz, Adam and Ciołkosz, Lidia. "Jan Czyński." In <u>Zarys Dziejów Socjalizmu Polskiego</u> 1 (London: Gryf Publications, Ltd., 1966): 199-222. (P)

2017 Danielewicz, J. "Jan Czyński and His Struggle for Equal Rights of the Jewish Population." <u>BŻIH</u> 11-12 (1954): 96-108. (P)

2018 Świerczewska, Krystyna. "Jan Czyński - Political Activist, Man of Letters and Publicist of the Great Emigration Days, 1801-1867." <u>Prace Polonistyczne Towarzystwa Literackiego im. Adama Mickiewicza Oddział w Łodzi</u> 8 (Wrocław-Łódź, 1951): 111-136. (P)

Dawidsohn, Joseph

2019 Frenk, Azriel Nathan and Zagorodski, Israel Chaim. <u>The Dawidsohn Family</u>. Warsaw: 1924. xxviii, 105p. illus. (Y)

Diamand, Bernard

2020 Brożek, Andrzej. "Materials to a Biography of Bernard Diamand, 1861-1921." <u>BŻIH</u> 4/28 (1982): 71-97. (P)

Diamand, Herman

2021 Piasecki, Henryk. "Herman Diamand in the Period 1890-1918." <u>BŻIH</u> 2/10 (1978): 33-49. (P)

2022 Piasecki, Henryk. "Herman Diamand in the Period of the Second Republic, November 1918 - May 1926." <u>BŻIH</u> 3/111, (1979): 63-72. (P)

2023 Piasecki, Henryk. "Henryk Diamand in the Period of the Second Republic, May 1926 - February 1931." <u>BŻIH</u> 1/113 (1980): 44-55. (P)

2024 Próchnik, Adam. "Herman Diamand: A Biography." <u>Kronika Ruchu Rewolucyjnego w Polsce</u>. 4, no. 1/13 (January, Februrary, March 1938): 181-188. (P)

Dickstein, Szymon (pseud. Jan Młot)

2025 Birkenmeier, Aleksander. "Szymon Dickstein." <u>Kwartalnik Historyczny</u> 53 (Warsaw, 1946): 477-479. (P)

2026 Krzywicki, Ludwik. "Jan Młot (Szymon Dickstein)." <u>Niepodległość</u> 1, no.1. (Warsaw: October 1929 - March 1930): 80-102. (P)

Dratner, Mendel

2027 Kanc, Szymon. <u>Mendel Dratner: A Report</u>. Warsaw: 1952. 52p. (Y)

Elchonon

2028 Shapiro, Chaim. "My Years with Reb Elchonon." The Jewish Observer 9, no.6. (1973): 12-17.

Eliezere Ben Jehuda

2029 Book to Commemorat Eliezere Ben Jehuda. New York: 1918. 92p. (H)

Elijah Ben Solomon Zalman

2030 Ben Sasson, H.H. "The Personality of Elijah Gaon of Vilno and His Historical Influence." Zion. 31, (Jerusalem: 1966): 36-86 et 197-216. (H)

2031 Schechter, Solomon. "Rabbi Elijah Vilna Gaon." Studies in Judaism: First Series. (Philadelphia, 1911): 73-98.

Elimelech R. from Lezajsk

2032 Landau, Bezalel. Rabbi R. Elimelech. Jerusalem: 1962. 329p. illus. (H)

Famous Jewish Women

2033 Citron, Samuel Loeb. Famous Jewish Ladies. Warsaw: 1928. 198p. (Y)

Feldman, Wilhelm

2034 Brückner, Aleksander et al. In Memory of Wilhelm Feldman. Kraków: Drukarnia Narodowa, 1922. 153p. (P)

2035 Finkelshtayn, Leo. "Wilhelm Feldman: Unforgotten Critic of Polish Literature." Literarisze Bleter 66, (Warsaw: August 7, 1925): 4-6. (Y)

Feivesh

2036 Bałaban, Majer. "Feivesh, Dictator of the Kahal in Krakow." YIVO Bleter 8, no.3. (Wilno, 1935): 223-234. (Y)

Felsenhardt, Rosalia

2037 Wawrzykowska-Wierciochowa, Danuta. "Rozalia Felserdt (1864-1887): Little Known Activist of the Great Proletariat." BŻIH 57 (1960): 105-120. (P)

Feuerman, Mosze

2038 Weinlos I. et al. Memorial Book to Honor Dr. Mosze Feuerman Hebrew Teacher in the Lwów Pedagogium. Lwów: 1926. 62p. (H)

Gepner, Abraham

2039 Lichten, Józef. "One of the Just: Abraham Gepner." THe Polish

Review. 14, no.1. (Winter, 1969): 40-52.

Gordon, Judah Leib

2040 Bader, Gershom. "I Meet the Mountain Lion." In GT (New York, 1984): 135-137.

Gottlieb, Maurycy

2041 Sandel, J. "Maurycy Gottlieb: Matejko's Pupil." BŻIH 8, (1953): 97-142. (P)

Gottlober, Abraham Ber

2042 Fridkin, Isaac. Abraham Ber Gottlober and His Epoch. Wilno: 1925. 2 vols. ed. by Fridckin and Z. Reisin. (Y)

Grosser, Bronisław

2043 Grinberg, Maria. "Bronisław Grosser, 1883-1912: On the Hundredth Anniversary of His Birth." BŻIH 2-3/126-127, (1983): 97-109. (P)

Grynbaum, Yizhak

2044 Mangel, Estera et al. "On the Fiftieth Birthday of Yizhak Grynbaum." Cyonistisze Bleter 29/54, (Warsaw, 1929): 421-448. (Y)

Gumplowicz, Ludwig

2045 Posner, Stanisław. Ludwik Gumplowicz, 1838-1909: Outline of His Life and Work. Warsaw: Towarzystwo Akcyjne S. Orgelbranda i Synów, 1911. 206p. illus. (P)

Guzikow, Jozef Michal

2046 Fuks, Marian. "Jozef Michal Guzikow: A Forgotten Musical Genius." BŻIH 2/78 (1971): 61-72. (P)

Hahn, Ryszard

2047 Torchalski, Ryszard. "Wiktor Hahn (1871-1959) - Historian of Literature, Bibliographer and Organizer of Scientific Life." Kwartalnik Historii Nauki i Techniki 15 (Warsaw, 1970): 71-79. (P)

Handelsman, Marceli

2048 Kuczyński, Stefan Krzysztof. "Bibliography of Marceli Handelsman's Works." Przeglad Historyczny 5 (Kraków, 1959): 116-121. (P)

2049 Moszczeńska, W. "Marceli Handelsman." Kwartalnik Historyczny 63, no.3. (1956): 111-150. (P)

Heilpern, Maksymilian

2050 Szulkin, Michał. "Maksymilian Heilperin: Socialist Activist and

Educator: On the 50th Anniversary of His Death." BŻIH 4/92 (1974): 3-13. (P)

Hirsch, Maurice Baron

2051 Schorr, Moses. Sage of the Heart: Homily Given in the Great Synagogue in the Tłumacki Square in Warsaw on Occasion of the Hundredth Anniversary of the Birth of Baron Maurice Hirsh, January 9, 1932. Warsaw: 1932. 16p. (P)

Horovitz, Jacob Isaak

2052 Alfassi, J. "The 'Seer' of Lublin and His Students." Sinai 59 (1966): 251-279. (H)

Infeld, Leopold

2053 Trautman, Andrzej. "Leopold Infeld." Acta Physica Poloniae 33 (1968): 165-170. (P)

Israel ben Shabbethai of Kozienice

2054 Rabinowitz, Zvi Meir. The Sage of Kos'nits. Jerusalem: 1947. 156p. illus. (H)

Jakubowiczowa, Judyta

2055 Eisenbach, Artur and Kosim, Artur. "Deed of the Estate of Judyta Jakubowiczowa." BŻIH 39 (1961): 88-143. (P)

Jogiches, Leon (pseud. Jan Tyszka)

2056 Leder, Zdzisław (pseud. of Władysław Fainstein). Biography of Leon Jogiches. Warsaw: Książka i Wiedza, 1976. 143p. (P)

Joselewicz, Berek

2057 Bałaban, Majer. Memorial Album to Honor Berek Joselewicz, Colonel of the Polish Army on the 125th Anniversary of His Heroic Death. Warsaw: Komitet Wileński ku Uczczeniu Pamięci Berka Joselewicza 1934. 208p. illus.

2058 Łuninski, Ernest. Berek Joselewicz. Kock: Komitet Obywatelski Budowy Pomnika-Szkoły Zawodowej i Powszechnej im. Pułk. Berka Joselewicza, 1928. 47p. illus. (P)

2059 Łuninski, Ernest. Berek Joselewicz and His Son: Historical Outline. Warsaw: Towarzystwo Akcyjne S. Orgelbranda i Synów, 1909. 136p. illus. (P)

Kacenelson, Icchak

2060 Novitch, Miriam. "Icchak Kacenelson." BŻIH 2-3/126-127 (1983): 127-134. (P)

Kalahora, Mattathias

2061 Bałaban, Majer. "The Kalahors: From Studies of Krakow Families." In His Z Historii Zydow w Polsce. (Warsaw, 1920): 90-103.

Klaczko, Julian

2062 Hoesick, Ferdynand. Julian Klaczko: His Life and Works. Warsaw: Trzaska, Evert i Michalski, 1934. 471p. (P)

2063 Tarnowski, Stanisław. Julian Klaczko. Kraków: Drukarnia Czasu, 1909. 2 vols (322 + 390 pp.) (P)

Klausner, Joseph

2064 Shohetman, Baruch and Elizedek, Bezalel. Biography of Joseph Klausner. Tel Aviv: 1937. 528p. (H)

Kleiner, Juliusz

2065 Kawyn, Stefan at al (eds). Jubilee Book to Commemorate Forty Years of Professor Doktor Juliusz Kleiner's Scholarly Work. Łódź: Towarzystwo Literackie im. Adama Mickiewicza, 1949. (P)

Korczak, Janusz

2066 Apenszlak, Pauline. Yanush Kortshak. Transl. from Polish by Diana Blumenfeld. Buenos Aires: Tsentral Farband fun Poilische Yidden, 1958. 361p. (Y)

2067 Bird, Thomas E. et al. "Janusz Korczak Symposium." The Polish Review 24, no.1 (New York, 1979): 22-45.

2068 Chiel, S. Janusz Korczak. "Assimilationist or Positive Jew?" Judaism 24 (1975) 319-328.

2069 Falkowska, Maria et al. (eds). A Chronology of the Life, Activities and Works of Janusz Korczak. Translated from Polish by E. Kulawiec. New York: The Kościuszko Foundation, 1980. 50p.

2070 Fuks, Marian. "Janusz Korczak's Mały Przegląd (Little Review)." BŻIH 1/105 (1978): 3-28. (P)

2071 Karren, Tamara (pseud. of T. Zagórska). Who Was That Man? A Piece on Janusz Korczak. London: Oficyna Poetów i Malarzy, 1981. 48p. (P)

2072 Lichten, Jozef. "Janusz Korczak and Poland." Wiadomości 32, no.6/1662 (London, February 5, 1978). (P)

2073 Olczakowa, Hanna (Mortkowicz). Mister Doctor: The Life of Janusz Korczak. Translated by Romuald Jan Kruk and Harold Gresswell. London: P. Davies, 1965. 227p.

2074 Piotrowski, Jan. Father of the Other Peoples' Children: Reminiscences About the Old Doctor Janusz Korczak. Łódź: Poligrafika,

1946. 55p. (P)

2075 Sakowska, Ruta. "On the Hundreth Anniversary of Janusz Korczak's Birthday." BŻIH 2/110 (1979): 93-96. (P)

2076 Szulkin, Michał. "Janusz Korczak as Educator: On the Hundredth Anniversary of His Birth." BŻIH 2/110 (1979): 21-31. (P)

2077 Szulkin, Michał. "Janusz Korczak - Contributor to the Pedagogical Periodical Szkoła Specjalna." BŻIH 1/105 (1978): 29-37 (P)

Koritzer, Pinkhas

2078 Heschel, Abraham J. "Reb Pinkhas Koritzer." YIVO Bleter 33 (1949): 9-48. (Y)

Kraushar, Aleksander

2079 Koczorowski, Stanisław Piotr. "Bibliography of Aleksander Kraushar's Works, 1861-1930." Przegląd Historyczny 30 (Kraków, 1930): 278-300. (P)

2080 Shatzky, Jacob. "Alexander Kraushar and His Road to Total Assimilation." YIVO Annual of Jewish Social Science 7 (New York, 1952): 146-174.

Krauss, Marie Augusta

2081 Whitby, H.A. Morton. Courage her Passport: The Story of Marie Augusta Krauss (alias Mary Josephine Van Hauweart). London: Frederick Muller, 1963. 204p. illus.

Krochmal, Nachman

2082 Rapoport, Solomon J. "On the Death of Nachman Krochmal." GT. (1984): 225-232.

Kronenberg, Leopold

2083 Doleżal, Franciszek et al (eds). Leopold Kronenberg: A Collective Monograph. Warsaw: Wydawnictwa Wychowanków b. Szkoły Handlowej, 1922. (P)

Kwiatek, Józef

2084 Piasecki, Henryk. "Józef Kwiatek - Organizer of The Armed Demonstration in 1904." BŻIH 2/90 (April-June, 1974): 47-61. (P)

Landowska, Wanda

2085 Gavoty, Bernard. Wanda Landowska. Geneva: R. Kister, 1956. 30p. illus. (F)

Lange, Antoni

2086 Borowy, Wacław. "Antoni Lange, 1862-1929." Pamiętnik Warszawski 1 (1929): 250-263. (P)

Lebenson, Micah Joseph

2087 Pitlik, Samuel. "Micah Joseph Lebenson: On the Hundreth Anniversary of His Death." Jewish Book Annual 11 (New York, 1952/1953): 164-168.

Leib, Nehemias Jehuda

2088 Lamm, Louis. Nehemias Jehuda Leib, Martyr for the Jewish Body Tax. Berlin: L. Lamm, 1910. 19p. (G)

Lestchinsky, Jacob

2089 Manor, Alexander. "Jacob Lestchinsky On His Eighty-Fifth Birthday." Jewish Journal of Sociology 4, no.1 (June, 1962): 101-106.

Lévy, Armand

2090 Borejsza, Jerzy W. Adam Mickiewicz's Private Secretary: Armand Lévy and His Time, 1827-1891. Warsaw: Państwowy Instytut Wydawniczy, 1969. 458p. (P)

Liberman, Aron Shmuel

2091 Piasecki, Henryk. "Aron Liberman (1844-1880): Pioneer of the Socialist Movement Among Jews." BŻIH 2/102 (1977): 17-34. (P)

Luxemburg, Rosa

2092 Ciołkosz, Adam. Roza Luksemburg and the Russian Revolution. Paris: Instytut Literacki, 1961. 257p. (P)

2093 Ettinger, Elżbieta. (ed. and transl.) Luxemburg, Rosa, 1871-1919: Comrade and Lover. Rosa Luxemburg's Letters to Leo Jogiches. Cambridge, Mass.: M.I.T. Press, 1979. xxxiv, 206 illus.

2094 Frölich, Paul. Rosa Luxemburg: Her Life and Work. Translated by Edward Fitzgerald. London: Victor Gollancz Ltd., 1940. 336p.

2095 Kochański, Aleksander. Róża Luxemburg. Warsaw: Książka i Wiedza, 1976. 416p. (P)

2096 Nettl, J.P. Rosa Luxemburg. New York: Oxford University Press, 1966. 2 vols (combined: xviii, 984).

2097 Richards, Michael D. "Rosa Luxemburg: Heroine of the Left." History Today 22 (London, 1972): 103-110.

2098 Schulze-Wilde, Harry. Rosa Luxemburg: I Was - I am - I will Be: Biography with Excerpts from Rosa Luxemburg's Speeches and Writings. Vienna: Molden, 1970. 264p. (G)

Maimon, Solomon

2099 Atlas, Samuel H. From Critical to Speculative Idealism: The Philosophy of Solomon Maimon. The Hague: Nijhoft, 1964. 335p.

2100 Jacobs, Noah J. "Solomon Maimon's Life and Philosophy." Studies in Bibliography and Booklore 4, no.2 (December, 1959): 59-67.

2101 Jacobs, Noah J. "Solomon Maimon's Relation to Judaism: An Annotated Bibliography." Kirjath Sepher 41 (1966): 145-262. (H)

Mark, Bernard

2102 Eisenbach, Artur. "Bernard Mark, 8.VI.1908-4.VII.1966." BŻIH 59 (July- September, 1966): 101-104. (P)

Medem, Vladimier

2103 Portnoy, Samuel A. The Life and Soul of a Legendary Jewish Socialist, Wladimir Medem. New York: KTAV Publishing House, 1979. xxxvi, 583p.

Meisels, Dob Berush

2104 Kamelhar, M. Rabbi Dov Ber Maizels: Great Scholar in the Holy Scriptures (Torah), Politician and Freedom Fighter. Jerusalem: 1970. 200p. illus. (H)

2105 Kupfer, Efraim F. Ber Meisels: His Part in the Struggle for Freedom of the Polish Nation and for Equal Rights for the Jews. Warsaw: Jiddish Bukh, 1952. 231p. (Y)

2106 Kupfer, Efraim F. Ber Meisels and His Part in Liberation Struggles of the Polish Nation: 1846, 1848 and 1863-1864. Warsaw: Żydowski Instytut Historyczny, 1953. 159p. (P)

2107 Szpet, N. "The Great Polish Patriot Ber Meisels." Ilustrierte Pojlisze Manczester. 5 (Łódź, 1930): 25-26. (Y)

Mendel, Menahem

2108 Gliksman, Pinnas Zelig. "Menahem Mendel's Hasidic Mode." GT. (1984): 103-107.

Menkes, Zygmunt

2109 Czapliński, Stanisław. "The Painters of Montparnasse." Przegląd Polski (New York: Oct. 10, 1985): 12-13. (P)

Morgenstern, Mendel (Kock Rabbi)

2110 Gliksman, Pinhas Zelig. The Kock Rabbi: The Learned Rabbi Mendl (of Blessed Memory) Morgenshtern, His Origin, Life, His Teachers, Friends and His Method in Instruction of Torah and Hasidism, His Children and Grandchildren. Piotrków: 1938/1939: 2 vol. (Y)

Nahman ben Simhah of Bracław

2111 Berger, A. "Approaches to Rabbi Nahman and his Tales." In Studies in Jewish Bibliography, History and Literature in Honor of I. Edward Kiev. New York: KTAV, 1971. pp. 11-20.

2112 Horodezky, Samuel Aba. Rabbi Nahman von Brazlaw: Contribution to the History of Jewish Mysticism. Berlin: M. Poppelauer, 1910. 87p. (G)

2113 Piekarz.M. "The Turning Point in the Literary Expression of Nahman of Bratzlav." Tarbiz 40, (1971): 226-254. (H)

2114 Piekarz, M. "The Uman Period in the Life of R. Nahman of Bratzlav and its Importance in the Development of Bratzlav Hasidic Thought." Zion. 36, (1971): 61-87. (H)

2115 Rappoport, A. "Two Sources of R. Nahman's Journey to the Holy Land." Kiriat Sefer. 46, (1970): 147-153. (H)

2116 Weiss, J. "R. Nahman of Bratzlav on the Dispute about Him." Gershom Sholem Jubilee Volume (1958): 232-245.

2117 Weiss, J. "R. Nahman of Bratzlav's Hidden Book on the Advent of the Messiah." Kiriat Sefer. 44, (1968/1969): 279-297. (H)

2118 Zeitlin, H. Rabbi Nahman of Bratslav: His Life and Teaching. New York: 1952. 302p. (H)

Namier, Sir Lewis (Bernstein-Namierowski)

2119 Rose, Norman. Lewis Namier and Zionism. New York: Oxford University Press, 1980. 192p.

Neufeld, Daniel

2120 Shatzky, Jacob. "Contribution to A Biography of Daniel Neufeld." YIVO Bleter. 7, (Wilno, 1934): 110-116. (Y)

Newachowicz, Judah Leib

2121 Kołodziejczyk, Ryszard. "Leon Newachowicz, 1776-1831." Rocznik Warszawski. 8, (1968): 143-173p. (P)

Nossig, Alfred

2122 Mendelsohn, Ezra. From Assimilation to Zionism in Lwow: The Case of Alfred Nossig." The Slavonic and East European Review 49, no. 117. (October, 1971): 521-534.

Orenstein-Braude

2123 Bałaban, Majer. Genealogy of the Orenstein-Braude Family. Warsaw: 1931. x. 47p. (H)

Ortwin, Ostap (Katzenelenbogen)

2124 Kleiner, Juliusz. "Ostap Ortwin." Pamiętnik Literacki (1946): 302-308. (P)

2125 Terlecki, Tymon. "Ostap Ortwin." In his (ed.) Straty Kultury Polskiej 2, (Glasgow, 1945): 342-373. (P)

Peltyn Samuel Hirsh

2126 Sokołow, Nahum. "S.H. Peltyn: Literary Effigy." Izraelita 46, (November 15, 1896): 1-4. (P)

Peretz, Isaac Leibush

2127 Meisel, Nachman. I. L. Peretz: His Life. New York: 1951. 404p. (Y)

2128 Meltzer, Shimsshon. (ed. and transl.) I.L. Peretz and His Works. Tel Aviv: 1960/1961. 2 vols in 1. (H)

2129 Nomberg, Hersh D. "Master of a Literary Generation." GT (1984): 286-297.

2130 Roback, Abraham Aaron. I.L. Peretz: Psychologist of Literature. Cambridge, Mass: Science-Art Publishers, 1935. 457p. illus.

2131 Samuel, Maurice. Prince of the Ghetto. Philadelphia: Jewish Publication Society of America, 1948. 294p.

2132 Trunk, Jehiel Isaiah. "Peretz at Home." GT (1984): 297-304.

Perl, Feliks

2133 Kielecki, W. Feliks Perl: An Attempt at A Biography. Warsaw: 1929. 88p. (P)

2134 Piasecki, Henryk. "Feliks Perl: Historian and Activist of the Polish Socialist Party (PPS)." BŻIH 4/92, (October-December, 1974): 59-70. (P)

2135 Wilczek, Ignacy. "Feliks Perl." Tydzień Polski (London: January 5, 1980). p. 4.

Perl, Yosef

2136 Friedman, Philip. "Yosef Perl as an Educational Activist in His School in Tarnopol." YIVO Bleter 31-32 (New York, 1948): 131-192. (Y)

Pollak, Roman

2137 Sajkowski, Alojzy. "Roman Pollak." Rocznik Towarzystwa Literackiego 3 (Warsaw, 1968): 125-132. (P)

Poznański, Samuel

2138 Bałaban, Majer. "Dr. Samuel Poznanski, 1864-1921: Biographical Outline." In Livre d'hommage a la Memoire du Dr. Samuel Poznanski. (Warsaw, 1927): ix-xxxiii. (P)

Pragier, Adam

2139 Ciołkosz, Adam. "Over the Grave of Adam Pragier." Wiadomości.

31, 34/35. (August 22-29, 1976): 1-2. (P)

Rabinovich, Sholem (pseud. Sholem Alejchem)

2140 Mark, Bernard. Szolem Alejchem, 1859-1916: His Era, Life and Works. Warsaw: Idisz Bush, 1959. 70p. (P)

Rapoport, Solomon Jehuda

2141 Barzilay, Issac. Shlomo Yehudah Rapoport [Shir] (1790-1867) and His Contemporaries: Some Aspects of Jewish Scholarship of the Nineteenth Century. Jerusalem: Massada Press Ltd., 1969. 214p.

2142 Kurlander, Aaron Tseki Hirsch. S. L. Rapoport: Biographical Study Based on Best Sources. Pest: Selbst-Verlag des Verfassers, 1868. 32p. (G)

Redlich, Henryk

2143 Podhorizer-Sandel, Erna. "Henryk Redlich - Engraver." BŻIH 1/77 (January-March, 1971): 65-78. (P)

Rokeach, Joshua

2144 Margoshes, Joseph. "Upholder of the Faith, the Rebbe of Bełz." GT (1984): 192-195.

Ringelblum, Emmanuel

2145 Szulkin, Michał. "Doctor Emmanuel Ringelblum: A Historian and Organizer of the Warsaw Ghetto's Undeground Archives." BŻIH 30 (1973): 111-125. (P)

Rubinsztejn, Ester

2146 Cytron, Szymon L. Book to Commemorate Ester Rubinsztejn. Wilno: 1926. 88p. (H)

Sadeger (Abraham Jacob Freedman)

2147 Ewen, Isaac. "The Golden Dynasty: Rebbe of Sadeger." GT (1984): 195-200.

Salomon, Haym

2148 Russell, Charles Edward. Haym Salomon and the Revolution. New York: Cosmopolitan Book Corporation, 1930. xv, 317p.illus.

Sandel, Jozef

2149 Podhorizer-Sandel, Erna. "Reminiscence About Jozef Sandel: On the 10th Anniversary of His Death." BŻIH 1/85 (1973): 111-119. (P)

Schiller, Leon

2150 Csato, Edward. Leon Schiller, 1887-1954. Warsaw: Państwowy Instytut Wydawniczy, 1968. 589p. (P)

Schneersohn, Menahem Mendel

2151 Hellman, Chaim Meir. "The Rebbe of Lubavich Bests Count Uvarov." GT (1984): 107-110.

Schorr, Moses

2152 Ginzberg, Louis and Weiss, Abraham (eds). Studies in Memory of Moses Schorr, 1874-1941. New York, 1944. xiii, 270p. (H)

Schulz, Bruno

2153 Ficowski, Jerzy. Regions of Great Heresy: Essays On the Life and Literary Output of Bruno Schulz. Kraków: Wydawnictwo Literackie, 1967. 247p. illus. (P)

Singer, Isaac Bashevis

2154 Allentuck, Maria Epstein. The Achievement of Isaac Bashevis Singer. Carbondale, Ill.: Southern Illinois University Press, 1969, xix, 177p.

2155 Sinclair, Clive. The Brothers Singer (Isaac Bashevis and Israel Joshua). New York: Allison and Busby, 1983. 176p.

Skikne, Larushka Misha (Laurence Harvey)

2156 Hickey, Des and Smith, Gus. The Prince: Being the Public and Private Life of Larushka Mischa Skikne, A Jewish Lithuanian Vagabond Player, Otherwise Known as Laurence Harvey. London: Frewin, 1975. 272p. illus.

Sochaczewski, Aleksander

2157 Podhorizer-Sandel, Erna. "Aleksander Sochaczewski: Painter, Exile, Originator of A Picture-Gallery From Martyrology of Siberian Exiles." BŻIH 75, (July-September, 1970): 75-84. (P)

Spektor, Isaac Elhanan

2158 Lipshitz, Jacob Halevy. "In the Service of Isaac Elhanan Spektor." GT (1984): 186-192.

Stern, Abraham

2159 Flis, Michal. "From the Ghetto in Hrubieszow to Science's Apex: Abraham Stern Self-taught Person - Inventor." Mówią Wieki 8, (Warsaw, 1966): 1-4. (P)

Szulman, Michał

2160 Lewandowski, Józef. " To Commemorate Michał Szulman, (Together with Excerpts of Recollections of Szulman by Tadeusz Wieniawa-Długoszewski)." Zeszyty Historyczne 18 (Paris, 1970): 130-133. (P)

Szyk Artur

2161 Morelowski, Marian. Artur Szyk - Illuminator and the Racial-Ethnic Problem in Poland. Wilno: Znicz, 1933. 24p. (P)

Tenenbaum, Aaron

2162 Shatzky, Jacob. "Aaron Tenenbaum: First Jewish Charade Expert." YIVO Bleter 20, (New York, 1942): 127-128. (Y)

Thon, Osias

2163 Grynbaum, Isaac. "Osias Thon: Statesman of Polish Jews." GT (1984): 482-492.

2164 Thon-Rostowa, N. Ozjasz Thon: A Daughter's Recollections. Lwów: Cofim, 1937. 54p. illus. (P)

Tuwim, Julian

2165 Głowinski, Michał. Tuwim's Poetics and Polish Literary Tradition. Warsaw: Polska Akademia Nauk, Instytut Badań Literackich, 1962. 274p. (P)

2166 Jedlicka, Wanda and Toporowski, Marian (joint eds.). Reminiscences About Julian Tuwim. Warsaw: Czytelnik, 1963. 467p. (P)

2167 Kryński, Magnus J. "Politics and Poetry: The Case of Julian Tuwim." The Polish Review 18, no.4. (New York, 1973): 3-33. et Ibid. 19, no.2 (1974): 113-117.

2168 Levine, Madeline G. "Julian Tuwim: 'We, the Polish Jews . . .'" The Polish Review. 17, no. 4. (Autumn, 1972): 82-89.

The Vilna Gaon (Elijah Ben Solomon Zalman)

2169 Schechter, Solomon. "Rabbi Elijah Vilna Gaon." In his Studies in Judaism, First Series. (Philadelphia, 1911): 73-98.

Weizman, Chaim

2170 Reinharz, Jehuda. The Making of a Zionist Leader. New York: Oxford University Press, 1985. 743p. illus.

Włodarski, Marek (Henryk Streng)

2171 Morawski, Karol. "Marek Włodarski (Henryk Streng), 1903-1960: Monographic Exhibition in the National Museum in Warsaw." BŻIH 1/125 (1982): 109-113. (P)

Wolfowicz, Zelman

2172 Zych, Franciszek. Zelman Wolfowicz. Lwów: Nakładem Autora, 1896. 44p. (P)

Zalman, Schneur

2173 Mindel, Nissam. Rabbi Schneur Zalman. Brooklyn, N.Y.: Chabad Research Center, 1969. 340p.

Zamenhof, Ludwik Lazar

2174 Boulton, Marjorie. Zamenhof, Creator of Esperanto. London: Rutledge and Paul, 1960. 228p. illus.

2175 Lapenna, Ivo (ed.). Memorial Book to Celebrate the Hundred Years From the Birth of Dr. L.L. Zamenhof. London: Universala Esperanto-Associo, Centrode esploro kaj dokumentado, 1960. 104p. (E)

2176 Privat, Edmoond. The Life of Zamenhof. Transl. from Esperanto by Ralph Eliott. London: G. Allen and Unwin Ltd., 1931. 123p.

Zelman

2177 Bałaban, Majer. "Zelman, Mayor of the Drohobycz Jewish Community A Historical Sketch." Hacefira (1911): 256-268. (H)

Zygielbojm, Szmul Mordechaj

2178 Hertz, Jacob Sholem (ed.) Zygielboym Book. New York: 1947. 408p. (Y)

2179 Stein, Abraham Samuel. Comrade Artur. Tel Aviv: 1953. 304p. (Y)

34
Town Communities and Shtetls

Aleksandrów

2180 Blumental, Nachman (ed.). Aleksander. Tel-Aviv: Association of Former Residents of Aleksandrów in Israel, 1968. 391p. illus. (H and Y)

Augustów

2181 Alexandroni, Ya'akov (ed.). Memorial Book of the Community of Augustów and Vicinity. Tel Aviv: Association of Former Residents of Augustów and Vicinity in Israel, 1966. 549p. (H and Y)

Baranowicze

2182 Baranowitz: A Memorial Book. Tel Aviv: Association of Former Residents of Baranowitz in Israel, 1953. 668p. (H and Y)

Baranów

2183 Blumental, Nachman (ed.). Baranow. Jerusalem: Yad Vashem, 1964. x, 439p. illus. (H)

2184 Franzos, Karl Emil. The Jews of Baranow: Stories. New York: Arno Press, 1975. xxii, 334p.

Bełchatów

2185 Belchatow Memorial Book. Buenos Aires: Association of Polish Jews in Argentine, 1951. 511p. (Y)

Bełz

2186 Guttman, Mathias, Ezekiel. Belz. Tel-Aviv: 1951/1952.

Beresteczko

2187 Singer, Mendel (ed.). There Was a Town: Memorial Book of Beresteczko and Vicinity. Haifa: Association of Former Residents of Beresteczko in Israel, 1961. 555p. (H and Y)

Berezno

2188 Bigil, G. My Town Berezne. Tel Aviv: Berezner Society in Israel, 1954. 182p. (H and Y)

Będzin

2189 Bendin Chronicle. Tel Aviv: 1959. 33p. (H)

Biała (Zulz)

2190 Rabin, Israel Abraham. The Jews in Zulz. Neustadt, Buchdrückerei der Neustadter Zeitung, 1926. 44p. illus. (G)

Biała Podlaska

2191 Feigenbaum, Moses Joseph. Book of Biala Podlaska. Tel Aviv: Kupat Gmilut Hesed of the Community of Biała Podlaska, 1961. 501p. (H and Y)

Białystok

2192 Eisenbach, Artur. "On the Situation of the Jewish Population in Białystok District in 1861." Rocznik Białostocki 6 (Białystok, 1966): 459-471. (P)

2193 Herschberg, Abraham Samuel. The Chronicle of Bialystok. New York: Bialystok Jewish Historical association, 1949-1950. 2 vols. (480 + 380p) (Y)

2194 Kalabiński, Stanisław. "Proclamations of the Białystok Committees of Worker Parties to the Jewish Proletariat in 1897-1900." BŻIH 56 (1965): 81-113. (P)

2195 Kalabiński, Stanisław. "Proclamations of the Białystok Committees of Worker Parties to the Jewish Proletariat in 1901-1903." BŻIH 57 (1966): 63-103. (P)

2196 Korzec, Paweł. Half a Century of the Revolutionary Movement Story in the Białystok Region, 1864-1919. Warsaw: Książka i Wiedza, 1965. 369p. (P)

2197 Korzec, Paweł. "Jewish Handicraft in Białystok at the Turn of XIX and XX Centuries." BŻIH 50 (1964)(: 23-35. (P)

2198 Linder, Menakhem. "The Ruin of Jewish Commerce in the Bialystok Region." Yidishe Ekonomik 1, (1937): 13-33. (Y)

2199 Sohn, David. (ed.). Bialystok Photo Album of a Renowned City and its Jews the World Over. New York: Bialystoker Album Committee, 1951. 386p. illus.

2200 Sokół, Zofia. "Jewish Public Librarianship in Białystok, 1918-1939." BŻIH 3/103 (1977): 15-26. (P)

2201 Zabłotniak, Ryszard. "Some Information About the Jewish Health

Service in Białystok." BŻIH 60 (1966): 111-116. (P)

Biecz

2202 Wagschal, Pinhas, ed. Memorial Book of the Martyrs of Biecz. Ramat-Gan: Association of Former Residents of Biecz and Vicinity in Israel, 1959/1960. 356p. illus. (H and Y)

Bielica

2203 Losh, L., ed. Book of Belitzah -Bielica. Tel Aviv: Former Residents of Bielica in Israel and the USA, 1968. 511p. illus. (H and Y)

Bielsk

2204 Leszczyński, Anatol. "Jewish Handicrafts in the Bielsk Region from Mid-XVII Century up to 1795." BŻIH 1/101 (1977): 17-39. (P)

2205 Leszczyński, Anatol. "Jewish Innkeepers and Publicans of the Bielsk Region from the Second Half of the XVII Century to 1795." BŻIH 2/102 (1977): 77-85. (P)

2206 Leszczyński, Anatol. Jews of the Bielsk Region from the Mid-XVII Century up to 1795: Study of Settlement, Legal and Economic Problems. Warsaw: 1980. 276p. (P)

2207 Leszczyński, Anatol. "The Jewish Settlement Movement in Bielsk District up to 1795: Introductry Remarks, Literature and Sources." BŻIH 4/92 (1974): 31--58. (P)

2208 Leszczyński, Anatol. "Legal Status of Bielsk Region Jews from the End of the XVth Century to 1795." BŻIH 4/96 (1975): 3-36. (P)

Bieżuń

2209 Memorial Book of the Martyrs of Bieżuń. Tel-Aviv: Former Residents of Bieżuń, 1956. 186p. (H and Y)

Bobrujsk

2210 Slutsky, Jehuda, ed. Bobroysk Memorial Book. Tel Aviv: 1967. 2 vols, 871p.illus. (H and Y)

Bochnia

2211 Kiryk, Feliks. "From the History of the Jews in Bochnia." BŻIH 114-115 (1980): 23-30. (P)

Bolechów

2212 Linder, M. "The Tannery in Bolechow." Jidisze ekonomick 1, (1937): 19 ff. (Y)

Borszczów

2213 Blumental, Nachman, ed. The Book of Borshtshiv. Tel-Aviv: Association of Former Residents of Borszczów in Israel, 1960. 341p. (H and Y)

Bóbrka

2214 Kallay, Sharaga Feivel, ed. Bobrka Memorial Book. Jerusalem: Association of Former Residents of Bobrka and Vicinity, 1964. 218p. (H and Y)

Brody

2215 Friedlander, Moriz. Five Weeks in Brody Among Jewish-Russian Emigrants: A Contribution to the History of Russian Persecution of Jews. Vienna: M. Weizner, 1882. 52p. (G)

2216 Gelber, Natan Michael. History of the Jews in Brody, 1584-1943. Jerusalem: Mosad Horaw Kuk, 1955. 437p. (H)

2217 Lutman, Tadeusz. Studies on the History of the Trade of Brody in the Years 1773-1880. Lwów: Kasa im. Rektora J. Mianowskiego, 1937. 363p. (P)

2218 Wischnitzer, Mark. "Position of the Jews of Brody in International Trade During the Second Half of XVIII Century." Dubnow-Festschrift (Berlin, 1930): 113-123. (G)

Brześć nad Bugiem

2219 Feinstein, Aryeh Loeb and Finkelnstein, Abraham Mordecai. The Renowned City. Warsaw: 1886. 239p. (H).

2220 Steinman, Eliezer, ed. The Brest Litowsk Volume. Jerusalem: Encyclopaedia of the Jewish Diaspora, 1954. 647p. (H)

2221 Tomaszewski, Jerzy. "Two Documents on the Pogrom in Brześć in 1937." BŻIH 49 (1964): 58-67. (P)

Brzeziny

2222 Alperyn, A. and Summer, N. The Brzeziny Memorial Book. New York: Brzeziner Book Committee, 1961. 288p. (Y)

Buczacz

2223 Kahan, I., ed. The Book of Buchacz: In Memory of a Martyred Community. Tel-Aviv: Am. Oved, 1956. 302p. (H)

Budzanów

2224 Siegelman, Yitshak, ed. The Book of Budzanow. Haifa: Former Residents of Budzanów and Israel, 1968. 319p. illus. (H and Y)

Bursztyn

2225 Kanz, S., ed. The Book of Bursztyn. Jerusalem: The Encyclopaedia of the Jewish Diaspora, 1960. 426p. (H and Y)

Busk

2226 Gelber, Natan Michael. A History of the Jews of Busk. Tel-Aviv: Olameynu, 1962. 120p. (H)

2227 Shayari, Abraham, ed. Busk: In Memory of Our Community. Haifa: Busker Organization in Israel, 1965. 343p. illus. (H and Y)

Bychawa Lubelska

2228 Adini, Ya'akov, ed. Bihavah: A Memorial to the Jewish Community of Bychawa Lubelska. Tel Aviv: Bychawa Organization in Israel, 1969. 636p. illus. (H and Y)

Bydgoszcz (Bromberg)

2229 Herzberg, Isaak. History of Jews in Bromberg: Also a Contribution to the History of Jews in the Poznań Province Restored from Printed and Unprinted Sources. Frankfurt a/Main: J. Kauffman, 1903. 106p. (G)

2230 Taubler, Eugen. "Naturalization Licences in the Bromberg District up to April 1838," Mitteilungen des Gesammtarchivs der deutschen Juden. 2, (1910): 26-28. (G)

Byteń

2231 Abramowich, D. and Bernstein M.W. (eds.) The Book of Byten. Buenos Aires: Former Residents of Byten in Argentina, 1954. 605p. (Y)

Bytom (Beuthen)

2232 Kopfstein, M. History of the Synagogue Community in Beuthen, Upper Silesia. Beuthen: M. Nothmann, 1891. 64p. (G)

Chełm

2233 Bakalczuk-Felin, Meilech, ed. The Commemoration Book of Khelm. Johannesburg: Former Residents of Chelm, 1954. vi, 751p. illus. (Y)

2234 Eidelberg, S. "About the Origins of the Chełm and Włodzimierz Communities." Zion 27 (1962): 116ff. (H)

2235 Simon, Solomon. The Heroes of Chełm. New York: Posy-Shoulson Press, 1942. 151p. illus. (Y)

2236 Simon, Solomon. The Wise Men of Helm and Their Merry Tales. New York: Behrman House, 1945. 135p. illus.

2237 Tenenbaum, Samuel. The Wise Men of Chelm. New York: T.Yoseloff, 1945. 176p. illus.

Chęciny

2238 "Letter of the Checiny Municipal Council to the King and His Ministry." MSC 6 (1967): 464-466. (P)

2239 Paulewicz, Marian. "Jewish Settlement in Checiny." BŻIH 2/94 (1975): 25-30. (P)

2240 Paulewicz, Marian. "The Struggle of the Jews for a Domicile in Checiny." BŻIH 1/101 (1977): 63-64. (P)

Chmielnik

2241 Baranowski, Jerzy. "The Synagogue in Chmielnik." BŻIH 36 (1960): 95-106. (P)

Chojnice (Konitz)

2242 Sutor, Gustav. The Chojnice Murder and Its Consequences: An Appeal to Common Sense. Berlin: H. Schildberger, 1900. 32p. (G)

Chorostków

2243 Sztokfisz, David, editor. The Horostkov Book. Tel-Aviv: Committee of Former Residents of Chorostków in Israel, 1968. 418p. illus. (H and Y)

Choroszcza

2244 Leszczyński, Anatol. "Jews in Choroszcza from the Middle of the XVI century to 1795." BŻIH 4/88 (1973): 3-31. (P)

2245 Leszczyński, Anatol. "Registration of Natural Statistics of the Jewish Population in the town of Choroszcza in 1882-1914 Period." BŻIH 2/82 (1972): 73-89. (P)

Chorzeł

2246 Losh, L. ed. Memorial Book of the Community of Horz'el. Tel-Aviv: Association of Former Residents of Chorzeł in Israel, 1967. 272p. (H and Y)

Chrzanów

2247 Bochner, Mordecai. Book of Chrzanow: The Life and Death of the Yiddish Shtetl. Regensburg: 1949. xiii, 377p. illus. (H)

Ciechanowiec

2248 Leoni, Elieser, ed. The Tsihanovits Memorial and Records. Tel Aviv: The Ciechanowitzer Immigrant Association in Israel and the USA, 1964. 936p. illus. (H and Y)

Ciechanów

2249 Jasny, A. Wolf, ed. Memorial Book of the Community of Ciechanov.

Tel- Aviv: Former Residents of Ciechanow in Israel and in the Diaspora, 1962. 535p. (H and Y)

Cieszanów

2250 Ravid, D. ed. Memorial Book of the Martyred Community of Cieszanow. Tel- Aviv: Former Residents of Cieszanów in Israel, 1970. 333p illus. (H and Y)

Chmielnik

2251 Memorial Book of Chmielnik. Tel-Aviv: Former Residents of Chmielnik in Israel, 1960. 1299 columns. (H and Y)

Częstochowa

2252 Mahler, Raphael, ed. The Jews of Częstochowa. New York: United Czestochower Relief Committee and Ladies Auxiliary, 1947. xii, 404p. illus. (Y)

2253 Shuzman, M. ed. Memorial Book of Chenstochow. Jerusalem: The Encyclopaedia of Jewish Diaspora, 1968. lxxvii, 542p. (H an Y)

2254 Singer, S.D. ed. Czenstochow: A New Supplement to the Book "Czenstokhover Yiddn." New York: United Relief Committee and Ladies Auxiliary in New York, 1958. viii, 356p. illus. (Y)

2255 Szymański, Stanisław. "To the History of the Jews in Czestochowa During the Constitutional Era of the Polish Kingdom, 1815-1830." BŻIH 39 (1961): 17-38. (P)

Czortków

2256 Austri-Dunn, Isaias, ed. Memorial Book of Czortkow. Tel-Aviv, Haifa: Former Residents of Czortków in Israel, 1967. 435p. illus. (H and Y)

Dąbrowa Górnicza

2257 Gelbert, M. ed. Memorial Book of Dombrovah Garnitsah. Tel-Aviv: Former Residents of Dąbrowa Górnicza, 696p. illus. (H and Y)

Dąbrowica

2258 Losh, L., ed. Book of Dombrovitsa. Tel Aviv: Association of Former Residents of Dombrowitsa in Israel, 1964. 928p. (H and Y)

Dawidgródek

2259 Idan, Y. et al eds. Memorial Book of Davidgrodek. Tel Aviv: Former Residents of Davidgrodek in Israel, 195-. 487p. (H and Y)

Dereczyn

2260 Derets'in Memorial Book. Tel Aviv: Deretchiners Societes in Israel and U.S.A. 1971. 494p. illus. (H and Y)

Dębica

2261 Leibl, D., ed. Book of Dembits. Tel-Aviv: Association of Former Residents of Dembica. 204p. (H and Y)

Dęblin-Modrzyc

2262 Sztokfisz, David, ed. The Demblin-Modrzyc Book. Tel-Aviv: Association of Former Residents, of Demblin-Modrzyc, 1969. 694p. (H and Y)

Dobre Miasto (Guttstadt)

2263 Halpern, Filix. History of the Jewish Community in Guttstadt: Contribution to the History of the Jews in Ermland (Warmia). Guttstadt: Buchdrückerei der Guttstadter Zeitung, 1927. 45p. (G)

Dobromil

2264 Gelbart, Mendl, ed. Memorial Book of the Dobromil Community. Tel-Aviv: The Dobromiler Society in New York and The Dobromiler Organization in Israel, 1964. 389p. illus. (H and Y)

Dobrzyń

2265 Berman, J. "The Jewish Problem in Dobrzyn." Junger Historyker 1 (Warsaw, 1926): 102-106. (Y)

2266 Harpaz, M. My Town: In Memory of the Communities Dobrzyn - Gollob. Tel-Aviv: Association of Former Residents of Dobrzyń-Golub. 1969. 459p. illus. (H and Y)

Dokrzyce-Parafianów

2267 Sztokfisz, David, ed. Dokshits-Parafyanow Book. Tel-Aviv: Association of Former Residents of Dokszyc-Parafianow in Israel, 1970. 350p. illus. (H and Y)

Drohiczyn Poleski

2268 Warshawsky, Dov B., ed. Drohitshin: Five Hundred Years of Jewish Life. Chicago: Book-Committee Drohichyn, 1958. viii, 424p. illus. (Y)

Drohobycz

2269 Catalogue of the Library of Jewish Homes in Drohobycz. 1928, 15p. (P)

2270 Gatkiewicz, Feliks. From Drohobycz Archives: Collection of Privileges, Legal Acts, Border Decrees, Illustrations, etc. Drohobycz, 1906. 407p. (P)

2271 Gelber, Naton Michael. Memorial to the Jews of Drohobycz, Boryslaw and Surroundings. Tel-Aviv: Association of Former Residents of Drohobycz, Borysław and Surroundings, 1959. 224p. illus. (H and Y)

2272 Wikler, Jerzy. "From the History of Drohobycz Jews: From 1648 to the Fall of First Republic." BŻIH 71-72 (1969: 39-63p. (P)

Drużkopol

2273 Our Town Druzkopol. Haifa: Former Residents of Droshkopol in Israel, 1956. 108p. (H)

2274 Boxer, A. (Ben-Arjeh), ed. The Story of My 'Stetele Droshkopol'. Haifa: S. Isenberg, 1962. 108p. (Y)

Dubno

2275 Adini, Y., ed. A Memorial to the Jewish Community of Dubno, Wołyń. Tel-Aviv: Dubno Organization in Israel, 1956. 752 columns. (H and Y)

Działoszyn

2276 Gelberg, Jakub and Wein, Adam. " Memorial Book of the Jewish Consistory in Działoszyn from the Second Half of the XVIII Century." BŻIH 53 (1965): 81-112 et 56 (1965): 59-79. (P)

Dzisna

2277 Bernstein, Dov and Tsirlin, Shalom, eds. Disna: Memorial Book of the Community. Tel-Aviv: Former Residents of Disna in Israel and the USA, 1969. 227p. (Y and H)

Ejszyszki

2278 Barkeli, Sh., ed. Ejszyszki, its History and Destruction. Jerusalem: Committee of the Survivors of Ejszyszki in Israel, 1960. 136p. (H and Y)

Falenica

2279 Shtokfish, D., ed. The Falenica Book. Tel-Aviv: Former Residents of Falenica in Israel, 1967. 478p. (H and Y)

Gdańsk (Danzig)

2280 Andrzejewski, Marek. "Comments About History of Jews in the Free City of Gdańsk in the Inter-War Period." BŻIH 4/112 (1979): 67-98. (P)

2281 Echt, Samuel. The History of the Jews in Danzig. Leer-Osffriesland: Rautenberg, 1972. 282p. (G)

2282 Lichtenstein, Erwin. The Jews in the Free City of Danzig Under the National - Socialist Rule. Tübingen: J.C.B. Mohr, 1973. xiii, 242p. illus. (G)

2283 Stein, Abraham. History of the Danzig Jews: From Their First Appearence in That Town up to Recent Time: Manuscript Sources Gathered for the First Time. Danzig: Backer, 1933. 65p. (G)

Gdynia

2284 Ropelewski, Andrzej. "Jewish Courses on Fishing in Gdynia, 1936-1939." BŻIH 1/117 (1981): 59-61. (P)

Gliniany

2285 Halpern, H., ed. The Book of Gline. New York: Former Residence of Gline, 1950. 307p. (Y)

Gniewoszów

2286 Sztokfisz, David, ed. Memorial Book of Gniewashow. Tel-Aviv: Association of Gniewashow in Israel and Diaspora, 1971. 533p. illus. (H and Y)

Gniezno (Gnesen)

2287 Posner, Abraham Bernard. The Annals of the Gnesen Community. Jerusalem: 1958. xviv, 69p. illus. (H)

Goniądz

2288 Ben-Meir, J.(Treshansky) and Fayans, A.L., eds. Our Hometown Gonyondz. Tel-Aviv: The Committee of the Goniondz Association in the USA and in Israel, 1960. xx, 808p. illus. (H and Y)

Gorlice

2289 Bar-On, M.Y., ed. The Gorlice Book: The Community at its Rise and Fall. Tel-Aviv: Association of Former Residents of Gorlice and Vicinity in Israel, 1962. 338p. (H and Y)

Gościa

2290 Fink, Reuben, ed. The Book of Hoszt - In Memoriam. Tel-Aviv: Society of Hoszt, 1957. 294p. illus. (Y)

Gostynin

2291 Biderman, I.M., ed. Book of Gostynin. New York: Gostynin Memorial Book Committees, 1960. 358p. (Y)

Goworowo

2292 Kossovsky, Dov. and Burstein, Aviezer, edts. Govorovo Memorial Book. Tel-Aviv: The Gorover Societies in Israel, the USA and Canada, 1966. xvi, 496p. illus. (H)

Góra Kalwaria

2293 Alfasi, Yitshak. Gur. Tel-Aviv: "Hidushe ha-Rim", 1954. 207p. (H)

Grodno

2294 Friedenstein, Simeon Eliezer. A City of Heroes. Wilno: 1880. 109p. (H)

Gródek Jagielloński

2295 Margel, Lejbisz Jehuda. Grejding Jagiellonski Book. Tel-Aviv: Former Inhabitants of Gródek Jagielloński, 1981. 128p. (P)

2296 Simon (Shemen), M. Horodok - In Memory of the Jewish Community. Tel-Aviv: Associations of Former Residents of Grodek in Israel and Argentina, 1963. 142p. (H and Y)

Gryce (Gritze)

2297 Alterman, I.B., ed. Memorial Book of Gritze. Tel-Aviv: Gritzer Association in Israel. 1955. iv, 408p. (H and Y)

Horochów

2298 Kariv, Joseph and Dan, Haim, eds. Horokhov Memorial Book. Tel-Aviv: Horchiv Committee in Israel, 1966. 357, 79p. illus. (H and Y)

Horodec

2299 Ben-Ezra, Akiva, ed. Horodec: History of a Town, 1142-1942. New York: Horodetz Book Committee, 1950. viii, 238p. illus. (Y)

Horodenka

2300 Meltzer, Shimshon, ed. The Book of Horodenka. Tel-Aviv: Former Residents of Horodenka and Vicinity in Israel and the USA, 1963. vii, 425p. illus. (H and Y)

Horodło

2301 Zawidowitch, Y. Ch., ad. The Community of Horodlo: Memorial Book. Tel-Aviv: Former Residents of Horodło in Israel, 1962. 324p. (Y)

Hoszcz

2302 Ayalon-Baranicka, B.H. and Yaron-Kritzmar, A., eds. Hoshtch-Wolyn: In Memory of the Jewish Community. Tel-Aviv: Former Residents of Hoshtch in Israel, 1957. 269p. (H)

Hrubieszów

2303 Kapliński, Boruch, ed. Memorial Book of Hrubieshov. Tel-Aviv: Hrubieshov Associations in Israel and the USA, 1962. xviii, 812 columns. (H and Y)

Husiatyn

2304 Avituv, Abraham Yitshak. From My Parents Home: Memorial

Chapter. Tel-Aviv: 1965. 155p (H)

2305 Diamond, Benjamin, ed. Husyatin. New York: Former Residents of Husiatin in America, New York, 1968. 269p. illus. (Y)

Ilja

2306 Kopilevitz, A., ad. The Community of Ilja. Tel-Aviv: Former Residents of Ilia in Israel, 1962. 466p. (H and Y)

Inowrocław (Hohensalza)

2307 Heppner, Aron and Herzberg, J. From the Past and Present of Jews in Hohensalza: After Printed and Unprinted Sources. Frankfurt a/ Main: J. Kauffmann, 1907. 68p. illus. (G)

2308 Kutzig, Heinrich. East German Jewry: Tradition of A Family. Stolp: Eulitz, 1927. vii, 164p. (G)

2309 Lewin, Louis. "History of the Jews in Inowroclaw." Zeitschrift der Histrischen Geselschaft fur die Provinz Posen 15 (1900): 43-94. (G)

Iwje

2310 Kaganovich, Moshe, ed. In Memory of the Jewish Community. Tel-Aviv: Association of Former Residents of Ivie in Israel and "United Ivier Relief" in America, 1968. 738p. illus. (H and Y)

Izaak Colony

2311 Salit, Salomon. Izaac Colony: Village of the Sokółka District. Warsaw: Państwowy Instytut Naukowy Gospodarstwa Wiejskiego w Puławach, 1934. 106p. illus. (P)

Jadów

2312 Jasny, A. Wolf, ed. The Book of Yadov. Jerusalem: 1966. xxiii, 472p. illus. (Y and H)

Janów Poleski

2313 Nafav, M. (Katzikowski), ed. Janow near Pinsk: Memorial Book. Jerusalem: Association of Former Residents of Janow near Pinsk in Israel, 1969. 420p. (H and Y)

Jasło

2314 Herzig, Jacov Joshua. My Wonders in War and Yaslo My Town. Tel-Aviv: Hamenora, 1964. 157p. (H)

Jędrzejów

2315 Yerushalmi, Shimson Dov, ed. Memorial Book of the Jews of Jedrzejow. Tel-Aviv: Former Residents of Jedrzejow in Israel, 1956. 490p. illus. (H and Y)

Jezierany

2316 Tennenblatt, M.A., ed. Memorial Book: Jezierany and Surroundings. Jerusalem: Encyclopaedia of the Jewish Diaspora, n.d. 498 columns. (H and Y)

Jezierna

2317 Siegelman, J., ed. Memorial Book of Jezierna. Haifa: Committee of Former Residents of Jezierna in Israel, 1971. 354p. (H and Y)

Kalisz

2318 Bet-Halevi, Israel David. History of the Jews of Kalisz. Tel-Aviv: 1960/1961. 448p. illus. (H)

2319 Lask, Israel Meir, ed. THe Kalish Book. Tel-Aviv: The Societies of Former Residents of Kalish and the Vicinity in Israel and the USA, 1968. 327p. illus.

2320 Lewin, Louis. "Contributions to the History of the Jews in Kalisch." In Festschrift zu Ehren des Dr. A. Harkavy. St. Petersburg: 1908: 141-176. (G)

2321 Pakentreger, Aleksander. "Economic Situation of the Jewish Population in Kalisz After World War I, 1918-1921: Demographic Situation of Kalisz Jews after Poland Gained Independence." BŻIH 1-2/129-130 (1984): 25-37. (P)

2322 Pakentreger, Aleksander. "The Jewish Press in Kalish, 1918-1939." BŻIH 1/89 (1974): 97-108. (P)

2323 Szczepaniak, Marian. "A Village Inn in the Kalisz District in the Second Half of the XVII and in the XVIII Century." Rocznik Kaliski 5 (1972): 91-111 illus. (P)

Kałuszyn

2324 Shimri, A. and Soroka, Sh., eds. Memorial Book of Kalushin. Tel-Aviv: Former Residents od Kalushin in Israel, 1961. 545p. (Y)

Karlin

2325 Naday, Mordehai. "The Communities of Pinsk and Karlin Between Hasidim and Mitnaggedim." Zion 34 (1969): 98-108. (H)

Katowice (Kattowitz)

2326 Cohn, Jacob. History of the Synagogue - Community of Katowice. Katowice: J. Herlitz, 1900. 46p. (G)

Kazimierz

2327 Sztokfisz, David, ed. Kazimierz - Memorial Book. Tel-Aviv: Former Residents of Kazimierz in Israel and the Diaspora, 1970. 655p. illus. (H and Y)

Kępno

2328 Zajczyk, Szymon. "The Synagogue in Kępno." BŻIH 43-44 (1962): 63-83. (P)

Kielce

2329 Meducka, Marta. "Jewish Cultural Institutions in Kielce, 1918-1939." BZIH 1-2/129-130 (1984): 61-73. (P)

2330 Zitron, Phinehas. History of the Community of Kielce. Tel-Aviv: Former Residents of Kielce in Israel, 1957. 328p. illus. (H and Y)

Kleck

2331 Stein, E. S., ed. A Memorial to the Jewish Community of Klezk - Poland. Tel-Aviv: Former Residents of Klezk in Israel, 1959. 385p. (H and Y)

Kłobucko

2332 The Book of Klobucko: In Memory of A Martyred Community which was Destroyed. Tel-Aviv: Former Residence of Klobucko in Israel, 1960. 439p. (Y)

Kobryń

2333 Schwartz, Bezalel and Bilecki, Srol, eds. Book of Kobrin: The Scroll of Life and Destruction. Tel-Aviv: 1951, 347p. (H)

Kobylnik

2334 Siegelman, Yitshak, ed. Memorial Book of Kobilnik. Haifa: Committee of Former Residents of Kobilnik in Israel, 1967. 296p. illus. (H and Y).

Kock

2335 Porath, Elijahu, ed. Memorial Book of Kotsk. Tel-Aviv: Former Residents of Kotsk in Israel, 1961. 424p. illus. (H and Y)

Kolbuszowa

2336 Biderman, Israel M., ed. Kolbushov Memorial Book. New York: United Kolbushover, 1971. 881p. illus. (H and Y)

Kolno

2337 Halevy, Benjamin and Remba, Issac, eds. Kolnah Memorial Book. Brooklyn and New York: Center of Jewish Books, 1971. 750p. illus. (H and Y)

Kolki

2338 Kac, Daniel. Shadows from the Ashes. Warsaw: Czytelnik, 1983. 400p. illus. (Y)

Town Communities and Shtetls 175

Koło

2339 Helter, M., ed. <u>Memorial Book of Kolo</u>. Tel-Aviv: Former Residents of Kolo in Israel and the USA, 1958. 408p. (H and Y)

Kołomyja

2340 Bickel, Shlomo. <u>Memorial Book of Kolomea</u>. New York: 1957. 448p. illus. (Y)

2341 Schutzman, Mark and Noy, Dov., eds. <u>Kolomeyer Memorial Book</u>. Tel-Aviv: Former Residents of Kolomey and Surroundings in Israel, 1972. 395p. illus. (H)

Komarno

2342 Yashar, Baruch. <u>Komarno Memorial Book: from its Foundation to its Destruction</u>. Tel-Aviv: 1965. 204p. illus. (H)

Konin

2343 Gelbart, Mendel, ed. <u>Memorial Book of Konin</u>. Tel-Aviv: Association of Konin Jews in Israel, 1968. 796p. illus. (Y)

Koprzywnica

2344 Ehrlich, Elhanan, ed. <u>Memorial Book of Koprzywnica</u>. Tel-Aviv: Former Residents of Koprzywnica in Israel, 1971. 351p. illus. (H and Y)

Korczyn

2345 England-Wasserstrom, Isaac and Zucker, Morris, eds. <u>Korczyna Memorial Book</u>. New York: Committee of the Korczyna Memorial Book, 1967. 495p. illus. (H and Y)

Korzec

2346 Leoni, Elieser, ed. <u>The Korets Book: In Memory of Our Community That is no More</u>. Tel-Aviv: Former Residents of Korets in Israel, 1959. 791p. illus. (H and Y)

Kosów Huculski

2347 Kressel, Getzel and Olitzky, Leib, eds. <u>Memorial Book of Kosow Huculski</u>. Tel-Aviv: Former Residents of Kosów and Vicinity in Israel, 1964. 430p. illus. (H and Y)

Kosów Poleski

2348 <u>Memorial Book of Kosow Poleski</u>. Jerusalem: Relief Organization of Former Residents of Kosów Poleski in Israel, 1956. 81p. (H)

Kostopol

2349 Lerner, Arie, ed. <u>Kostopol: The Life and Death of a Community</u>.

Tel-Aviv: 1967. 386p. illus. (H)

Kowel

2350 Baler, B., ed. Memorial Book of Kowel. Buenos Aires: Former Residents of Kowel and Surroundings in Argentina, 1951. 511p. (Y)

2351 Leoni-Zopperfin, E. Kowel: Testimony and Memorial Book of Our Destroyed Community. Tel-Aviv: Former Residents of Kowel in Israel, 1959. 539p. (H and Y)

Kozienice

2352 Kapliński, Baruch, ed. Memorial Book of the Community of Kozshenits. Tel-Aviv: Former Residents of Kozieniec in Israel, 1969. 516p. illus. (H and Y)

Kraków (Cracow)

2353 Bałaban, Majer. Guide to the Jewish Antiquities in Kraków. Kraków: Stowarzyszenie Solidarność B'nei B'rith, 1935. viii, 125p. illus. (P)

2354 Bałaban, Majer. History of the Jews in Kraków and in Kazimierz, 1304-1868. Kraków: Towarzystwo Szkoły Żydowskiej, 1936. 2 vols. xxxiv, 800p. illus. (P)

2355 Bauminger, Arieh L. et al eds. Memorial Book of Kraków: Mother and Town in Israel. Jerusalem: The Rav Kuk Institut and Former Residents of Crakow in Israel, 1958/1959. 429p. illus. (H)

2356 Freudenheim, Mieczysław. "Recollection About Two Kraków Bookstores." BŻIH 1/117 (1981): 83-94. (P)

2357 Frejlichowna, J. "The Problem of Liquidating the Debts of the Kazimierz (Kraków) Community After the Third Partition, 1795-1809 and Under the Republic of Kraków, 1817-1929." M. Żyd. 3 (Warsaw, 1932): 467-478. (P)

2358 Friedberg, Bernhard. A Hebrew Printing Shop in Kraków. Kraków: Verlag des Verfassers, 1900. 46p. (H)

2359 Friedberg, Bernhard. Epitaphs Containing Biographies of the Kraków Rabbis, Learned Men, and Consistory Superintendents, from the Beginning of the 16th Century to the Present: Contribution to the History of Jews in Poland and Germany. Frankfurt a/Main: J. Kauffmann. 1904. viii, 122, 14. (H)

2360 Gelber, Nathan Michael. Essays on Jewish History in the Kraków Commonwealth, 1815-1846. Kraków: Nowy Dziennik, 1924. 61p. (P)

2361 Lewi, Hirsch David. The Speech of the Kazimierz Rabbi, of October 16, 1820 to the People Gathered on Occasion of the Erection of Tadeusz Kościuszko's Monument transl. from Hebrew by Samuel Baum. Kraków: 1820. 4p. (P)

2362 Raczka, Jan Wladyslaw. The Kazimierz District of Kraków. Warsaw: 1982. 120p. illus. (P)

2363 Wettstein, Feivel Hirsch. An Exchange of Letters Between A.J. Weizenfeld and Rappoport, et al.; A Contribution to the History of Jewish Enlightenment in Kraków. Kraków: 1900. 100p. (H)

2364 Wettstein, Feivel Hirsch. From the Diary of the Kraków Community. Breslaw (Wrocław): 1900. 2 vols. (H)

2365 Wettstein, Feivel Hirsch. Sources for History of Jews in Poland, particularly in Kraków. Kraków: A. Faust, 1892. 66p. (G)

2366 Zunz, Jehiel Mattathias. The City of Justice: History of the Kraków Rabbinate from Beginning of the XVI Century up to Present, as a Contribution for the History of Jews in Poland. Lwów: A. Faust, 1874. x, 190p. illus. (H)

Krasnobród

2367 Kusznir, M., ed. Krasnobrod: A Memorial to the Jewish Community. Tel-Aviv: Former Residents of Krasnobrod in Israel, 1956. 526p. (H and Y)

Kraśnik

2368 Morgensztern, Janina. "Common Struggle of the Kraśnik Burghers and Jews in the XIX Century for Abolishment of the Feudal Dependence." BŻIH 50 (1964): 11-21. (P)

2369 Morgensztern, Janina. "Participation of Jews in the Economic Life of Kraśnik." Bleter fűr Geschichte 15 (Warsaw, 1962-1963): 3-48. (Y)

Krotoszyn

2370 "Document Inventory of the Krotoszyn Synagogue Community." Nitteilungen des Gesammtarchives der deutsche Juden, 2 (1910): 48-50. (G)

2371 Berger, Heinrich. History of the Jews in Krotoschin. Krotoschin: A. Alkalay and Sohm, 1907. 24p. (G)

Krynki

2372 Korzec, Paweł. "The First Strikes in Krynki." BŻIH 43-44 (1962): 48-59. (P)

2373 Rabin, Dov, ed. Memorial Book of Krinki. Tel-Aviv: Former Residents of Krinki in Israel and in thge Diaspora, 1970. 374p. illus. (H and Y)

Krzemieniec

2374 Stein, Abraham Samuel, ed. Memorial Book of Kremeniec. Tel-Aviv: Former Residents of Kremeniec in Israel. 1954. 453p. illus. (H and Y)

Kurów

2375 Grossman, Moishe, ed. Memorial Book of Our Home Town Kurow. Tel-Aviv: 1955. 1152 columns. illus. (H)

Kurzeniec

2376 Meyerowitz, A., ed. The Scroll of Kurzeniec. Tel-Aviv: Former Residents of Kurzeniec in Israel and in the USA, 1956. 335p (H)

Kutno

2377 Sztokfisz, David, ed. The Book of Kutnah and Surroundings. Tel-Aviv: Former Residents of Kutno and Surroundings in Israel and the Diaspora, 1968. 591p. illus. (H and Y)

Kuty

2378 Husen, Eisig, ed. Kuttiver Memorial Book. New York: Kuttiver Sick and Benevolent Society in New York, 1958. 240p. (Y)

Lachowicze

2379 Rubin, J., ed. Memorial Book of Lachowicze. Tel-Aviv: Association of Former Residents of Lachowicze, 1959. 395p. (H and Y)

Lesko

2380 Mark, Natan and Friedlander Shimon, eds. Memorial Book Dedicated to the Jews of Linsk, Istrik . . . and Vicinity who Perished in the Holocaust in the Years 1939-1944. Tel-Aviv: Book Committee of the "Libai" Organization, 1965. x, 516p. illus. (H and Y)

Leszno (Lissa)

2381 Lewin, Louis. History of the Jews in Lissa: Published with Support of the Society for Spreading Knowledge About Jewry. Pniewo: N. Gundermann, 1904. 401p. (G)

2382 Washinsky, Emil. "Jewish Musicians in Lissa." Historische Monatsblätter fur die Provinz Posen. (Poznan, 1917): 29-30. (G)

Leżajsk

2383 Rabin, Haim, ed. Lezansk: Memorial Book of the Martyrs of Lezajsk who Perished in the Holocaust. Tel-Aviv: Former Residents of Leżajsk in Israel, 1970. 495p. illus. (H and Y)

Lida

2384 Manor, Alexander and Ganusovitch, Itzchak, eds. The Book of Lifa. Tel-Aviv: Former Residents of Lida in Israel and the Relief Committee of the Lida Jews in USA, 1970. xvii, 438p. illus. (H and Y)

Lipniszki

2385 Lewin, Awner, ed. Memorial Book of the Community of Lipniszki.

Tel-Aviv: Former Residents of Lipniszki in Israel, 1968. 206p. illus. (H and Y)

Lublin

2386 Bałaban, Majer. "The Ghettos of Polish Cities: Lublin." <u>Nowe Życie</u> 2 (Warsaw, 1924): 61-67. (P)

2387 Bałaban, Majer. <u>The Jewish Town of Lublin</u>. Berlin: Jüdischer Verlag, 1919. 112p, illus. (G)

2388 Blumental, N. and Korzeń, M., eds. <u>The Lublin Volume</u>. Jerusalem: The Encyclopaedia of the Jewish Diaspora, 1957. 816 columns. (H and Y)

2389 Ćwik, W. "Jewish Population of Royal Towns in the Lublin Region in the Second Half of the XVIII Century." <u>BŻIH</u> 59 (1966): 29-62. (P)

2390 Friedberg, Bernhard. <u>History of Hebrew Typography in Lublin</u>. Kraków: by the author, 1890. 12p. (H)

2391 Friedman, Phillip. "The Lublin Reservation and the Madagascar Plan." <u>YIVO Annual</u>, 8, (New York, 1953): 151-177.

2392 Fuks, Marian. "The Jewish Press in Lublin and in the Lublin Region, 1918-1939." <u>BŻIH</u>, 4/112, (November-December, 1979): 49-66. (P)

2393 Kruk, Stefan. "The Jewish Theatre in Lublin in the Years 1916-1917." <u>BŻIH</u>, 3-4/123-124 (1982): 49-63. (P)

2394 Kruk, Stefan. "Lublin Performances of the Jewish National Theatre from Odessa, August 22-September 17, 1883." <u>BŻIH</u> 1/105, (1978): 69-81. (P)

2395 Lewin, Yitshak. "Academy of the Lublin Sages." <u>Sefer ha-shana yorbukh</u> (1967): 381-388. (Y)

2396 Mandelsberg-Szyldkraut, Bela. <u>On the History of Lublin Jewry</u>. Tel-Aviv: 1965. 210p. illus. (H)

2397 Roszgold, Mosze. <u>The Memorial Book of Lublin</u>. Paris: Former Residents of Lublin in Paris, 1952. 685p. illus. (Y)

2398 Nissenbaum, Solomon Baruch. <u>History of the Jews in Lublin</u>. Lublin: 1920. iv, 196p. (H)

2399 Opas, Tomasz. "Jews in Towns Owned by Nobles in the Lublin Region in the XVIII Century." <u>BŻIH</u> 67, (1968): 3-37. (P)

2400 Seidman, Hillel. <u>On the Path of Talmudic Learning: Judaic Scholarhsip and the Higher Talmudic School in Lublin</u>. Warsaw: F. Hoesick, 1934. 81p. illus. (P)

2401 Shemen, Nachman (Nathan Boimoil). <u>Lublin: City of Torah, Rabbinism and Piety, (A Study in Jewish Culture)</u>. Toronto: Pomer Publishing, 1951. 541p. illus. (Y)

2402 Shapira, Meyer. "The Teaching of Torah: Religious Academies and Yeshiva Sages in Lublin." Der Yud 38 (Nov. 2, 1928): 7-8. (Y)

Ludwipol

2403 Ayalon, N., ed. Ludvipol (Wołyń): In Memory of the Jewish Community. Tel-Aviv: Ludwipol Relief Society of Israel, 1965. 335p. illus. (H and Y)

Lutomiersk

2404 Goldberg, Jakub. "Jewish Population of Lutomiersk in the Second Half of the XVIII Century and Her Struggle Against Feudal Oppression." BŻIH, 15-16 (1955): 189 ff. (P)

2405 Zelkovitch, Joseph. "A Picture of the Communal Life of a Jewish Town in Poland in the Second Half of the Nineteenth Century: The Philanthropic Association in Lutomiers." YIVO Annual 6 (1951): 253-266.

Lwów (Lviv, Lemberg)

2406 Al Hamiszmar (On Guard Duty). Anniversary Issue to Celebrate 10 Years of Jewish Grammar and High Schools in Lwów. Lwów: 1929, 60p. (P)

2407 Bałaban, Majer. History of the Progressive Synagogue in Lwów. Lwów: Nakładem Zarządu Synagogi Postępowej, 1937. 386p. illus. (P)

2408 Bałaban, Majer. The Jewish Quarter, Its History and Remains. Lwów: Towarzystwo Miłośników Przeszłości Lwowa, 1909. 99p. illus. (P)

2409 Bałaban, Majer. "Memories of the Jewish Theatre in Lwów and its Founder, A. Goldfadn." Bibliothek fun YIVO New York, 1940: 17-21. (Y)

2410 Bałaban, Majer. Speech of January 6, 1901 on Occasion of the Opening of the Jewish Community's Library in Lwow. Lwów, 1901. 13p. (G)

2411 Berliner, A. From the Manuscripts of the Jolles Brothers of Lwów. Berlin: 1909. xii. 48p. (H)

2412 Byk, Emil. Speech Given at the Occasion of the Opening of the New Building of the Jewish Community in Lwów on October 26, 1899. Lwów: 1899. 15p. (P)

2413 Caro, Jecheskel. History of the Jews in Lwow, from the oldest Times up to Poland's Partition in the Year 1792 (sic) Based on Chronicles and Archival Sources. Kraków: J. Fischer, 1894. 181p. (G)

2414 Chajes, Wiktor. Six Years of the Jewish Consistory Commune in Lwów, 1929-1934. Lwów: Nakładem Autora, 1935. 31p. (P)

2415 Dembitzer, Hayyim Nathan. A Book on the Aureole of Beauty: History of Lwów Rabbis. New York: 1960. 2 vols in 1. (H)

2416 Gewurz, Salomon. Lwów: A Critical Exposure of Jewish Pogroms from November 21st to 23rd in 1918. Berlin: L. Lamm, 1919. 13p. (G)

2417 Inquiry into the Polish-Jewish Question Held in the Days of February 2, 3, 4, 9 and 16th in 1919 in Lwów Together with Conclusions of the Special Board of Inquiry, Appointed by the Provisional Ruling Committee on January 1, 1919. Lwów, 1919. 203p. (P)

2418 Jaworski, Franciszek. "About the Past of Lwów Jews: Report on M. Bałaban's Lectures." Tydzień 10 (1903): 78-79. (P)

2419 K.I. "Fragments of Memoirs: the Lwów Circle in 1902, First Association named 'Poalej Syon', Lwów 1903." Jidiszer arbeter-pinkas 1 (Warsaw, 1927): 365-371. (Y)

2420 Krysiak, Franciszek Salezy. From the Days of Threat in Lwów (from November 1-22, 1918). Notes from Memoirs: Testimony, Proofs, Documents -- the Jewish Pogrom in Lwow in Light of Truth. Kraków: Gebethner i S-ka, 1919. 142p. (P)

2421 Mendelsohn, Ezra. "From Assimilation to Zionism in Lvov: The Case of Alfred Nossig." THe Slavonic and East Europoean Review 49, no. 117, (London: October, 1971): 521-534.

2422 Mendelsohn, Ezra. "Wilhelm Feldman and Alfred Nossig: Assimilation and Zionism in Lwów." Gal Ed. 2, (1975): 89-111.

2423 Schall, Jakób. Guide to the Jewish Art Relic in Lwow: History of Lwów Jews in Outline. Lwów: "Ever", 1935. 74p. illus. (P)

2424 Tennenbaum, Joseph. The Lwów Pogrom, November 1918 - January, 1919. Vienna - Brno: M. Hickl, 1919. 167p. illus. (G)

2425 Tomaszewski, Jerzy. "Lwów, November 22, 1918." Przegląd Historyczny 75, no.2, (1984): 279-285. (P)

2426 Twenty-fifth Anniversary of the Jewish Merchants Association in Lwów, 1904-1929. Lwów: 1929. 88p. (P)

2427 Wittlin, Józef. My Lwów. New York: Biblioteka Polska, 1946. 42p. illus. (P)

Łanowce

2428 Rabin, Haim, ed. Lanovits: Memorial Book of the Martyrs of Lanovic who Perished During the Holocaust. Tel-Aviv: Association of Former Residents of Łanowce, 1970. 440p. illus. (H and Y)

Łańcut

2429 Walzer, Michael and Kudish, Naton, eds. Lansut: The Life and Destruction of a Jewish Community. Tel-Aviv: Association of Former Residents of Lanzut in Israel and USA, 1963.lix, 465 illus. (H and Y)

Łask

2430 Tsurnamal, Zeev, ed. Memorial Book of Lask. Tel-Aviv: Association of Former Residents of Lask in Israel, 1968. 902p. illus. (H and Y)

Łęczyca

2431 Frenkel, Itzhak Yedidia, ed. Memorial Book of Lentshits. Tel-Aviv: Former Residents of Leczyca and Israel, 1953. 224p. illus. (H)

Łódź

2432 Bałaban, Majer. "Preface to A. Alperin's Jews in Łódź: Beginnings of Jewish Community, 1780-1822." Rocznik Łódzki 1 (1928): 147-150. (P)

2433 Baranowski, Krzysztof. "Jewish High Schools in Lodz, 1918-1939." BŻIH 3/119 (1981): (P)

2434 Friedman, Filip. "History of the Burial Society in Łódź." Stary Cmentarz Żydowski (Łódź, 1938): 37-111. (P)

2435 Friedman, Filip. History of the Jews in Łódź from the Beginning of Their Settlement until 1863: Demographic Relations, Economic Life, Social Relations. Łódź: Łódzki Oddział Towarzystwa Krajoznawczego w Polsce, 1935. 391p. (P)

2436 Friedman, Filip. "Industrialization and Proletarization of Jews in Łódź in the Years 1860-1914." Lodzer Visnshaftlecher Shriften 1 (Lodz, 1938): 63-132. (Y)

2437 Friedman, Filip. "The Tombstones of the Old Jewish Cementery in Łódź." Stary Cmentarz Żydowski (Łódź, 1938): 5-115. (H)

2438 Hertz, Jacob Sholem. History of the Jewish Labor Bund in Łódź. New York: Ferlag Unser Tsait, 1958. 503p. illus. (Y)

2439 Jasny, A. Wolf. The History of the Jewish Labor Movement in Lodzsh. Lodz: 1937. 427p. (Y)

2440 Tenenbaum, Arazi Abraham. Lodz and its Jews. Buenos Aires: 1956. 393p. illus. (Y)

Łomza

2441 Lewiński, Yom-Tow. Lomza - In Memory of the Jewish Community. Tel-Aviv: Former Residents of Łomża in Israel, 1952. x, 377p. illus. (H)

2442 Sabatka, H., ed. The Rise and Fall of Łomża. New York: American Committee for the Book of Lomza, 1957. 371p. (Y)

2443 Shapiro, Chaim. "Lomza: A Yeshiva Grew in Poland." The Jewish Observer 9, no.10 (1974): 13-16 illus.

Łosice

2444 Shener, M. Losice: In Memory of a Jewish Community, Exterminated by Nazi Murderers. Tel-Aviv: Former Residents of Losice in Israel. 1963. 459p. (H and Y)

Łowicz

2445 Shaiak, G., ed. Lowicz, a Town in Mazowia: Memorial Book. Tel-Aviv: Former Residents of Łowicz in Melbourne and Sydney, Australia, 1966. xxii, 395p. (H and Y)

Łuck

2446 Sharon, Nathon, ed. The Memorial Book of Lutzk. Tel-Aviv: Former Residents of Lutzk in Israel, 1961. 608p. (H and Y)

2447 Ullmann, F. "The Jewish Community in Luck and its Fall." Zeitschrift für die Geschichte der Juden (1966): 117-123. (G)

Łuków

2448 Heller, Binem, ed. The Book of Łuków: Dedicated to a Destroyed Community. Tel-Aviv: Former Residents of Łuków in Israel and the USA, 1968. 652p. illus. (H and Y)

Łuniniec

2449 Zeevi (Wilk), Yosef et al, eds. Memorial Book of the Community of Luniniec/Kozhanhorodok. Tel-Aviv: Association of Former Residents of Luniniec/Kozhanhorodok, 1952. 268p. illus. (H and Y)

Maków Mazowiecki

2450 Brat, Itzhak, ed. Memorial Book of the Community of Makov-Mazovitsk. Tel-Aviv: Former Residents of Makow Mazowiecki in Israel, 1969. 505p. illus. (Y)

Miechów

2451 Blumental, N. and Ben-Azar, A.(Broshy), eds. Miechov Memorial Book, Charsznica, and Ksiaz. Tel-Aviv: Former Residents of Miechov, Charshnitza and Kshoynge, 1971. 314p. (H and Y)

Miedzybór

2452 Opas, Tomasz. "Tomasz Kurdwanowski's Proposal in 1828 Concerning Improvement of the Situation of the Jewish Population in Miedzybor." BŻIH 2/94 (1975): 31-40. (P)

Miedzyrzec

2453 Ayalon-Baranick, Benzion Hayyim, ed. Mezhirith - Wolyn: In Memory of the Jewish Community. Tel-Aviv: Former Residents of Mezhiritch, 442 columns illus. (Y)

2454 Horn, Y., ed. The Mezeritch Volume. Buenos Aires: Association of Former Residents of Mezeritch in Argentina, 1952. 635p. (Y)

2455 Yaari, A. "Hebrew Printing at Mezyrow." Kiriat Sefer 42 (1967): 258-268. (H)

Międzyszyn

2456 "A Child in Medem's Convalescent Home in Międzyszyn." Życie Dziecka 1-2 (Warsaw, 1932/1933): 228-236. (P)

Mława

2457 Shatzky, Jacob, ed. Memorial Book of Mława. New York: Association of Former Residents of Mława, 1950. 546p. illus. (Y)

Młynów

2458 Siegelman, Yitshak, ed. Młynów-Muravica Memorial Book. Haifa: Former Residents of Młynów-Muravica in Israel, 1970. 511p. illus. (Y and H)

Mordy

2459 Wein, Adam. "The Book of the Burial Society in Mordy." BŻIH 63 (1967): 57-64. (P)

Nasielsk

2460 Wein, Adam. "The Book of the Guild of Jewish Taylors, Furriers and Haberdashers." BŻIH 42 (1962): 128-130. (P)

Nieśwież

2461 Damesek, Solomon. In Those Years: Notes and Images from My Home Town Niesvich. New York: 1950. 160p. (Y)

Nowogródek

2462 Yerushalmi, Eliezer et al, eds. Navaredok Memorial Book Tel-Aviv: Navaredker Relief Committee in the USA and in Israel, 1963. 419p. (H and Y)

Nowy Dwór

2463 Ringelblum, Emmanuel. "Johann Anton Kriger-Printer of Hebrew Books in Nowy Dwór: About His Activity in the Years 1781-1795." BŻIH 42 (1962): 45-60. (P)

2464 Shamri, Aryer and Berish, eds. Novi-Devor Memorial Book. Tel-Aviv: Organization of Former Residents of Novy Dvor Jews in Israel, the US, Canada, Argentina, Uruguay and France, 1965. xix, 556p. illus. (Y)

Nowy Sącz

2465 Mahler, Raphael, ed. The Book of the Jewish Community of Sants. New York: Former Residents of Sants in New York, 1970. 886p. illus. (H and Y)

2466 Mahler, Raphael. "Chapters in the History of the Jews in Nowy Sącz." BŻIH 55 (1965): 3-32. et BŻIH 56 (1965): 28-58p. (P)

2467   Mahler,   Raphael.   Sources to the History of the Jewish Community in Poland (Sandz).   Tel-Aviv: Tel-Aviv University, 1964.   886p.   illus. (H)

Olszany

2468   Kaplan, Shabetai.   The Life and Destruction of Olshan.   Tel-Aviv: Former Residents of Olshan in Israel, 1965.   567p.   illus.   (H and Y)

Opatków

2469   Yasheev,   Zvi,   ed.   A Town Which Does Not Exist Any More.   Tel-Aviv: The Apt Organizations in Israel,   USA,   Canada and Brasil,   1966. 461p. illus.   (H and Y)

Opole

2470   Bąk,   Maria.   "Jewish   Cemeteries   in the Opole Province."   BŻIH 4/128 (1983): 119-122.   (P)

2471   Dziewulski,   Władysław.   "Jews Accepted to Municipal Law in Opole in the Years 1814-1851."   BŻIH   2/118 (1981): 3-13.   (P)

Orla

2472   Leszczyński,   Anatol.   "The Orla Jewish Consistory Law of October 27, 1780."   BŻIH   2/98 (1976):   113ff.   (P)

Ostrołęka

2473   Ivri, Y., ed.   Book of Kehilat Ostrolenka.   Tel-Aviv: Association of Former Residents of Ostrolenka, 1963.   579p.   (H and Y)

Ostrowce

2474   Ostrovtse: Dedicated   to the Memory of Ostrovtse, Apt. . . .. Buenos Aires: Former Residents of Ostrovtse in Argentina, 1949.   217p. illus.   (Y)

Ostrowo

2475   Freimann,   Aron.   History   of   the   Jewish   Ostrowo Community. Ostrowo: J. Haym, 1896.   26p.   (G)

Ostróg

2476   Ayalon-Baranick, Benzion Hayyim,   ed.   Ostróg-Wołyń: In Memory of the   Jewish   Community.   Tel-Aviv: Association of Former Residents of Ostrog, 1960.   640 columns.   (H and Y)

2477   Biber, Menahem Mendel.   To Commemorate the Learned Men in Torah of Ostrah.   Ostróg: 1907. 346p.   (H)

Ostrów Mazowiecka

2478   Margalit, A.   Memorial Book of the Community of Ostrów-Mazowiecka.

Tel-Aviv: Association of Former Residents of Ostrow-Mazowieck, 1960. 653p. (H and Y)

Oszmiana

2479 Gelbart, Mendl, ed. Oshmana Memorial Book. Tel-Aviv: Oshmaner Organization in Israel and the Oshmaner Society in the USA, 1969. 768p. illus. (H and Y)

Otwock

2480 Kanc, Shimon, ed. Memorial Book of Otvozk and Kartshev. Tel-Aviv: Former Residents of Otvozk-Kartshev, 1968. 1086 columns. (H and Y)

Ożarów

2481 A Jewish Cemetery in Ożarów (Tarnobrzeg District). Kielce: 1978. 67p. illus. (P)

2482 Penkalla, Adam. "A Jewish Community and Cemetery in Ożarow." BŻIH 2/110 (1979): 35-68. (P)

Pabianice

2483 Jasny, A. Wolf. Memorial Book of Pabianice. Tel-Aviv: Former Residents of Pabianice in Israel, 1956. 419p. (H and Y)

Parysów

2484 Granatsztajn, Jechie, ed. A Memorial to the Jewish Community of Parysow - Poland. Tel-Aviv: Former Residents of Parysów in Israel, 1971. 625p. illus. (H and Y)

Pinczów

2485 Shinar, Mordechai, ed. A Book of Memory of the Jewish Community of Pinczów - Poland. Tel-Aviv: Former Residents of Pinczow in Israel and in the Diaspora, 1970. 480p. illus. (H and Y)

Pińsk

2486 Feinstein, Abraham Asher. The History of Misfortune. Tel-Aviv: 1929. 297p. illus. (H)

2487 Hoffman, Benzion, ed. A Thousand Years of Pińsk. New York: 1941. xv, 500p. illus. (Y)

2488 Nadav, Morehai. History of the Jews in Pińsk. Jerusalem: 1964. iv, 33. (H)

2489 Shohat, Azriel. "The Story of the Pińsk Pogrom on April 5, 1919." Gal-Ed 1 (1973): 135-173. (H)

2490 Tamir, Machman, ed. Pińsk: Second Volume. Tel-Aviv: Former Residents of Pińsk-Karlin in Israel, 1966. 655p. illus. (H and Y)

Piotrków Trybunalski

2491 Baranowski, Jerzy and Jaworowski, H. "The History and Development of the Synagogue in Piotrków Trybunalski." BŻIH 57 (1966): 121-133. (P)

2492 Feinkind, Mojżesz. History of the Jews in Piotrków and Vicinity from the Oldest Times until Present. Piotrków: Nakład Własny, 1930. 88p. (P)

2493 Fijalek, Jan. "Concerning the Problem of Jewish Hospitals in Piotrków Trybunalski in Mid-XIX Century." BŻIH 31 (July-September, 1959): 38-56. (P)

2494 Melz, Y. and Lau (Lavy), N., eds. Piotrków Trybunalski and Vicinity. Tel-Aviv: Former Residents of Piotrków Tryb. in Israel, 1965. lxiv, 1192p. (H and Y)

Płock

2495 Eisenberg, Eliyahu, ed. Plotzk: A History of an Ancient Jewish Community in Poland. Tel-Aviv: World Committee for the Plotzk Memorial Book, 1967. 780p. illus. (H and Y)

2496 Greenspan, Sol. Jews in Plotzk. New York: S. Greenspan, 1960. 325p. illus. (Y)

2497 Trunk, Isaiah. The History of Jews in Płock. Warsaw: 1939. lxiii, 174p. (Y)

Płonsk

2498 Semah, Sh., ed. Memorial Book of Płonsk and Vicinity. Tel-Aviv: Former Residents of Płonsk in Israel, 1963. 775p. (H and Y)

Pniewy (Pinne)

2499 Lewin. Louis. From the Past of the Jewish Community in Pinne. Pinne: Gunderman, 1903. 24p. (G)

Poczajów

2500 Gelernt, H., ed. Memorial Book Dedicated to the Jews of Pitchayev-Wohlyn Executed by the Germans. Philadelphia: The Pitchayever Wohliner Aid Society, 1960. 311p. (Y)

Poznań (Posen)

2501 Bloch, Ph. "First Cultural Aspirations of the Jewish Community in Poznań under Prussian Rule." Jubelschrift H. Grätz. (Breslau, 1871): 194-217. (G)

2502 Avron, Dov, ed. Register of the Obligations of the Poznań Consistory, 1621-1835. Jerusalem: 1966. 478p. (H)

2503 Heppner, Aaron and Herzberg, Isaak. From the Past and Present

Time of the Jews in the Jewish Communities of the Poznań District, Based on Printed and Unprinted Sources. Koschmin: 1909. 1034p. illus. (G)

2504 Kaufmann, David. "Duties of the Poznań Consistory During the Rabbinate of Rabbi Isak b. Abraham." Monatschrift für Geschichte und Wissenschaft des Judentums 38, (Breslau, 1894): 184-192. (G)

2505 Kollenscher, Max. Jewish Problems During the German-Polish Transition Period, 1918-1920. Berlin: H. Werner, 1925. 223p. (G)

2506 Kupfer, F. "Register of the Records of Electors of the Poznań Jewish Consistory." BŻIH 2-3 (1953): 56-121. (P)

2507 Lambert, M. "Safe Conduct Tax and the Kosher Meat Duty: Two Special Taxes of Poznań Jews." Monatschrift für Geschichte und Wissenschaft des Judentums 67 (1923): 273-278. (G)

2508 Landsberger, J. "Regulations on the Debt of the Jewish Community in the Years 1774-1780." Historische Monatsblätter für die Provinz Posen 3 (1902): 38-45. (G)

2509 Perles, Joseph. The History of Jews in Posen. Breslau: Verlag der Schletter'schen Buchhandlung, 1865. 155p. (G)

2510 Strzelecki, A. "A Posen Voivode for the Jews." Historische Monatsblatter fur die Provinz Posen 3 (1902): 125-130. (G)

Pruszków

2511 Brodsky, David, ed. Memorial Book of Pruszków, Nadzin and Vicinity. Tel-Aviv: Former Residents of Pruszkow in Israel, 1966. 334p. illus. (H and Y)

Prużana

2512 Bernstein, Mardoqueo and Forer, David, eds. Memorial Book of Five Destroyed Communities of the Towns of Prużana, Bereza, Malch, Scherschev and Seltz: Their Origin, Development and Annihilation. Buenos Aires: Former Residents of Pruzana atc., 1958. 972p. (Y)

Przemyśl

2513 Bałaban, Majer. "From the Przemyśl History: A Sketch of Jewish History." In his Z Historii Żydow w Polsce: Szkice i Studia (Warsaw, 1920): 147-154. (P)

2514 Menczer, Arie, ed. Przemyśl Memorial Book. Tel-Aviv: Former Residents of Przemyśl in Israel, 1964. 552p. illus. (H and Y)

2515 Schorr, Moses. From the Jewish History in Przemyśl: A Sketch. Vienna: R. Löwitt, 1915. 28p. (G)

2516 Schorr, Moses. Jews in Przemyśl Until the End of the XVIII Century: Elaboration and Publication of Archival Material. Lwów: Nakładem Funduszu Konkursowego, 1903. 294p. (P and H)

2517 Warschauer, Adolf. "The Jews" In <u>Catalogue of the Archives of Old Documents of the Town of Przemyśl</u>. (Przemyśl, 1927): 190-198. <u>et</u> 591-594. (P)

Przytyk

2518 Penkalla, Adam. "A Jewish Cemetery in Przytyk." <u>BŻIH</u> 1-2/129-130 (1984): 175-182. (P)

2519 Sztokfisz, David, ed. <u>Book of Pshitik: A Memorial to the Jewish Community</u>. Tel-Aviv: 1973. 461p. illus. (H and Y)

2520 Tsimbalista, Israel. "We Were Ready to Resist." In <u>Sefer Pshitik</u> (Tel-Aviv, 1973): 200-202. (Y)

Puławy

2521 Bernstein, Mardoqued, ed. <u>Memorial Book of Pulav</u>. New York: Pulawer Yiskor Book Committee, 1964. 494p. illus. (Y)

Raciąż

2522 Zoref, Efraim, ed. <u>Memorial Book of the Community of Racionz</u>. Tel-Aviv: Former Residents of Raciąż, 1965. 493p. illus. (H and Y)

Radom

2523 Penkalla, Adam and Szczepański, Jerzy. "The Jewish Public Buildings in the Towns of Radom Province in the Mid XIX Century." <u>BŻIH</u> (1977): 77-83. (P)

2524 Perlov, Isaac, ed. <u>Memorial Book of Radom</u>. Tel-Aviv: Former Residents of Radom in Israel and the USA, 1961. lxxviii, 451p. illus. (Y)

2525 Waks, Szymon. "The Tanning Industry in Radom." <u>Jidisze Ekonomok</u> 3-4 (1938): 152ff. (Y)

Radomsk

2526 Losh, L., ed. <u>Memorial Book of the Community of Radomsk and Vicinity</u>. Tel-Aviv: Former Residents of Radomsk, 1967. 603p. illus. (H and Y)

Radomyśl Wielki

2527 Harsshoshanim, Hilel and Turkow-Grudberg, Isaac, eds. <u>Radomyśl Wielki and Neighborhood Memorial Book</u>. Tel-Aviv: Former Residents of Radomyśl and Surroundings in Israel, 1971. 1167 columns, illus. (H and Y)

Radoszkowice

2528 Rabinson, Markus, ed. <u>Radoshkowitz: A Memorial to the Jewish Community</u>. Tel-Aviv: Former Residents of Radoshkowitz in Israel, 1953. 222p. illus. (H)

Radziwiłłów

2529 Adini, Jacakov, ed. <u>A Memorial to the Jewish Community of Radziwiłłów</u>. Tel-Aviv: The Radziwillow Organization in Israel, 1966. 438p. illus. (H and Y)

Raków

2530 Abramson, H., ed. <u>Memorial Book of the Community of Raków</u>. Tel-Aviv: Former Residents of Raków in Israel and the USA, 1959. 184p. (H and Y)

Ratno

2531 Botoshansky, Jacobo and Yanasovich, Isaac, eds. <u>Memorial Book of Ratno: The Life and Destruction of a Jewish Town in Wolyń</u>. Buenos Aires: Former Residents of Ratno in Argentina and the USA, 1954. 806p. illus. (Y)

Rawicz

2532 Cohn, John. <u>History of the Jewish Community in Rawitsch</u>. Berlin: L. Lamm, 1915. 122p. (G)

2533 Posner, Arthur Bernhard. <u>The Annals of the Ravitsh Community</u>. Tel-Aviv: 1962. xvi, 84p. illus. (H)

Rohatyn

2534 Amihai, Mordekhai, ed. <u>Rohatyn: The History of a Jewish Community</u>. Tel-Aviv: Former Residents of Rohatyn in Israel, 1962. 362p. (H and Y)

Rokitno

2535 Leoni, Elieser, ed. <u>Rokitno-Wolyn and Surroundings: Memorial Book and Testimony</u>. Tel-Aviv: Former Residents of Rokitno in Israel, 1967. 495p. illus. (H and Y)

Rozwadów

2536 Blumental, Nachman, ed. <u>Rozwadów Memorial Book</u>. Jerusalem: Former Residents of Rozwadów in Israel, 1968. xix, 349p. illus. (H and Y)

Równe

2537 Avatihi, Aryeh, ed. <u>Rowno: A Memorial to the Jewish Community of Rowno, Wołyn</u>. Tel-Aviv: Former Residents of Rowno in Israel, 1956. 591p. illus. (H)

Różana

2538 Sokolowsky, M., ed. <u>Różana: A Memorial to the Jewish Community</u>. Tel-Aviv: Former Residents of Rozhinoy in Israel, 1957. 232p. (H and Y)

Rypin

2539 Huberband, Shim'on. Sacrificed for Faith. Tel-Aviv: 1969. 354p. illus. (H)

2540 Kanc, Shimon, ed. Ripin: A Memorial to the Jewish Community of Ripin-Poland. Tel-Aviv: Former Residents of Ripin in Israel and in the Diaspora, 1963. 993p. illus. (H and Y)

Rzeszów

2541 Yaari-Wold, Moshe, ed. Rzeszów Jews: Memorial Book. Tel-Aviv: Former Residents of Rzeszów in Israel and the USA, 1967. 620p. (H and Y)

Sanok

2542 Sharvit, Elazar, ed. Memorial Book of Sanok and Vicinity in Israel. Jerusalem: Former Residents of Sanok and Vicinity in Israel, 1970. 686p. illus. (H and Y)

Sarnaki

2543 Shuval, Dov, ed. Memorial Book of the Community of Sarnaki. Haifa: Former Residents of Sarnaki in Israel, 1968. 415p. illus. (H and Y)

Sarny

2544 Kariv, Joseph, ed. Memorial Book of the Community of Sarny. Tel-Aviv: Former Residents of Sarny and Vicinity in Israel, 1961. 508p. illus. (H and Y)

Serock

2545 Gelbart, Mendel, ed. The Book of Serock. Tel-Aviv: Former Residents of Serock in Israel, 1971. 736p. illus. (H and Y)

Siedlce

2546 Goldshtein, S. "From the Past of Siedlce." J.St. 4 (1911): 125-129. (R)

2547 Grünberg, Abraham. Jewish-Polish-Russian Jubilee: The Great Siedlce Pogrom in 1906. Prague: "Grafia", 1916. 47p. (G)

2548 Jasny, A. Wolf, ed. Memorial Book of the Community of Siedlce. Buenos Aires: Former Residents of Siedlce in Israel and Argentina, 1956. xvi, 813p. illus. (H and Y)

2549 Kaspi, Isaac. Chronicle of the Shedlits Pogrom in 1906. Tel-Aviv: 1947. (H)

2550 Twenty-Fifth Anniversary of the 'Jidisz Kunst' in Siedlce. Siedlce: 1925. 57p. (Y)

Siedliszcze

2551 Haruvi, B., ed. Memorial Book of the Community of Siedliszcze and Vicinity. Tel-Aviv: Former Residents of Siedliszcze in Israel, 1970. 360p. (H and Y)

Siemiatycze

2552 Tash, Eliezer, ed. The Community of Semiatich. Tel-Aviv: Association of Former Residents of Semiatich in Israel and the Diaspora, 1965. xiii, 449p. (H and Y)

Sierpc

2553 Talmi, E., ed. The Community of Sierpc: Memorial Book. Tel-Aviv: Former Residents of Sierpc in Israel and Abroad, 1959. 603p. (H and Y)

Skałat

2554 Braunstein, Chaim, ed. Skałat: Memorial Volume of the Community which Perished in the Diaspora. Tel-Aviv: The Yaacov Krol School in Petah-Tikva and Former Residents of Skałat in Israel, 1971. 160p. illus. (H)

Skierniewice

2555 Perlow, Isaac, ed. The Book of Skiernievitz. Tel-Aviv: Former Residents of Skernievtz in Israel, 1955. 772p. illus. (Y)

Słonim

2556 Lichtenstein, Kalman, ed. Memorial Book of Słonim: Record and Face of a Town, Ruin of the Community: In Memorial. Tel-Aviv: Former Residents of Słonim in Israel, 1961. 2 vols. (H and Y)

Słuck

2557 Epsztejn, A. "Records and Recollections from my Home Town Słuck." Rszumot 4, (Odessa, 1926): 231-242. (H)

Smorgonie

2558 Tash, E. (Tur-Shalom), ed. Smorgonie, District Vilna: Memorial Booknd Testimony. Tel-Aviv: Association of Former Residents of Smorgonie in Israel and USA, 1965. 584p. illus. (H and Y)

Sochaczew

2559 Stein, A. Sh. and Weissman, G., eds. Memorial Book of Sochaczew. Jerusalem: Former Residents of Sochaczew in Israel, 1962. 843p. (H and Y)

Sokal

2560 Chomet, Abraham, ed. Memorial Book of Sokal, Tartakow and

Surroundings. Tel-Aviv: Former Residents of Sokal and Surroundings, 1968. 576p. illus. (H and Y)

Sokołów Podlaski

2561 Gelbart, Mendl, ed. Memorial Book of Sokolow-Podlask. Tel-Aviv: Former Residents of Sokolow-Podlask in Israel and in the USA, 1962. 785p. illus. (Y and H)

Sokoły

2562 Grossman, Moishe, ed. Memorial Book of the Martyrs of Sokoly. Tel-Aviv: Former Residents of Sokoły in Israel, 1962. 625p. illus. (Y)

Sokółka

2563 Mishkinski, Ester, ed. Memorial Book of Sokolkah. Jerusalem: The Encyclopaedia of the Jerwish Diaspora, 1968. 768 columns, illus. (H)

Sosnowiec

2564 Klajner, A. "Small Industry in Sosnowiec." Jidisze Ekonomik 5-6 (1938): 270ff. (Y)

Stanisławów

2565 Streit, Leon. Armenians and Jews in Stanislawow in the XVII and XVIII Centuries: Historical Essay. Stanisławów: Kolo Naukowe Towarzystwa Przyjaciół Uniwersytetu Hebrajskiego w Jerozolimie, 1936. 16p. (P)

2566 Weitz, Emmy. On Your Ruins Stanisławów. Tel-Aviv: 1947. 112p. illus. (H)

Staszów

2567 Erlich, E., ed. The Staszów Book. Tel-Aviv: Former Residents of Staszów in Israel and in the Diaspora, 1962. 690p. (H and Y)

Stoczek

2568 Rosenthal-Stopnicka (Heller), Celia. "Deviation and Social Change in the Jewish Community of a Small Jewish Town." American Journal of Sociology 60, no.2 (September, 1954): 177-181.

Stolin

2569 Avatihi, Aryeh and Ben-Zaccai, Johana, eds. Stolin: A Memorial to the Jewish Communities of Stolin and Vicinity. Tel-Aviv: Former Residents of Stolin and Vicinity in Israel, 1952. 263p. illus. (H)

Stołpce

2570 Hinitz, Nahum, ed. Memorial Volume of Steibtz-Swerznie and the

Neighboring Villages: Rubeziewicz, Derewno, Nalybok. Tel-Aviv: Former Residents of Steibtz in Israel, 1964. xxiii, 537p. illus. (H and Y)

2571 Shazar, Schneur Zalman. "Defenders of the City." GT (New York, 1984): 383-388.

Stryj

2572 Kudish, Natan et al, eds. Memorial Book of Stryj. Tel-Aviv: Former Residents of Stryj in Israel, 1962. 328p. illus. (H and Y)

Stryków

2573 Bartys, J. "Materials to Wooden Architecture and to the Socio-Professional Structure of the Jewish Population in Stryków in the XVIII Century." BŻIH 11-12 (1954): 89-96. (P)

Strzegowo

2574 Memorial Book of Strzegowo. New York: United Strzegower Relief Committee, 1951. xi, 135p. (H and Y)

Strzyżów

2575 Berglas, Yitshak and Yahalomi, Solomon, eds. Memorial Book of Strzyżów and Vicinity. Tel-Aviv: Former Residents of Strzyżów in Israel and Diaspora, 1969. 480p. illus. (H and Y)

Suchowola

2576 Steinberg, Hannah et al., eds. Memorial Book of Suchowola. Jerusalem: The Encyclopaedia of the Jewish Diaspora, 1957. 616 columns, illus. (H and Y)

Suwałki

2577 Kahan, B., ed. Memorial Book of Suwalk. New York: The Suwalk and Vicinity Relief Committee of New York, 1961. 825 columns. (Y)

Święciany

2578 Kanc, Shimon, ed. Swintzian Region Memorial Book in Memory pf Twenty-three Jewish Communities. Tel-Aviv: 1965. 954 columns, illus. (H)

Świr

2579 Swironi (Drutz), Hanoch, ed. Our Townlet Svir. Tel-Aviv: Former Residents of Svir in Israel and in the United States, 1959. 240p. (H and Y)

Świsłocz

2580 Ain, Abraham. "Swislocz: Portrait of a Jewish Community in Eastern Europe." YIVO Annual of Jewish Social Science 4 (New York, 1949): 86-114.

2581 Rabin, H., ed. The Community of Świsłocz, Grodna District. Tel-Aviv: Former Residents of Swislocz in Israel, 1961. 159p. (H and Y)

Szczecin (Stettin)

2582 The Catalogue of the Synagogue-Consistory's Library in Stettin. Stettin: 1930. 44p. (G)

Szczekociny

2583 Schweizer, J., ed. A Memorial Book to the Jewish Community of Szczekociny. Tel-Aviv: Former Residents of Szczekociny in Israel, 1959. 276p. (H and Y)

Szczuczyn

2584 Losh, L., ed. Memorial Book of the Communities Szczuczyn and Wasiliszki. Tel-Aviv: Former Residents of the Communities Szczuczyn, Wasiliszki, 1966. 456p. illus. (H and Y)

Szrańsk

2585 Rimon (Granat), Joseph Zvi, ed. The Jewish Community of Shrensk and Vicinity: A Memorial Volume. Jerusalem: Former Residenmts of Shrensk in Israel, 1960. 588p. illus. (H and Y)

Szumsk

2586 Rabin, Haim, ed. Shumsk: Memorial Book of the Martyrs of Shumsk. Tel-Aviv: Former Residents of Szumsk in Israel, 477p. illus. (H and Y)

Szydłów

2587 Penkalla, Adam. "The Synagogue and Jewish Community in Szydłów." BŻIH 1-2/121-122, (1982): 57-70. (P)

Targowica

2588 Siegelman, I., ed. Memorial Book of Trovits. Haifa: Former Residents of Targowica in Israel, 1967. 452p. (H and Y)

Tarłowo

2589 Wyrobisz, A. "Jewish Population in Tarlowo : From the middle of the XVIth to the End of the XVIIIth Century." BŻIH 89 (1974): 3-17. (P)

Tarnogród

2590 Kanc, Sh., ed. Book of Tarnogrod: In Memory of the Destroyed Jewish Community. Tel-Aviv: Organization of the Former Residents of Tarnogrod and Vicinity in Israel, United States and England, 1966. 592p. (H and Y)

Tarnopol

2591 Korngruen, Philip, ed. Tarnopol. Jerusalem: Encyclopaedia of the Jewish Diaspora, 1955. 474 columns. (H and Y)

Tarnów

2592 Catalogue of the Jewish Library in Tarnów. Tarnów: 1924. 108p. (P)

2593 Chomet, Abraham, ed. Torne: The Life and Decline of a Jewish City. Tel-Aviv: Association of Former Residents of Tarnów, vol.1 xx, 928p; vol 2 (eds Chomet A. and Kornilo, Y) 1968. 433p. (H and Y)

2594 Cienciała, Teodor. " Jewish Hospital in Tarnów." BŻIH 50 (1964): 83-90. (P)

2595 Ruta, Zygmunt. "From the History of Jewish High-School Education in Tarnów." BŻIH 3/103 (1977): 27-34. (P)

Telechan

2596 Sokoler, Sh. ed. Telekhan Memorial Book. Los Angeles: Telekhan Memorial Book Committee, 1963. 204p. (H and Y)

Tłuste

2597 Alfasi, Yitshak. The Book of Sages. Tel-Aviv: 1961. 136p. (H)

2598 Lindberg, Gavriel, ed. Memorial Book of Tlustah. Tel-Aviv: Association of Former Residemts of Tłuste and Vicinity in Israel and USA, 1965. (H and Y)

Tłuszcz

2599 Gelbart, Mendel, ed. Memorial Book of the Community of Tlusht. Tel-Aviv: Association of Former Residents of Tlusht, 1971. 340p. illus. (H and Y)

Tomaszów Lubelski

2600 Memorial Book of Tomshover (Lubelski). New York: Tomashover Relief Committee, 1965. 912p. (Y)

Tomaszów Mazowiecki

2601 Wajsberg, Moshe, ed. A Memorial to the Jewish Community of Tomashov-Mazovitsk. Tel-Aviv: Tomashov Organization in Israel, 1969. 648p. illus. (H and Y)

Troki

2602 Troki. Tel-Aviv: 1934. 79p. (H)

Trzcianka (Schonlanke)

2603 Bambarger, Mose Loeb. History of Schönlanke Jews. Berlin: L. Lamm, 1912. 44p. (G)

Trzebinia

2604 Goldwasser, P. et al., eds. The Community of Trzebinia. Haifa: Committee of Trzebinians in Israel, 1969. 435p. (H)

Tuczyn

2605 Ayalon-Baranick, Hayyim, ed. Tutshin-Krippe, Wolyn: In Memory of the Jewish Community. Tel-Aviv: Tutchin and Krippe Relief Society in Israel, 1967. 384 columns, illus. (H and Y)

Turka

2606 Siegelman, Yitshak, ed. Memorial Book Committee of Turka on the Stryj River and Vicinity. Haifa: Former Residents of Turka (Stryj) in Israel, 472p. (H and Y)

Turobin

2607 Geshuri, Meir Simon, ed. Turbin Book: In Memory of the Jewish Community. Tel-Aviv: 1967. 397p. illus. (Y)

Tykocin

2608 Bar-Yuda, M. and Ben--Nachum, Z., eds. Memorial Book of Tiktin: History of the Jewish Population, its Growing and Upbringing, its Destruction and Devastation. Tel-Aviv: Former Residents of Tiktin in Israel, 1959. 606p. illus. (H)

2609 Baranowski, Jerzy. "On the Antique Synagogue in Tykocin." BŻIH 34, (1960): 158-170. (P)

2610 Gaworin, Abram. "The Jewish Community in Tykocin." Bleter far Geszychte 13, (1960): 60-102. (Y)

Tyszowce

2611 Shtern, Yekhiel. "A Cheder in Tishevits." YIVO Annual of Jewish Social SDcience (New York: 1950): 152-157.

2612 Zipper, Jacob, ed. Tishovits Book. Tel-Aviv: Association of Former Residents of Tiszowic in Israel, 1970. 324p. illus. (H and Y)

Uściług

2613 Avinadav, Aryeh, ed. The Growth and Destruction of the Community of Uściług. Tel-Aviv: Association of Former Residents of Uściług, 334p. (H and Y)

Wadowice

2614 Jakubowicz, David, ed. Memorial Book of the Communities Vadovitsah, Anfrikhov, Kalvaryah, Mishenits, Sucha. Masada, Ramat-Gan: Former Residents of Wadowice etc., 1967. 454p. illus. (H and Y)

Warka

2615 Kalish, Ita. "Life in a Hassidic Court in Russian Poland Toward the End of the XIXth and Early XXth Centuries." YIVO Annual 13 (1965): 264-278.

Warszawa (Warsaw)

2616 Anenkiel, Anrzej. "Jewish Community in Interwar Warsaw." BŻIH 3-4/107-108 (1978): 65-71. (P)

2617 Auerbach, Rachella. A Warsaw Testament: Encounters, Activity and Vicissitudes. Tel-Aviv: Israel Buch, 1974. 355p. (Y)

2618 Bałaban, Majer. "The First Attempt to Establish a Hebrew Printing Press in Warsaw." In his Z Historii Żydów w Polsce 3, (Warsaw: 1925): 85-89. (P)

2619 Bałaban, Majer. "Warsaw, the Greatest Jewish Community in Europe." Haynt Jubilee Book (1928): 117-120. (Y)

2620 Baumgarten, Leon. "The First Circle of Jewish Revolutionary Youth in Warsaw." BŻIH 63, (July-September, 1967): 65-88. (P)

2621 Berkowicz, Sz. "Jewish Workers in Warsaw's Small Industry and Size of Those Enterprises." Das wirtszaftleche lebn 1, (Warsaw, 1935): 40ff. (Y)

2622 Bloch, Bronisław. "Spatial Evolution of the Jewish and General Population of Warsaw." In U.O. Schmelz et al eds. Papers in Jewish Demography (Jerusalem, 1973): 209-234.

2623 Blum-Bielicka, Luba. "Nursing School at the Hospital of Orthodox Jewish Community in Warsaw." BŻIH 40 (October-December, 1961): 66-77. (P)

2624 Carlebach, Alexander. "A German Rabbi Goes East: Emanuel Carlebach's Letters from Warsaw, 1916-1918." Leo Baeck Institute Yearbook 6 (New York, 1961): 60-121.

2625 Chromiński, Kazimierz. "Explanation of the Laws for Free Habitation and Commerce of Jews in Warsaw." MSC 6 (1969): 27-46. (P)

2626 Datner, Szymon. "Activities of the Warsaw Jewish Consistory as Reflected by the Documents of the Underground Archive of the Warsaw Ghetto." BŻIH 73 (1970): 101-132. (P)

2627 Duker, Abraham Gordon. "Ghettos for Jewish Students in Warsaw Colleges." School and Society 46 (New York, 1937): 591ff.

2628 Eisenbach, Artur. "Aleksander Kraushar in the Matter of a Memorandum of the Stock-Exchange Committee in Warsaw, in 1886." BŻIH 1/109 (1979): 73-75. (P)

2629 Eisenbach, Artur. "Distribution and Dwelling Conditions of the Jewish Population in Warsaw in Light of the 1815 Census." BŻIH 20 (1956): 50-86. (P)

2630 Eisenbach, Artur. "Legal Status of the Jewish Population in Warsaw in the End of 18th and the Begining of 19th Century. BŻIH 39 (1961): 3-16. (P)

2631 Eisenbach, Artur. "The Structure of the Jewish Population in Warsaw in Light of 1810 Census. BŻIH 13-14 (1958): 73-121. (P)

2632 Frendenson, W. "The New Hospital of the Orthodox Jews in Czyste Suburb of Warsaw." Gazeta Lekarska 37, no.50 (Warsaw, 1902): 1257-1263 et no. 51, pp.1287-1291. (P)

2633 Frenk, Ezriel Nathan. "The Struggle with Agnosticism in Old Warsaw." Almanach-Moment (Warsaw, 1921): 95-114. (Y)

2634 Fuks, Marian. The Jewish Press in Warsaw, 1823-1939. Warsaw: Państwowe Wydawnictwo Naukowe, 1979. 362p. illus. (P)

2635 Goldstein, Bernard. Twenty Years with The Jewish Labor Bund in Warsaw, 1919-1939. New York: Verlag Unser Tsayt, 1960. xvi, 328. (Y)

2636 Gruenbaum, J., ed. Warsaw Memorial Volumes. 2 vols. Jerusalem: Encyclopaedia of the Jewish Diaspora, 1953, 1959. 816p., 698 columns. Illus. (H)

2637 Hersch, L. "Linguistic Assimilation of Jewish Students in Warsaw High Schools." YIVO Bleter 2 (1931): 441-444. (Y)

2638 Hirschhorn, Samuel. "The Warsaw Pogrom." In his History of Jews in Poland. (Warsaw, 1921): 222-236. (P)

2639 "Humble Request of Warsaw Jews." MSC, 6 (Warsaw. 1969): 129-132. (P)

2640 Ignotus (pseud. of Adolf Peretz). Warsaw Finanacial Circles, 1870-1925. Warsaw: 1926. 128p. (P)

2641 The Jewish Press in Warsaw: From Recent Past. Vol. II of From Recent Past. New York: 1956. viii, 538p. (Y)

2642 Jewish "Thatched Roof" for University Students. Warsaw: Centrala Żydowskich Stowarzyszeń Samopomocowych Środowiska Warszawskiego, 1932. 63p. (P)

2643 Kaganowski, Efraim. Warsaw Tales. Trans;. from Yiddish by Stanisław Wygodzki. Warsaw: Iskry, 1958. 267p. illus. (P)

2644 Kantor-Lichtensztejn, R. "Jewish Bakers' Trade in Warsaw." YIVO-

bleter (Wilno, 1936) p. 86ff. (Y)
2645 Katz, P., et al., editors. Book of Warsaw: Memorial Book On the Jewish Population of the City of Warsaw. Buenos Aires: Former Residents of Warsaw and Surroundings in Argentina, 1955. lvi. 1351 columns. (Y)

2646 Kermisz, Józef. "Jewish Representation in the Warsaw City Council, 1919-1938." GGŻ 2, no. 10-11 (1938): 318-321. (P)

2647 Kieniewicz, Stefan. "The British Consul in Warsaw and Moses Montefiore." BŻIH 1-2/121-122 (1982): 103-108. (P)

2648 Kowalska-Glikman, Stefania. "The Jewish Population of Warsaw in Light of Civil Status Acts." BŻIH 2/118 (1981): 37-49. (P)

2649 Kraushar, Alexander (pseud. Alkar) Warsaw Tradesmen: An Outline of their Five Centuries' Long History: Historico-Moral Monograph based on Archival Sources. Warsaw: F. Hoesick, 1929. 245p. (P)

2650 Krongold H. and Segal, M. "Origin of the Warsaw 'Young Guard' Association." Hazak we'emac nol (January, 1919): pp. 41ff.

2651 Kroszczor, Henryk. "The Bersohns and Baumans' Hospital for Children." BŻIH 73 (1970): 67-86 et 74, (April-June, 1970): 59-80. (P)

2652 Kroszczor, Henryk. "The Great Synagogue at Tłumacki Square." BŻIH 3/95 (1975): 3-16. (P)

2653 Kroszczor, Henryk. "The Main Library of Jewish Historical Documents." BŻIH 2/78 (1971): 3-10. (P)

2654 Kroszczor, Henryk and Zabłotniak, Ryszard. "Jewish Anti Tuberculosis Society 'Brijus-Zdrowie." BŻIH 1/89 (1974): 83-96. (P)

2655 Kroszczor, Henryk and Zabłotniak, Ryszard. "Jewish Sanitary Help Committee in Warsaw, 1914-1915." BŻIH 1/81 (1972): 91-97. (P)

2656 Kroszczor, Henryk and Zabłotniak, Ryszard. "Social Anti-Tuberculosis Organizations of the Jewish Population in Warsaw." BŻIH 4/112 (1979): 35-48. (P)

2657 Kroszczor, Henryk and Zimler, Henryk. The Jewish Cemetery in Warsaw. Warsaw: Państwowe Wydawnictwo Naukowe, 1983. 114p. illus. (P)

2658 Kublicki, Stanisław. "Income-Tax from Jewish Long-Time Residents of Warsaw." MSC 6 (1969): 43-43. (P)

2659 "Letter in the Matter of the Persecution of Warsaw Jews." MSC 6 (1969): 191-193. (P)

2660 Levinson, Abraham. History of the Warsaw Jews. Tel-Aviv: 1952/1953. 415p. illus. (H)

2661 Lewandowski, Stefan, "Origin of Samuel Orgelbrand's Business, 1830-1868." Rocznik Warszawski 10 (1971): 113-141. (P)

2662 Lewestam, F.H. "On Invention of Printing, Development of the Art of Printing, and on the Establishment of Samuel Orgelbrand." Kalendarz Warszawskiego Towarzystwa Dobroczynności, 1983. 77-88. (P)

2663 Lewin, Sabina. " The Warsaw Orphanage (Shelter Home) in the XIXth Century." BŻIH 3-4/123-124 (1982): 31-47. (P)

2664 Mahler, Raphael. "Jewish Vendors of Cracknels in Warsaw in Light of an Inquiry." Zagadnienia Gospodarcze 1-2 (1935): 115ff. (P)

2665 Marek, Lucjan. "The Beginnings of the Unionist Movement Among Jewish Salesmen in Warsaw." BŻIH 58 (1966): 81-105. (P)

2666 Muratowicz, Szl. "Response from Szl. Muratowicz." MSC 6 (1969): 193-206. (P)

2667 Neuman, I.M. "Looking at the Nalewki." Menorah Journal 9, no.3, (August, 1923): 230-234.

2668 Nussbaum, Hilary. Historical Sketches from Jewish Life in Warsaw, Starting with the First Traces of Their Settlement in that City up to Present Times. Warsaw: K. Kowalewski, 1881. iv, 269p. (P)

2669 Ostersetzer, I. "Institute of Jewish Higher Learning in Warsaw." M.Żyd. 2 (Warsaw, 1931): 262-273. (P)

2670 Podhorizer-Sandel, Erna. "Jewish Historical Documents in the National Museum in Warsaw." BŻIH 2/78 (1971): 55-60. (P)

2671 Reports from the First National Convention of the 'Toz' Society, held on June 24-25, 1928. Warsaw: 1929. xxxv. 206p. (Y)

2672 Ringelblum, Emmanuel. Jews in Warsaw. Warsaw: Towarzystwo Miłośników Historji, 1932. (P)

2673 Rozenowicz, Ch. "Jews in the Council of the Capital City's Defense." GGŻ 2, no. 10-11, (Warsaw,1938): 245-246. (P)

2674 Sawicki, Aron. " School for Rabbis in Warsaw." M. Żyd. 1, (1933): 246-276. (P)

2675 The School System: Vol. I, From the History of the Orthodox Jewish Commune in 19th Century Warsaw. Warsaw: 1907. 284p. illus. (P)

2676 Schorr, Moses. Inaugural Homily Rendered in the Great Synagogue in Tlumacki Square on the Eve of December 7, 1923. Warsaw: Komitet Wielkiej Synagogi na Tłumackiem, 1924. 28p. (P)

2677 Schorr, Moses. "Our Requests." GGŻ 2, no.10-11 (1938): 232-233. (P)

2678 Seidmen, Hillel. "Archives of the Jewish Consistory in Warsaw." Almanach Gminy Żydowskiej 1 (Warsaw, 1939): 70-75. (P)

2679 Schiper, Ignacy. "Jewish Population in Warsaw During the XIXth Century." Krajoznastwo 2 (Warsaw,1935): 4-5. (P)

2680 Shatzky, Jacob. History of the Jews in Warsaw. New York: 1947-1953. 3 vols. (Y)

2681 Shatzky, Jacob. "Institutional Aspects of Jewish Life in Warsaw in the Second Half of the XIXth Century." YIVO Annual 10 (New York: 1955): 9-44.

2682 Shatzky, Jacob. "The Jewish Role in Economic Life of Warsaw in the Years 1863-1896." Transl. from Yiddish by A. Rutkowski. BŻIH 30 (1959): 12-49. (P)

2683 Shatzky, Jacob. "Warsaw Jews in Polish Cultural Life of the Early 19th Century." YIVO Annual 5 (1950): 41-54.

2684 Shneiderman, Samuerl Loeb. The Warsaw Heresy. New York: Horizon Press, 1959. 253p.

2685 Słonimski, Antoni. "What is my tie with Warsaw?" Stolica 45, (Warsaw, 1966): 16-17. (P)

2686 Sokołow, Nahum. "Henri Bergson's Old-Warsaw Lineage." GT (New York,1984): 349-359.

2687 "Special Request of the Warsaw Brotherhood of Merchants and Guilds." MSC 6 (1969): 283-292. (P)

2688 Tartakower, Arieh. "The Institute of Jewish Studies in Warsaw." In Ginzberg, Louis and Weiss, Abraham, eds. Studies in Memory of Moses Schorr. (New York, 1944): 163-176.

2689 Teitelbaum, Abraham. Backyards of Warsaw. Buenos Aires: 1947. 207p. illus. (Y)

2690 Tomaszewski, Jerzy. "Jewish Workers in Interwar Warsaw: A Statistical Outline." BŻIH 1/81 (1972): 71-84. (P)

2691 Trunk, Isaiah. "The Library of the Jewish Historical Institute." BŻIH 2 (1950): pp. 24ff. (P)

2692 Tych, Feliks. "Rosa Luxemburg's Last Sojourn in Warsaw." Warszawa Popowstaniowa, 1864-1918 1, (Warsaw, 1968): 229-255. (P)

2693 Vaykhert, Mikhal. Memoirs from Warsaw. 2 vols. Tel-Aviv, 1961. (Y)

2694 Warszawski, S. "City Militia of Warsaw During the November Uprising." M. Żyd. 1 (1930):55-67.

2695 Warszawski, S. "Social and Economic Structure of Warsaw Jewry in the year 1840." M.Żyd. 3 (1931): 245-262. (P)

2696 Wein, Adam. "Jews Outside the Jewish District in Warsaw, 1809-1862." BŻIH 41 (1962): 45-70. (P)

2697 Wein, Adam. "Purchasing and Building of Houses by Jews in Warsaw, 1821-1862." BŻIH 64 (1967): 33-53. (P)

2698 Wein, Adam. "Restrictions on the Jewish Influx into Warsaw, 1815-1862." BŻIH 49 (1964): 3-34. (P)

2699 Zabłotniak, Ryszard. "Scientific Circle of Physicians at the Jewish Hospital in Warsaw, 1903-1939." BŻIH 71-72 (1969): 65-72. (P)

2700 Zilbersztejn, Sara. "The Progressive Synagogue at Daniłowiczowska Street in Warsaw: A Contribution to the XIXth Century Histoiry of Polish Jewry's Culture." BŻIH 74 (1970): 31-57. (P)

Węgrów

2701 Tamari, Moshe, ed. Community of Węgrów: Memorial Book. Tel-Aviv: Former Residents of Węgrów in Israel, 1961. 418p. illus. (H and Y)

Wieluń

2702 Goldberg, J. "Agriculture Among Jews of the Wielun District in the Second Half of the XVIIIth Century." BŻIH 23 (1958): 63 ff. (P)

2703 Wieluń Memorial Book. Tel-Aviv: Wieluń Organization in Israel and the Memorial Book Committee in USA, 1971. 558p. illus. (H and Y)

Wieruszów

2704 Goldberg, J. "A Jewish Community Owned by a Nobleman: Jews in Old Wieruszów." BŻIH 59, (1966): 3-28. (P)

2705 Wierushow Memorial Book. Tel-Aviv: Former Residents of Wieruszów Book Committee, 1970. 907p. illus. (H and Y)

Wierzbnik

2706 Schutzman, Mark, ed. Wierzbnik-Starachowitz Memorial Book. Tel-Aviv: 1973. 606p. illus. (H and Y)

Wilno (Vilnius)

2707 Cohen, Israel. Vilna: History of Jews in Vilna. Philadelphia: Jewish Publication Society of America, 1943. xxiii, 527p.

2708 Dworzecki, Mark. Lithuania's Jerusalem: Its Growth and its Destruction. Tel-Aviv: 1951. 430p. illus. (H)

2709 Friedenstein, Simeon Eliezer. The City of Heroes. Wilno: 1880. 109p. (H)

2710 Funn, Samuel Joseph. Kiryah Neeman's Book 'Faithful City'. Wilno: 1860. xxiv, 333p. (H)

2711 Gotlober, A.B. Jewish Work. Wilno: 1927. xxii, 257p. (Y)

2712 Jeshurin, Ephraim M., ed. Vilne: A Collective Book Dedicated to the City of Wilno. New York: Vilna Branch of the Workmen Circle, 1935. x, 1012p. illus. (Y)

2713 Jewish Central Committee for Education. Wilno: 1924. 387p. illus. (P)

2714 Klausner, Israel. History of the Old Cemetery in Wilno. Wilno: 1935. 144p. illus. (H)

2715 Kon, Pinchas. "Letter of a Wilno Student from the Year 1822." Jinger Historyker 2 (1929): 143-148 (Y)

2716 Kon, Pinchas. A Recovered Part of Old Wilno Kehillot's Archives. Wilno: Ateneum Wileńskie, 1929. 20p. (P)

2717 Łuński, Ch. "Matisjohu Straszun's Library in Wilno." Bicher Welt (Mińsk, 1922): 263-268. (Y)

2718 Maggid, Hillel Noah. City of Vilna. Wilno: 1900.xiv, 304p. (H)

2719 Magid, D.G. "From My Archives: 1. On History of Jewish Deputies During Tsar Alexander I; 2. Jewish Self-government in the Thirties of the Last Century." Pierez 4 (1913): 181-211. (R)

2720 Novogrodsky, Emanuel. "Jewish Labor 'Bund' in Lithuanian Jerusalem." Farois 18, (Mexico City, October 1957): 12-15. (Y)

2721 Ran, Leyzer. Jerusalem of Lithuania: Illustrated and Documented. 3 vol. New York: The Vilno Album Committee, 1974.

2722 Ran, Leyzer and Koriski, L., eds. Pages About Vilna: A Compilation. Łódź: Association of Jews from Vilna in Poland, 1947. xvii, 77p. (Y)

2723 Reisen, Zalman, et al., eds. Chronicle of Wilno During the Years of War and Occupation . Wilno: Żydowskie Towarzystwo Historyczno-Etnograficzne, 1922. 472p. (Y)

2724 "Representation from the Creditors to the Wilno Kehillot ." MSC 6 (1969): 13-27. (P)

2725 "Request of the Wilno Kehillot to the King and Diet." MSC 6 (1969): 9-13. (P)

2726 "Response of Wilno Jews." MSC 6, (1969): 105-113. (P)

2727 Sevela, Efraim. Legends from Invalid Street. Transl. from French by Anthony Kahn. London:Robson Books, 1974. 212p.

2728 Steinberg, O.N. "Count Murawew and his Attitude to the Wilno Jewry." Russkaia Starina 2, (1901):" 305-320. (R)

2729 Szabad, C. Elections to the Sejm (Parliament) in Wilno held on January 8, 1922. Wilno: Generalny Komitet Wyborczy, 1922. 172p. (P)

2730 Szabad, C. Movement of the Jewish Population (Birthrate and Mortality) in Wilno, 1911-1926. Wilno: Pogoń, 1927. 33p. (P)

2731 Worobeichic, Moise. The Ghetto Lane Vilno. Zurich: Orell Fussli Publishers, 1931. 65p. illus. (H)

2732 Weinreih, Max. The Yiddish Scientific Institute (YIVO): Its Aims and Achievements. New York: 1936. 19p.

2733 Weisbord, Chana. "The Children's Library of the Jewish Central Educational Committee in Wilne." Pinkas Wilno (1922): 767-772. (Y)

Wiślica

2734 Aizenberg, Yitshak, ed. Book of Wiślica. Tel Aviv: Association of Former Residents of Wiślica, 1971. 299p. illus. (H, Y and P)

Wiśniowiec

2735 Rabin, Hayim, ed. Wiśniowiec: Memorial Book of the Martyrs of Wiśniowiec who Perished in the Nazi Holocaust. Tel-Aviv: Former Residents of Wiśniowiec, 1970. 540p. illus. (H and Y)

Włodawa

2736 Rovner, D., ed. In Memory of Włodawa. Haifa: 1968. 211p. (H, Y and P)

Włocławek

2737 Tchorsh, Katriel Fishel and Korzen, Meir, eds. Włocławek and Vicinity: Memorial Book. Tel-Aviv: Association of Former Residents of Włoclawek in Israel and the USA, 1967. xvi, 1032 columns illus. (H and Y)

Włodzimierz Wołyński

2738 Wolynsk Wladimir. In Memory of the Jewish Community. Tel-Aviv: Former Residents of Wladimir in Israel, 1962. 624 columns. (H and Y)

Wojsławice

2739 Kanc, Sh., ed. Yizkor Book in Memory of Voislavize. Tel-Aviv: Former Residents of Voislavitze, 1970. 515p. (H and Y)

Wolbrom

2740 Geshuri, Meir Simon, ed. Our Town Wolbrom. Tel-Aviv: Association of Former Residents of Wolbrom in Israel, 1962. 909p. (H and Y)

Wołkowysk

2741 Einhorn, Moses, ed. Memorial Book of Wolkovisk. New York: 1949. 2 vols, 990p. (Y)

Wołożyn

2742 Cytron, Sz.L. "Dynastic Struggle in the Wolozyn Yeshiva (Jewish Institute of Higher Learning)." Rszumot 1 (Odessa, 1925): 125-135. (H)

2743 Leoni, Elieser, ed. Wolozin: The Book of the City and of the Etz Hayyim Yeshiva. Tel-Aviv: Former Residents of Wolozin in Israel and the USA, 1970. 679p. illus. (H and Y)

Wrocław (Breslau)

2744 Brann, Marcus. History of the Jewish Theological Seminary in Breslau: Festschrift for the Fiftieth Anniversary of the Institute. Breslau: von T. Schatzky, 1904. lii, 209p. illus. (G)

2745 Brilling, B. "Archives of the Jewish Breslau Community." Jahrbuch der schlesischen Friedrich-Wilhelms Universität zu Breslau 18, (Berlin-München, 1973): 258-284. (G)

2746 Hoffman, Zygmunt. " Crystal Night in the Wrocław District of SS." BŻIH 2/98 (1976): 75-96. (P)

Wrzeszcz (Langfurth)

2747 Kupfer, Franciszek Efraim. "Chronicle of the Jewish Commune in Wrzeszcz," BŻIH 22, (1957): 26-44. (P)

Wysock

2748 Our Town Wysock: Memorial Book. Haifa: Association of Former Residents of Vysotsk in Israel, 1963. 231p. (H and Y)

Wyszków

2749 Stokfisch, David, ed. Vishkov Book. Tel-Aviv: Association of Former Residents of Wishkow in Israel and Abroad, 1964. 351p. illus. (H and Y)

Wyszogród

2750 Rabin, Haim, ed. Vishogrod: Dedicated to the Memory of the Vishogrod Martyrs who Died by the Hands of the Nazis and Their Henchmen. Tel-Aviv: Former Residents of Vishogrod, 1971. 366p. illus. (H and Y)

Zabłotów

2751 A City and the Dead: Zablotov Alive and Destroyed. Tel-Aviv: Former Residents of Zabłotów in Israel and the USA, 1949. (H and Y)

Zabłudów

2752 Asaf, Sz. "Zabłudów Chronicle." Kirjat Sefer 1, (1924/1925): 307-317. (H)

2753 Zesler, Sh et al., eds. Zabłudów Memorial Book. Buenos Aires:

Zabłudowo Book Committee, 507p. (Y)

Zambrów

2754 Lewiński, Yom Tov, ed. The Book of Zambrów: Memoirs of Our Town which had been Annihilated by the Nazis and does not exist any more. Tel-Aviv: The Zambnrover Societies in USA, Argentina and Israel. 1963. 696p. illus. (H and Y)

Zamość

2755 Baranowska, Zofia and Baranowski, Jerzy. "The Jewish Quarter and Synagogue in Zamość." BŻIH 63 (1967): 39-56. (P)

2756 Bernstein, Maroqued, ed. Zamość Chronicle: Dedicated to the Sacred Memory of the Jewish Community of Zamość. Buenos Aires: 1957. 1265p.illus. (Y)

2757 Klausner, I.A. "Zamoshts - City of J.L. Perec." He-Avar, 13 (1966): 98-117. (H)

2758 Kupfer, Franciszek Efraim. " Chronicle of the Burial and Philanthropic Society in Zamość." BŻIH 2, (1951): 47-80. (P)

2759 Sawa, Bogumiła. "A Contribution to the Legal Status of Zamosc Jews in the XVIth -XVIIIth Centuries." BŻIH 3/99 (1976): 27-40. (P)

2760 Szyszka, Bogdan. "From the History of Jewish Schools in Interwar Zamość." BŻIH 4/112 (1979): 79-86. (P)

2761 Tamari, Moshe, ed. The Rise and Fall of Zamosc. Tel-Aviv: Former Residents of Zamość in Israel, 1953. 327p. illus. (H and P)

Zaromb

2762 For Eternal Remembrance: The Jews of Zaromb. New York: United Zaromber Relief, 1947. 68p. (Y)

Zawiercie

2763 Spivak, Sh., ed. Memorial Book of the Martyrs of Zawiercie and Vicinity. Tel-Aviv: Former Residents of Zawiercie and Vicinity, 1948. 570p. (H and Y)

Zborów

2764 Berger, Solomon. The Jewish Commonwealth of Zborów. New York: Regsol Publishing Co., 1967. xiv, 154p. illus.

Zduńska Wola

2765 Erlich, Elchanan, ed. The Zdunska-Wola Book. Tel-Aviv: Zdunska Wola Associations in Israel and in the Diaspora, 1968. 55p. (H and Y)

Zetel

2766 Kapliński, Baruch, ed. Zetel Chronicle: A Memorial to the Jewish

Community of Zetel. Tel-Aviv: Zetel Association in Israel, 1957. 482p. illus. (H and Y)

Zgierz

2767 Baum, D. "The Textile Industry in Zgierz 1936." Yidisze ekonomik 2-3 (1937): 4-5. (Y)

Złoczów

2768 Book of Zlots'ev. Tel-Aviv: Community of the Association of Former Residents of Zloczew, 1971. 432p. illus. (Y)

2769 Perski, Jakub. "Material to the History of Jewish in Złoczów." BŻIH 1/81 (1972): 85-90 et 1/93 (1975): 97-100. (P)

Żarki

2770 Lader (Lederman), Yitshak, ed. The Community of Żarki: Life and Destruction of a Town. Tel-Aviv: Former Residents of Żarki in Israel, 1959. 324p. illus. (H and Y)

Żelechów

2771 Jasny, A., ed. Memorial Book of the Community of Żelechów. Chicago: Former Residents of Żelechów in Chicago, 1953. xxiv, 398p. illus. (Y)

Żołądź

2772 Avinadav, A., ed. Memorial Book of the Community of Zoludzk in Israel. Tel-Aviv: Association of Former Residents of Zoludzk in Israel, 1970. 188p. (H and Y)

Żołudek

2773 Meyerowitz, A., ed. The Book of Żołudek and Orłowa: A Living Memorial. Tel-Aviv: Former Residents of Żołudek in Israel and the USA, n.d. (H and Y)

Żółkiew

2774 Bałaban, Majer. "Zolkiew." In His Z Historii Zydow w Polsce. (Warsaw, 1920): 42-48. (P)

2775 Bałaban, Majer. "Hebraic Printing Shops in Żółkiew and Lwów." in his Z Historii Żydów w Polsce. (Warsaw, 1920): 72-84. (P)

2776 Buber, Salomon. Famous City: Biographies and the Gravestone Inscriptions of the Outstanding Men, Rabbis and the Communal Superintendents of the City of Żółkiew, arranged in alphabetical order as a Contribution to the History of Jews in Żółkiew. Kraków: 1903. 128p. (G)

2777 Belber, Natan Michael and Ben-Shem Y., eds. Memorial Book of Z'olkiv. Jerusalem, Encyclopaedia of the Jewish Diaspora, 1969. 844

columns. illus. (H)

Żyrardów

2778 Bernstein, M. W., ed. <u>Memorial Book of Żyrardów, Amszynów and Wiskit</u>. Buenos Aires: Association of Former Residents in the USA, Israel, France and Argentina, 1961. 69p. (Y)

Author and Editor Index

(References are to entry numbers in the bibliography, not page numbers.)

Abraham of Szarogrod 1154
Abramovitch, Raphael R. (1880–1963) 821, 1329
Abramowich, D. 2231
Abramsky, Chimen 27, 1294
Abramson, H. 2530
Ackerberg, Armand 648
Adini, Ya'akov 2228, 2275, 2529
Adler, Cyrus (1863–1940) 1506
Adler, Max (1873–1937) 1380
Adler-Rudel, Salomon (b.1894) 178
Adus, Maurice 1721
Aescoly, Aaron Ze'ev (1901–1948) 731
Agnon, Shmuel Yosef (1888–1970) 50
Ain, Abraham 2580
Ainsztein, Reuben 348
Aisene, Benjamin 349
Aizenberg, Yitshak 2734
Alef, Gustaw (pseud. Bolkowiak) 1696
Alejchem (Rabinowitz), Szalom (1859–1916) 913, 1960, 1961, 1962, 1963
Aleksandrova, H. 457
Alexandroni, Ya'kov 2181
Alexandrow, H.B. 179
Alfasi, Yitshak 732, 2293, 2597
Alfassi, J. 649, 2052
Allentuck, Marcia Epstein (b.1928) 2154
Allerhand, Mauryey (1863–1942) 616
Almi, A. (pseud. of Elias Sheps) (1892–1963) 271
Alpersohn, Marcos (b.1860) 1449
Alperyn, A. 2222
Alsberg, P.A. 1
Altbauer, M. 914, 915
Alter, Leon 1450
Alter, M. 650
Alter, Wiktor (1890–1942) 1220, 1722
Alterman, I.B. 2297
Amihai, Mordekhai 2534
Andreski, Stanislaw 1723
Andrzejewski, Jerzy 1724
Andrzejewski, Marek 2280
Anenkiel, Andrzej 2616
Ansky, S.A. (pseud. of Solomon Zaynal Rapaport) (1863–1920)
995, 996, 1651, 1863, 1864
Antonow, M. 516
Appenszlak, Jacob 1604
Appenszlak, Pauline 2066
Arnsberg, Paul 1155
Arnstein, Marc (pseud. Andrzej Marek) (b.1879) 1125
Aron, Izaks 1865
Aron, Milton 733
Aronson, Grigori (1887–1968) 1330, 1347
Aronson, Michael 1183
Assaf, Michael (b.1896) 1381, 2752
Asch, Sholem (1880–1957) 917, 918, 919
Ashkenazy, Abraham ben Shmuel 651
Askenazy, Szymon (1867–1935) 180, 181, 1382
Assaf, Simhah (1889–1953) 653
Asz, Nachum 652
Atlas, Samuel H. (b.1899) 2099
Aubac, Stephane 567, 1527
Auerbach, Julian 1295, 1697
Auerbach, Rachella 2617
Austri-Dunn, Isaias 2256
Avatihi, Aryeh 2537, 2569
Avidan, Moshe 51
Avinadav, Aryeh 2613, 2772
Avituv, Abraham Yitshak (b.1898) 2304
Avron, Dov 2502
Ayalon-Baranick, Benzion Hayyim (b.1901) 2302, 2453, 2476, 2605
Ayalon, N. 2403
Axer, Erwin (b.1917) 1866

Bacon, Gershon C. 2
Bacon, I. 734
Bader, Gershom (1868–1953) 52, 1867, 2040
Baer, Yitzhak Fritz (b.1888) 735
Bak, Maria 2470
Bakalczuk-Felin, Meilech 2233
Baler, B. 2350
Balaban, Majer (1877–1943) 3, 28, 29, 30, 53, 54, 148, 149, 150, 151, 182, 183, 184, 185, 272, 273, 274, 275, 276, 277, 568, 617, 618, 619, 620, 654,

655, 736, 822, 823, 824, 825,
826, 827, 828, 829, 920, 921,
922, 1027, 1156, 1157, 1158,
1221, 1222, 1223, 1451, 1730,
2036, 2057, 2061, 2123, 2138,
2177, 2353, 2354, 2386, 2387,
2407, 2408, 2409, 2410, 2432,
2513, 2618, 2619, 2774, 2775
Bałucki, Michal (1837-1901)
1028
Bamberger, Mose Loeb (1869-1924)
2603
Banasiak, A. 1549
Baranowska, Zofia 2755
Baranowski, Jerzy 2241, 2491,
2609, 2755
Baranowski, Krzysztof 2433
Bardichevski, Aharon 1383
Barkeli, Sh. 2278
Bar-On, M.Y. 2289
Baron, Salo W. (b.1895) 1452
Bartoszewicz, Kazimierz (1852-1930) 152, 1184
Bartoszewicz, Włodzimierz 1029
Bartyś, Julian 517, 518, 519, 2573
Bar-Yuda, M. 2608
Barzilay, Issac 2141
Baskerville, Beatrice C. 488
Batault, Georges 1731
Bauer, Yehuda 1508
Baum, D. 2767
Baumfeld-Boleski, Andrzej 56
Baumgarten, Leon 1528, 1698, 1699, 1700, 2620
Bauminger, Arieh L. (b.1913) 2355
Becker, Rafal 1224, 1225
Beer, Max (1864-1949) 1453
Begey, Atille 1030
Behr, Isachar Falkensohn (1746-1791); 153, 923, 924
Beilin, Asher (1881-1946) 278
Belber, Natan Michael 2777
Belmont, Leo 925, 1031, 1185
Bełza, Władysław (1847-1913)
1032
Benari, Yehuda 1430, 1454
Ben-Azar, A. (Broshy) 2451
Bender, Ryszard 279
Ben-Ezra, Akiva 2299
Ben-Meir, J. (Treshansky) 2288
Ben-Nachum, Z. 2608
Ben Sasson, Haim Hillel (b.1914)
2030
Ben-Shem, Y. 2777

Ben-Yeruham, H. 1384
Ben-Zaccai, Johana 2569
Ber of Bolechów (Birkenthal)
(1723-1805) 1868
Beregowski, Moses Yakovlevich
(1892-1961) 830
Berenson, Leon (1885-1943) 1869
Berger, A. 2111
Berger, Heinrich 2371
Berger, Solomon (b.1857) 2764
Berglas, Yitshak 2575
Bergmann, Eugen von (b.1857)
458
Berkovicz, Sh. 1509, 2621
Berliner, Abraham (1833-1915)
1870, 2411
Berman, Adolf Abraham (1906-1978) 1871
Berman, Jacob (b.1901) 1159, 2265
Bernfeld, Simon (1860-1940) 55, 1872
Bernstein, Dov 2277
Bernstein, Herman (1876-1935)
1550, 1734
Bernstein, M.W. 2231, 2778
Bernstein, Mardoqueo 2512, 2521
Berstein, Maroqued 2756
Bershadskii, Sergei Aleksandrovich (1850-1896) 186
Bersohn, Mathias (1823-1908)
154
Bet-Halevi 2318
Bialik, Hayyim Nahman (1873-1934) 926, 927
Biber, Menahem Mendel 2477
Bickel, Shlomo (b. 1896-1969)
2340
Biderman, Israel M. (1911-1973)
31, 2291, 2336
Bielecki, Tadeusz 187
Bierman, Jacob 1873
Bierzanek, Remigiusz 351
Bigil, G. 2188
Bird, Thomas E. 2067
Birkenmeier, Aleksander 2025
Birnbaum, Nathan (pseud. Mathias
Acher) (1864-1937) 1226, 1385
Bischoff, Erich (1865-1936)
1227
Blaustein, Miriam Umstadter
1874
Blit, Lucjan 1735
Bloch, Bronisław 2622
Bloch, Hayim I. (1864-1948) 737
Bloch, Joseph Samuel (1850-1923)

1605, 1876
Bloch, Philipp (1841-1923) 280, 569, 2501
Blum, Eliezer (pseud. B. Alkawit) (1896-1963) 281
Blum, Hillel (1868-1943) 1875
Blum-Bielicka, Luba 2623
Blumenstrauch, B. 489
Blumental, Nachman 2180, 2183, 2213, 2388, 2451, 2536
Bochner, Mordecai 2247
Bohm, Adolf (1873-1941) 1386
Bojarski, J.P. 1228
Bojomir-Mileski, Waclaw 1736
Borejsza, Jerzy W. 2090
Bornstein, I.L. 490, 554, 1229, 1230
Borochow, Ber (1881-1917) 928, 929, 930
Borowy, Wacław (1890-1950) 1033, 2086
Borski, Jan M. 1529
Borwicz, Michał Maksymilian (Boruchowicz) (b.1911) 57, 1737
Borzemińska, Zofia 831
Bosak, Meir (b.1912) 1160
Botoshansky, Jacob (1892-1964) 2531
Boulton, Marjorie 2174
Boxer, A. (Ben-Arjeh) 2274
Brafman, Iakov Aleksandrovich (1825-1879) 621
Brainin, Reuben (1862-1939) 1877, 1878
Brandes, Leo 570
Brandstaetter, Roman (b.1906) 282, 931, 1034
Brandys, Kazimierz (b.1916) 932
Brann, Marcus (1849-1920) 2744
Brat, Itzhak 2450
Braunstein, Chaim 2554
Brawer, Michael (b.1862) 738
Breier, Alois 832
Breslauer, Bernhard (1851-1928) 1455
Brilling, Bernhard (b.1906) 2745
Brodsky, David 2511
Brodowski, Feliks (1964-1934) 1035
Bronikowski, Alexander 1036
Bronisławski, Jerzy 571
Bronsztejn, Szyja 459, 1231
Bross, Jacob (1883-1942) 1296
Brożek, Andrzej 188, 2020

Brückner, Aleksander (1856-1939) 58, 2034
Brustin-Berenstein, Tatiana 1701, 1702
Brutzkus, Boris Dov (1874-1938) 520
Buber, Martin (1878-1965) 739, 740, 741, 742, 743, 744, 745, 746, 1232
Buber, Salomon (1827-1906) 2776
Buchbinder, Nahum Abramovich (b.1895) 1297
Buchner, Abraham (1789-1869) 657
Buchweitz, R. 352
Buczkowski, Leopold 1037
Buell, Raymond Leslie (1896-1946) 353
Bujak, Franciszek (1875-1953) 59
Bunam, Simha (1762-1827) 747
Bunimowicz, J. 1879
Burchard, Przemyslaw 555
Burstein, Aviezer 2292
Burszta, Józef 1233
Bursztyn, Michael (1896-1945) 933
Butrymowicz, Mateusz Topór (1892-1964) 155, 1653, 1654
Buzek, Józef (b.1973) 460
Byk, Emil (1845-1906) 1606, 1607, 1880, 2412
Bystroń, Jan Stanisław (1892-1964) 833

Cahan, Abraham (1860-1951) 1881
Cang, Joel 354, 1608
Carlebach, Alexander 2624
Carmoly, Eliakim (1802-1875) 189
Caro, Jesechel (1844-1916) 2413
Caro, Leopold (1864-1939) 536, 1234
Castellan, Georges 1235
Cederbaum, Henryk 283
Centnerszwerowa, Rosa 834, 934, 1551
Chaimowicz, Pejsak 1655
Chajes, Chaim 748
Chajes, Wiktor 2414
Chajn, Leon (b.1910) 1552, 1609
Chankowski, Stanisław 284
Chasanowich, Leon (pseud. of Katriel Shub) (18820-1925) 1738
Chciuk, Andrzej (1920-1978)

1038
Cherykower, A. 1298
Chicherin, Boris Nikolaevich
 (1828-1904) 60
Chiel, S. 2068
Chmielewski, Samuel 355
Chojnowski, Andrzej 356
Chołoniewski, Antoni (1868-1924)
 357, 1553, 1554, 1656, 1739
Chomet, Abraham (b.1892) 2560,
 2593
Chones, Simon Moses 659
Christiani, W. 285
Chromiński, Kazimierz 2625
Cięciała, Teodor 2594
Ciołkosz, Adam (1901-1978) 358,
 1334, 2016, 2092, 2139
Ciołkosz, Lidia 2016
Citron, Samuel Loeb 2033
Cohen, Israel (1879-1961) 359,
 360, 1740, 1882, 2707
Cohn, Adam 491
Cohn, Eduard 935
Cohn, J. 936
Cohn, Jacob 2326
Cohn, John 2532
Cohn, Norman Rufus Collin 1741
Crowe, David 5
Csato, Edward (b.1921) 2150
Cutter, Charles 4
Ćwik, Władysław 461, 2389
Cynberg, J. 286
Cytron, Szymon L.
 622, 660, 2146, 2742
Czacki, Michał 1657
Czacki, Tadeusz (1765-1813)
 1555
Czajkowski, P. 835
Czajkowski, R. 1742
Czapliński, Stanisław 2109
Czapska, Maria 1039
Czarny, D. 1883
Czarny, J.J. 1884
Czechowski, Michał B. (b.1818)
 572
Czekanowski, Jan (b.1882) 1237
Czerikower, A. 661
Czerniakow, Adam (1880-1942)
 361
Czyński, Jan (1801-1867) 61,
 62, 190, 191, 937

Damesek, Solomon 2461
Dan, Haim 2298
Dan, Joseph (b.1935) 749
Danielewicz, J. 192, 2017

Daniłowski, Gustaw (1872-1927)
 1040
Datner, Szymon 63, 287, 2626
David, Janina (b.1930) 1885
Davidowicz, David (b.1905) 836,
 837
Davies, Norman (b.1939) 64,
 362, 1510
Dawidowicz, Lucy S. 65, 838
Dawidsohn, Jozef 623
Dawison, Bogumił (1818-1872)
 1886
De Courtenay, Jan Baudoin 1556
Deiches, Ernest 156
Dembiński, Henryk 1558
Dembitzer, Hayyim Nathan (1820-
 1892) 2415
Detko, Jan 1041
Deutsch, Helene (b.1884) 1186
Deutscher, Isaac (1907-1967)
 1187
Diamand, Herman (1860-1930)
 1610, 1887
Diament, Jozef 492
Diamond, Benjamin (b.1895) 2305
Didier, Stanislaw 1162
Diner, Sz. 1511
Dinur, Benzion (b.1884) 750
Dmowski, Roman (1864-1939)
 1743, 1744, 1745
Dobroszycki, Lucjan (b. 1925)
 839
Dobrzyński, Bernard 521
Doleżal, Franciszek 2083
Doumont, Eduard 1746
Dresdner, K.R. 850
Dresner, Samuel H. 751
Drobner, Bolesław (1883-1968)
 1888
Drohojowski, Jan 1747
Droujanoff, Abraham Alter (1870-
 1938) 1388
Drozdowski, Marian Marek 573
Droździński, Aleksander 840
Drymmer, Wiktor Tomir 363
Dubanowicz, Edward (1881-1943)
 194
Dubnov, Simon (1860-1941) 32,
 66, 157, 752, 753, 754, 1389
Duker, Abraham Gordon (b.1907)
 67, 196, 197, 198, 199, 200,
 201, 288, 289, 290, 291, 364,
 1042, 1043, 1044, 1163, 1164,
 1748, 2627
Dutkiewicz, Jozef 2000
Dworak, Stanisław 1335

Dworzecki, Mark 2708
Dykman, Shlomo (1917-1965) 938
Dziewulski, Władysław 2471
Dzwonkowski, Władysław 68, 202, 365

Echt, Samuel 2281
Eck, Nathan 366
Eden, S. 367, 841
Efrosy, Ch. 69
Eger, Feliksa 1749
Ehrenkranz, Benjamin Wolf (1819-1884) 755, 939
Ehrlich, Elhanan 2344
Eidelberg, S. 2234
Eile, Henryk 292
Einhorn, Moses (1896-1966) 2741
Eisenbach, Artur 70, 158, 159, 203, 204, 205, 206, 207, 208, 293, 294, 462, 463, 493, 522, 574, 575, 576, 1188, 1189, 1238, 1559, 1611, 1658, 2055, 2102, 2192, 2628, 2629, 2630, 2631
Eisenberg, Eliyahu 2495
Eisenstein, A.E. 368
Eisenstein, Miriam 369
Eitzen, D. Stanley 1239
Elenbogen, Herman 1889
Eliasberg, Alexander (1878-1924) 940
Eliasberg, Ya'kov 1390
Eliaszew (pseud. of Baal Machszowis) 1456
Elimelech of Leżajsk (1717-1787) 756, 757, 1890
Elizedek, Bezalel 2064
Elmer, Aleksander 1391
Endres, Franz Carl 1392
England-Wasserstrom, Isaac 2345
Epstein Baruch Ha-Levi (1860-1942) 1891
Epstein, Melech (b.1889) 1892
Epsztejn, Abraham (1880-1952) 2557
Erckmann, Émille (1822-1899) 1126
Erik, Max (pseud. of Zalman Merlin) (1898-1937) 1127
Erlich, E. 2567, 2765
Erlich, Henryk (1882-1941) 1337, 1338, 1339, 1340
Ertel, Rachel 1240
Erter, Isaac (1791-1851) 662, 941
Ettinger, Elżbieta 942, 2093

Ettinger, Solomon (1803-1856) 758, 1893
Ettinger, Solomon 1128
Ettinger, Samuel 370, 1281
Everett, Leila P. 209
Ewen, Isaac (1861-1925) 2147

Fajersztejn, J. 1894
Fajnhauz, Dawid 210, 295, 1045
Falkowska, Maria (1878-1942) 2069
Fallek, Wilhelm (1888-1941) 943, 1046, 1047
Farbstein, Joshua Heshel (1870-1948) 1612
Farmer, Kenneth C. 5
Fater, Isaschar 842
Fayans, A.L. 2288
Federbush, Simon (1892-1969) 759
Feigenbaum, Moses Joseph 2191
Feinberg, Nathan (b.1895) 577
Feinkind, Mojżesz 71, 2492
Feinstein, Abraham, Asher 2486
Feinstein, Aryeh Loeb (1821-1903) 2219
Feldhorn, Juliusz 944, 1048
Feldman, E. 663
Feldman, Eliezar 464
Feldman, Wilhelm (1868-1919) 72, 211, 212, 945, 1129, 1130, 1190, 1613
Feldstejn, Herman 73, 371, 494
Fenster, A.H. 946
Fermi, Laura 1457
Ficowski, Jerzy 2153
Fijałek, Jan 2493
Fine, David M. 1458
Fink, Reuben 2290
Finkelshtayn, Leo 2035
Finkelstein, Abraham Mordecai 2219
Fishberg, Maurice (1872-1934) 1241
Fishman, Joshua Aaron (b.1926) 373, 1751
Fiszer, Artur 843
Fleischer, Ziegfried 1299
Flinker, David 844
Flis, Michał 2159
Flugjan, Cwajfel Fin. 1895
Fogelson, S. 465
Forer, David 2512
Fraenkel, Jacob Emanuel 664
Frank, Bruno (1887-1945) 947
Frank, M.Z. 33

Frank-Kapłanowa, B. 1049
Franzos, Karl Emil 2184
Fredro, Aleksander (1793-1876)
 1050
Freimann, Aron (1871-1948) 2475
Frejlichowa, J. 2357
Frendenson, W. 2632
Frenk, Ezriel Nathan (1865-1924)
 74, 75, 160, 213, 466, 1191,
 2019, 2633
Frenkel, Itzhak Yedidia 2431
Frenkel, Jeremiasz 665, 666,
 760, 761, 948
Frenkel, Jonathan 1341
Freudenheim, Mieczysław 2356
Freytag, Lucjan 1560
Fridkin, Isaac 2042
Friedberg, Bernhard (1876-1961)
 845, 2358, 2359, 2390
Friedeberger, Hans 2015
Friedenstein, Simeon Eliezer
 2294, 2709
Friedländer, Israel (1876-1940)
 76
Friedländer, Moritz (1849-1919)
 2215
Friedlander, Shimon 2380
Friedman, Philip (1901-1960)
 34, 214, 215, 374, 523, 578,
 2136, 2391, 2434, 2435, 2436,
 2437
Friedmann, Lazarus 1192
Fritz, Georg 1393
Frölich, Paul (b.1884) 2094
Frostig, M. 495, 1242
Frydman, A. Zisha 667
Frydman, Ber 668
Fuks, Marian 77, 78, 375, 376,
 439, 846, 847, 848, 1342,
 1703, 2046, 2070, 2392, 2392,
 2634
Funn, Samuel Joseph 2710
Fuszkof, P. 1896

Gabara, Edward 1300
Gabel, Henryk 1614
Gadon, Lubomir (1831-1908) 1660
Gainer, Bernard 1459
Gajewski, Kazimierz 1753, 1754
Galant, I. 762
Gamska, Larysa 1704
Ganszyniec, Ryszard (1886-1958)
 1561
Ganusovitch, Itzchak 2384
Garfeinowa-Garska, Matylda Maria
 (1869-1932) 949

Garncarska-Kadari, Bina 1301
Gąsiorowska, Natalia (b.1881)
 216
Gaster, Theodor Herzl (b.1906)
 849
Gatkiewicz, Feliks 2270
Gavoty, Bernard 2085
Gaworin, Abram 2610
Gawroński, Franciszek (1846-
 1930) 1051
Gawze, Aaron 1897
Gejler, Lazarz 1300
Gelbart, Mendel (b.1898) 2264,
 2343, 2479, 2545, 2561, 2599
Gelber, Nathan Michael (1891-
 1966) 161, 162, 297, 298,
 299, 467, 468, 669, 1166,
 1394, 1395, 1562, 1661, 1662,
 2011, 2216,2226, 2271, 2360
Gelberg, Jakub 2276
Gelbert, M. 2257
Gelernt, H. 2500
Gershuni, Henry 1167
Geshuri, Meir Simon (1897-1977)
 2607, 2740
Gewurz, Solomon 2416
Giertych, Jędrzej 1755, 1756
Gilbert, Martin (b.1936) 6
Gillon, Adam (b.1921) 1052
Ginzberg, Asher (pseud. Haam
 Achad) (1858-1927) 1898
Ginzberg, Louis (1873-1955)
 2152
Glanz, Rudolf 1460
Glass, Montagu Mardsen (1877-
 1934) 1131
Glatman, Ludwik 163, 1615
Glatstein, Jacob (1896-1971)
 950
Glicksman, William M. 496, 624,
 951, 952, 1243
Gliksman, Jerzy G. (b.1902)
 497, 1244, 1245
Gliksman, Pinnas Zelig (1869-
 1942) 2108, 2110
Glikson, Paul (1921-1983) 7
Glock, Charles Y. 1757
Głowacka-Maksymiuk, Urszula
 1530
Głowiński, Michał 2165
Golczewski, Frank 217, 1758
Goldberg, Jacob Alter (b.1890)
 625, 2702, 2704
Goldberg, Jakub 164, 165, 166,
 1193, 2404
Goldfaden, Abraham (1840-1908)

1132, 1133
Goldman, Pierre (d.1944) 1899
Goldmann, Nahum (1895-1982)
   1246, 1900, 1901
Goldshtein, S. 2546
Goldstein, B. 2635
Goldstein, M. 1663
Goldstein, Maksymiljan 850
Goldwasser, P. 2604
Gołuchowski, Józef 1664
Gomer, Abba (b.1894) 851
Gomulicki, Wiktor Teofil (1850-1919) 1053
Goodheart, Arthur Lehman (b.1891) 579
Gordin, Jacob (1853-1909) 1134
Gordon, Aaron David (1865-1922) 953
Gordon, David (1831-1886) 1396
Gordon, Jakub (1825-1894) 1902
Gordon, Judah Leib (1831-1892) 1903, 1904, 1905
Górewicz, R. 377
Gorin, Bernard (1868-1925) 1135
Gorni, Yosef 1302
Gotlober, A.B. 2711
Gottesfeld, Chone (1890-1964) 1906
Gottlieb, Samuel Noah 670
Grabowski, Ignacy (b.1878) 1759, 1760
Graetz, Heinrich (1817-1891) 1168
Granatsztajn, Jechie 2484
Graubart, Judah Leib (1861-1937) 1907
Greeley, Andrew 1247
Greenberg, Eliezer (b.1896) 956, 957
Greenspan, Sol 2496
Grinberg, Maria 1303, 1563, 2043
Grines, M. 1908
Gronowicz, Antoni (1913-1985) 1564
Grosser, Bronislaw (1883-1912) 1909
Grossman, Kurt Richard (b.1897) 1461
Grossman, Moishe 2375, 2562
Groth, Alexander J. 378, 1616
Grotte, Alfred (b.1872) 852, 853, 854
Gruber, Henryk (b.1892) 1910
Grubiński, Wacław (b.1883) 1054
Gruenbaum, J. 2636

Gruinski, Stanislaw 469
Grünbaum, Yitzhak (1879-1970) 79, 379, 380, 1397, 1617
Grünberg, Abraham (1871-1953) 2547
Grunwald, M. 300
Grydzewski, Mieczysław (1894-1970) 1565
Grynbaum, Isaac 2163
Grynberg, Henryk (b.1936) 1055, 1761, 1911
Grynberg, Michal 537
Grynsztejn, M. 580
Grynzburg, Isaac (b.1879) 1912
Grzybowski, Konstanty 301
Gulkowitsch, Lazar (b.1899) 763, 764
Gumplowicz, Ludwig (1838-1909) 581, 1248, 1249, 1665
Günzburg, Mordecai Aaron (1795-1846) 1913
Günzenhauser, Max von 3
Gurland, Hayyim Jonah (1843-1890) 1762
Guterman, Jozef 9
Guttman, Mathias Ezekiel 765, 2186

Haberman, Abraham Meir (b.1901) 2010
Haesler, Wolfgang 218
Hafftka, Aleksander 127, 556, 562, 582, 855, 1618, 1619, 1620
Hagani, Baruch (b.1885) 1194
Hagen, William W. 219
Halevy, Benjamin (b.1913) 2337
Halicki, Wacław 1705
Halperin, I. 1250
Halpern, Filix 2263
Halpern, H. 2285
Halpern, Israel 80, 81
Halpern, L. 1621
Handelsman, Marceli (1882-1945) 220
Handlin, Oscar (b.1915) 1512
Hanecki, Michał 1622
Harkavy, W.O. 1914
Harpaz, M. 2266
Harsshoshanim, Hilel 2527
Hartglas, Maksymilian Apolinary Meir (1883-1953) 583, 1623
Haruvi, B. 2551
Hasman, R. 221
Hass, Ludwik 1462, 1566
Haupt, G. 1763

Hauptmann, Zygmunt 1764
Healy, Ann E. 1765
Hecht, Gedo 381, 382
Heiman, H. 856
Hekker, Helena 470, 1666, 1766
Heller, Binem (b.1908) 2448
Heller, Celia Stopnicka 383, 1195, 1196, 1251, 1252, 1253
Heller, Eliezer 557
Hellman, Chaim Meir (b.1856) 2151
Helter, M. 2339
Hemar (Heschels), Marian 1197
Henish, M. 1463
Hensel, J. 1198
Heppner, Aron (1865-1938) 222, 2503
Hersch, Pesuch Liebman (1882-1955) 384, 385, 2637
Herschberg, Abraham Samuel (1858-1943) 2193
Hertz, Aleksander (d.1983) 857, 858, 1254, 1255, 1567
Hertz, Benedykt (1872-1952) 1056
Hertz, Jacob Sholem (b.1893) 1256, 1304, 1343, 1344, 1345, 1346, 1347, 1915, 2178, 2438
Hertz, S. 1348
Hertzberg, Arthur (b.1921) 1398
Herzberg, Isaac 2229, 2503
Herzberg, J. 302, 2307
Herzig, Jacob Joshua (1887-1956) 2314
Herzl, Theodor (1860-1904) 1399
Herzog, Elizabeth 1291
Herzog, Marvin I. 859
Heschel, Abraham Joshua (b.1907) 671, 860, 2078
Hessen, Julius Isidorovich (1871-1940?) 223
Hickey, Des 2156
Hiliewski, Krzysztof 1667
Hinitz, Nahum 2570
Hirschhorn, Samuel (1876-1942) 82, 303, 584, 2638
Hirszfeld, Ludwik (1884-1954) 1916
Hirszhorn, S. 224
Hirszowicz, Abraham 1668
Hochberg, Leo 11
Hoesick, Ferdynand (1867-1941) 2062
Hoffman, Benzion (pseud. "Zivion") (1874-1954) 2487

Hoffman, Zygmunt 12, 2746
Hollaenderski, Leon (1808-1878) 83, 84, 954, 955, 1257, 1767
Hollender, Tadeusz 1057
Horain, Juljan 1464
Horak, Stephan (b.1920) 585
Horn, Maurycy 2005
Horn, Y. 2454
Horodezky, Samuel Aba (1871-1957) 672, 673, 766, 767, 2112
Horowitz, David (b.1899) 1400, 1401, 1402, 1917
Horowitz, Leon 225
Horwitz, Max H. 85
Hourwitz, Zalkind (c.1740-1812) 1465
Howe, Irving (b.1920) 956, 957
Hrabyk, Klaudiusz 1769
Hryniewiecki, Kajetan 1669
Huberband, Shim'on 2539
Hubman, Franz (b.1914) 1258
Husen, Eisig 2378

Idan, Y. 2259
Ignotus (pseud. of Adolf Peretz) 2640
Indelman, M. 1624
Infeld, Leopold (1898-1968) 1918, 1919, 1920
Iranek-Osmecki, Kazimierz (d.1984) 86
Isbitzki, Joseph (pseud. Beinish Michalewicz) 1922
Ivri, Y. 2473
Iwański, G. 1706
Iwenicki, Abraham 1921

Jacobs, Louis (b.1920) 768, 769, 770, 1995
Jacobs, Noah J. 675, 2100, 2101
Jacobsohn, Jacobi 167, 626
Jakubowicz, David 2614
Jamiński, Z. 862
Janecki, Marcelli 1259
Jankielewicz, Michał 524
Jankielewicz, Mowsza (pseud. Jan Kamienski) 1670
Janowsky, Oscar Isaiah (b.1900) 87, 586, 587
Janulaitis, Augustinas 226
Jaros, Jerzy 558
Jasiewicz, Krzystof 1260
Jasny, A. Wolf 2249, 2312, 2439, 2483, 2548, 2771
Jastrow, Markus (1829-1903) 88,

227, 304
Jaszuński, J. 958
Jaworski, Franciszek 2418
Jedlicka, Wanda 2166
Jeleński, Jan (1845-1909) 1770
Jeshurin, Ephraim M. 2712
Jeske-Choiński, Teodor (1854-1920) 89, 627, 1059, 1169, 1771, 1772, 1773
Johnpoll, Bernard K. 35, 1349
Jolles, Zechariah Isaiah (1816-1852) 1923
Jonicz, Stefan 1775
Josefowicz, Herszel 1673
Joseph, Samuel (1881-1959) 1466

Kac, Daniel 2338
Kacyzne, Alter (1885-1941) 959
Kaffe, Ph. 1625
Kaganovich, Moshe 2310
Kaganowski, Efraim (1893-1958) 2643
Kahan, B. 2577
Kahan, I. 2223
Kahan, Jacob 306
Kahana, Shmuel Zanwil (b.1905) 676
Kahn, Alexander (1881-1962) 388
Kalabiński, Stanisław 2194, 2195
Kalish, Ita 2615
Kallay, Sharaga Feivel 2214
Kallen, Horace Meyer (b.1882) 1467
Kamelhar, M. 2104
Kamińska, Ida (1899-1980) 1136, 1924
Kanc, Szymon 2027, 2480, 2540, 2578, 2590, 2739
Kandel, Dawid 228, 229, 230, 231, 232, 307, 308, 498, 629, 1925
Kantor-Lichtensztejn, R. 2644
Kantorowicz, N. 1404
Kanz, S. 2225
Kapelow, I. 1926
Kapiszewski, Andrzej 1468
Kaplan, Jonathan 13
Kaplan, Shabetai 2468
Kapliński, Baruch 2303, 2352, 2766
Kaplun-Kogan, Wladimir Wolf (b.1888) 92, 960
Kariv, Joseph 2298, 2544
Karpiński, Franciszek (1741-1825) 1674

Karren, Tamara (pseud. of T. Zagórska) 2071
Kaspi, Isaac 2549
Kasprowicz, Jan (1860-1926) 1060
Katz, Alfred 1350
Katz, Ben-Zion (1875-1958) 93
Katz, Jacob (b.1904) 863, 1170, 1199, 1261, 1776
Katz, Moses (1885-1960) 389
Katz, P. 2645
Kaufman, David 2504
Kaufman, Michal 1626
Kaufman, Mojżesz (pseud. Mojsie Mezryczer) 1531, 1532
Kaufmann, Fritz Mordecai (1888-1921) 1262
Kawyn, Stefan 2065
Kazenelson, L. 1405
Kazhdan, Khaim Shloyme (b.1883) 390, 1351, 1352
Kazis, Israel Joseph 771
Kaznelson, Mejer 37
Kelles-Krauz, Kazimierz 1568
Kempiński, Israel 309
Kempner, R. 630
Kermisz, Jozef 2646
Khayes, S. 961
Kiel, Mark 1627
Kielecki, W. 2133
Kieniewicz, Stefan 233, 2647
Kinderfreund, Aleksander (1862-1941) 962
Kirschenblatt-Gimblatt, Barbara 839
Kirszrot, Jacob 588
Kirszrot, Jan 94
Kirton, I. 1200
Kiryk, Feliks 2211
Kirznic, A.D. 1305
Klajner, A. 2564
Klatzkin, Jacob (1882-1948) 1777
Klausner, I.A. 2757
Klausner, Israel (b.1905) 1406, 1407, 1927, 2714
Klausner, J. 772
Kleiner, Juliusz (1886-1957) 2124
Kleinmann, Moshe (1870-1948) 1408
Kligsberg, Moshe 391, 1263
Kochański, Aleksander 2095
Koczorowski, Stanisław Piotr 2079
Kohn, Hans (1891-1971) 1409

Kołakowski, Leszek 1778
Kolat, Yisrael 1707
Kollenscher, Max (b.1875) 631, 2505
Kołodziejczyk, Ryszard 2121
Kon, Pinchas 310, 2715, 2716
Koneczny, Feliks (1862-1949) 1779
Konic, Władysław 311, 312
Koniuszyński, Eugeniusz 1780
Konopczyński, Władysław (1880-1952) 1781, 1782
Konopnicka, Maria (1842-1910) 1061
Kopff, Wiktor 1928
Kopfstein, M. 2232
Kopilevitz, A. 2306
Korboński, Stefan (b.1901) 1569, 2008
Korczak, Janusz (pseud. of Goldszmit, Henryk) (1878-1942) 963, 964, 965
Koriski, L. 2722
Korkis, Abraham Adolf (1865-1921) 471
Korngruen, Philip 2591
Korobkow, Chaim 313, 314, 472, 499, 500, 539
Korsch, Rudolf (pseud. of Kazimierz Krippendorf) 1708
Korzec, Paweł 392, 393, 589, 1628, 1763, 1783, 1784, 2196, 2197, 2372
Korzeń, M. 2388, 2737
Korzeniowski, Józef (1797-1863) 1062
Kościałkowska, Janina 1063
Kościesza, Zbigniew 1785, 1786
Kosim, Artur 2055
Kossovsky, Vladimir (pseud. of Nahum Mendel Levinsohn) (1867-1941) 1353
Kossovsky, Dov 2292
Kot, Stanisław (b.1885) 1064
Kotarbiński, Tadeusz (1886-1981) 1570, 1571
Kotik, Abraham (b.1867) 1929
Kotik, Ezekiel (1847-1921) 1930
Kovalsky, S. 1787
Kowalczyk, K. 315
Kowalska-Glikman, Stefania 1264, 1265, 2648
Kozłowski, Jozef 1137, 1138, 1354
Koźminski, Tadeusz 590
Krajewska, Monika 864

Kramstyck, Izaak 677
Krasiński, Wincenty Korwin (d.1858) 1065
Krasiński, Zygmunt (1812-1859) 1066
Krasnowski, Zbigniew (b.1889) 1788
Kraszewski, Józef Ignacy (1812-1889) 1067, 1068
Kraus, Samuel 678
Kraushar, Aleksander (pseud. Alkar) (1843-1931) 95, 966, 1171, 1931, 2649
Kremer, M. 559
Kressel, Getzel (b.1911) 2347
Krevets'kyi, Ivan 394
Kridl, Manfred (1882-1957) 1572
Krochmal, Abraham (1823-1895) 679, 680, 681, 682, 683
Krochmal, Nachman (1785-1840) 684, 685
Król, Michał 1533
Kronenberg, Leopold (1812-1878) 1932
Krongold, H. 2650
Kroszczor, Henryk 686, 1266, 1267, 1513, 2006, 2651, 2652, 2653, 2654, 2655, 2656, 2657
Kruk, Abraham 1469
Kruk, Stefan 2393, 2394
Kruszyński, Jozef (1877-1953) 865, 967, 1069, 1629, 1789, 1790, 1791, 1792, 1793, 1794, 1795
Kryński, Magnus J. 1070, 2167
Krysiak, Franciszek Salezy 2420
Krzywicki, Ludwik (1859-1941) 2026
Kubiakowa, A. 866
Kublicki, Stanisław 2658
Kuczyński, Stefan Krzysztof 2048
Kudish, Natan 2429, 2572
Kukiel, Marian (b.1885) 2001
Kulczyński, Stanisław (1895-1969) 1573
Kulka, Erich 316
Kupfer, Efraim F. 968, 2105, 2106, 2506, 2747, 2758
Kurländer, Aaron 2142
Kurtzig, Heinrich (b.1865) 2308
Kuśniewicz, Andrej 1071
Kusznir, M. 2367

Kutrzeba, Stanisław (1876-1946) 96
Kwiatek, Józef 1534

Lader (Lederman), Yitshak 2770
Ladier, Salomon 687
Lambert, M. 2507
Lamm, Louis (b.1871) 2088
Landau, Bezalel 774, 2032
Landau, Moshe 395, 396, 397, 1630, 1631
Landau, Saul Rafael (1870-1943) 1306, 1632
Landes, Ruth (b.1908) 1268
Landmann, Salcia (b.1911) 1269
Landsberger, J. 501, 525, 1201, 2508
Lange, Antoni (1861-1929) 1574
Lange, Nicholas D. 14
Langer, Mordecai G. (1894-1943) 773
Langnas, Saul 398
Langsam, A. 688
Lapenna, Ivo 2175
Lapkes, Y. 526
Lapradelle, Albert Geouffre de (1871-1955) 591
Laserson, Max M. (1887-1951) 592
Lask, Israel Meir (b.1905) 2319
Laskowski, Kazimierz 1307
Lau, (Lavy) N. 2494
Laubert, Manfred 234, 235, 473, 540
Laudyn, Stephanie 1796, 1797
Lauer, Bernard 97
Lebensohn, Abraham Dob Baer (1794-1878) 689, 969, 1139
Lebensohn, Michah Joseph (1828-1852) 867, 970, 971
Lech, Marian J. 236
Leder, Zdzisław (pseud. of Władysław Fainstein) 2056
Leftwich, Joseph (b.1892) 972
Leibl, Daniel (1891-1967) 2261
Lelewel, Joachim (1786-1861) 237, 1576
LeMoal, Francoise 1575
Lengyel, Emil (b.1895) 1798
Lenin, Vladimir I. (1870-1924) 1355
Leoni-Zopperfin, Elieser 2248, 2346, 2351, 2535, 2743
Lerner, Arie 2349

Lerski, George J. (b.1917) 38, 238, 1577
Lestchinsky, Jacob (1876-1966) 399, 474, 502, 503, 504, 505, 506, 507, 973, 1270, 1470, 1471, 1514, 1799, 1800
Leszczyński, Anatol 2204, 2205, 2206, 2207, 2208, 2244, 2245, 2472
Leszczyński, Józef (pseud. Chmurner) (1884-1935) 1333, 1933
Levin, Nora 1356
Levine, Madeline G. 1072, 2168
Levinsohn, Isaac Baer (1788-1860) 1140
Levinson, Abraham 2660
Levit, Tonja 870
Lew, Aba 1801
Lew, Myer S. 98
Lewandowski, Józef 2160
Lewandowski, Stefan 2661
Lewandowski, W. 317
Lewestam, F.H. 2662
Lewi, Hirsch David 2361
Lewin, Aron (1879-1941) 1633
Lewin, Awner (b. 1909) 2385
Lewin, Epstein A. 1410
Lewin, Isaac 593, 632, 690, 868, 1634
Lewin, Jacob Ha-Levi 318
Lewin, L. 691
Lewin, Louis (1850-1929) 239, 240, 2499
Lewin, Louis (1868-1941) 869, 2309, 2320, 2381
Lewin, Sabina 2663
Lewin, Yitszak 2395
Lewiński, Yom-Tov (b.1899) 2441, 2754
Lewinsky, A. 1202
Lewinsohn, Isaac Baer 692, 693, 694
Lewinson, Abraham 1411
Lewinzon, J. 475
Lewit, Tonja (b.1904) 870
Lewitter, I.R. 1802
Lewitz, L. 1472
Lichten, Joseph L. 400, 1203, 1473, 2039, 2072
Lichtenstein, Erwin 2282
Lichtenstein, Kalman 2556
Lichtensztejn, M. 594
Liebman, Hersch 1271, 1474
Liev, Ziskind 1803
Lifschütz, Ezekiel 401

Lilienthal, Regina 695, 1272
Lin, Joseph 1934
Lindberg, Gavriel 2598
Linder, M. 2212
Linder, Menachem 1475, 1476, 477, 2198
Linetzki, Isaac Joel (1839-1915) 974
Lipp, Adolf 541
Lipski, Jan Józef 99, 1578
Lipsky, Louis (1876-1963) 1412
Lipschitz, Jacob Lipman 1935
Lipshitz, Jacob Halevy (1838-1921) 2158
Lipszic, S. 241
Liptzin, Solomon (b.1901) 975
Lisser, Michal 595, 633
Litman, A. 1635
Liwerant, Elia Boruch 319
Locker, Berl (b.1887) 1936
Loew, Chaim 1073, 1074
Loewenstein, Stanislaw 1204
Losh, L. 2203, 2246, 2258, 2526, 2584
Lowenkopf, Anne N. 775
Lozynskyj, M. 242
Lubliner, Ludwig Osias (1809-1868) 100
Lukashevich, Olga 1075
Lukomskii, Georgii (1884-1954) 871
Lunski, Ch. 596, 2717
Lunsky, Haykel 1999
Lutman, Tadeusz 2217
Luxemburg, Rosa (1871-1919) 1536
Lvavi, Jacob 527
Łastik, Salomon 696, 976, 977, 1205
Łukasiński, Walerian (1786-1868) 1579
Łukaszewski, Witold 1076
Łuninski, Ernest (1870-1931) 320, 2058, 2059
Łypacewicz, Wacław 1675

Macartney, Carlile Aylmer (b.1895) 597
Madison, Charles A. 978
Maggid, D.G. (1862-1942) 776, 2719
Maggid, Hillel Noah 2718
Mahler, Raphael (b.1899) 101, 102, 402, 403, 404, 405, 476, 777, 1273, 1478, 1636, 1804, 2252, 2465, 2466, 2467, 2664

Maimon, Judah Leib (1875-1962) 778
Maimon, Salomon (1753-1800) 1937, 1938, 1939
Majer, Dawid 872
Majerowicz, M.L. 1940
Majzel, E. 697
Majzel, N. 1941
Makuszyński, Kornel (1884-1953) 1077
Mandel, Arnold (b.1913) 779
Mandel, Arthur 1173
Mandelsberg-Szyldkraut, Bela (1901-1943) 2396
Mangel, Estera 2044
Manor, Alexander 2089, 2384
Mantel, Feliks 1942
Mapu, Abraham (1808-1867) 979, 980, 981
Marchlewski, Julian (1866-1925) 1805
Marcus, Joseph (b.1923) 406
Marek, Lucjan 542, 1308, 1709, 2665
Marek, P.S. 634, 698, 780, 781
Margalit, A. 2478
Margalit, Elkana 1413, 1414, 1710
Margalith, Aaron M. 1506
Margel, Lejbish Jehuda 2295
Margolin, Arnold Davidovich (b.1877) 103
Margoshes, Joseph 1943, 2144
Mark, Bernard (1908-1966) 104, 1309, 1310, 2140
Mark, Natan 2380
Mark, Yudel (b.1897) 982
Marrus, R. 1206
Marstejn, Michal 873
Marylski (Łuszczewski), Antoni (1865-1932) 105
Mauersberg, Stanislaw 407
Mayzel, Maurycy 408, 1515
Mazowiecki, Tadeusz 1806
Medem, Vladimir Davidovich (1879-1923) 1357, 1358, 1359, 1944
Meducka, Marta 2329
Mehnan, M. 1141
Meisel, Nachman 1945, 2127
Meisl, Josef (b.1882) 106, 699
Meizel, Eliahu Chaim 1946
Melcer, Wanda (b.1897) 1078
Meltser, Emanuel 409
Meltzer, Shimshon (b.1909) 983, 2128, 2300

Author and Editor Index   *223*

Melz, Y. 2494
Menczer, Arie 2514
Mendelsohn, Ezra 411, 412, 413, 1208, 1209, 1210, 1311, 1312, 1416, 1417, 1637, 1638, 2122, 2421, 2422
Mendelssohn, Moses (1729-1786) 598
Mendes-Flohr, Paul R. 108
Menes, Abraham 1360
Merowitz, Morton J. 15
Merunowicz, Teofil (1846-1927) 109, 110, 414
Merwin, Bertold (b.1879) 321
Merzan, Ida 1516, 1517, 1518
Metzer, Emmanuel 1479
Meyer, David 1313
Meyerowitz, A. 2376, 2773
Meyersohn, Malwina 984
Mickiewicz, Adam (1798-1855) 1079
Miedziński, Boguslaw 1807
Mieses, Mathias (b.1885) 322, 874, 985, 1080, 1211
Mill, Joseph Solomon 1947
Mill, Josif (1870-1952) 1314
Milwicz, Edmund 1808
Mindel, Nissam 2173
Mintsin, Y. 1639
Miodunka, Władysław 875
Mirkin, Menahem 415
Miron, D. 986
Mirsky, Samuel Kalman (1899-1967) 700, 876
Mishkinski, Ester 2563
Mishkinsky, Moshe 39, 1315
Młodzieniec, Stanisław 1142
Młot, Jan (pseud. of Szymon Dickstein) 1711
Modras, Ronald 111
Morawski, Karol 16, 2171
Morawski, Kazimierz 1809
Morelowski, Marian 2161
Morgensztern, Janina 2368, 2369
Morgenthau, Henry (1856-1941) 416
Mościcki, Henryk 169
Moskowitz, Moses 701, 1810, 1811
Mosse, George 141
Moszczeńska, Izabella (1864-1941) 243, 1580
Moszczeńska, W. 2049
Moszkowicz, Bronisław 1316, 1317, 1318
Motzkin, Leo (1867-1933) 1812

Mozes, Samuel R. 417
Mroczkowski, Stanisław 1813
Mstislawskaja, S. 323
Mulkiewicz-Goldberg, O. 877
Muratowicz, Szl. 2666
Mus, E. 1361

Nachman, Ben Sim Hah 782, 783
Nadav, Mordehai 784, 2488
Naday, Mordehai 2325
Nadel, Beniamin 324
Nafav, M. (Katzikowski) 2313
Nahman, Rabbi of Bracław 702
Nathan, Paul (1857-1927) 1274
Nettl, J.P. 2096
Neubach, Helmut 244, 1480
Neuman, I.M. 1481, 2667
Neumann, Salomon 1482
Newachowicz, Jehuda L. 703
Newman, Louis Israel (b.1893) 785
Newerly, Igor 1948
Niborski, Itzok 1990
Niebudek, Stefan 1814
Niemcewicz, Julian Ursyn (1758-1841) 1081, 1082
Niemojewski, Andrzej (1864-1921) 1083, 1815, 1816
Nissenbaum, Isaac (1868-1942) 1949
Nissenbaum, Salomon Baruch (1866-1926) 112, 2398
Nomberg, Hersh David (1876-1927) 2129
Nomberg-Przytyk, Sara 987
Nordon, Haskell 1950
Norwid, Kamil Cyprian (1821-1883) 1084
Nossig, Alfred (b.1864) 418, 988, 1418, 1677, 1678
Novitch, Miriam 2060
Novogrodsky, Emanuel 1362, 2720
Nowaczyński, Adolf (1876-1944) 1817
Nowak, Jan (b.1913) 1581
Nowakowski, Marian Antoni 1818
Nowicki, Stefan 1819
Noy, Dov 2341
Noylens, Joseph 419
Nussbaum, Hilary (1821-1895) 113, 989, 1951, 2668

Oberländer, Ludwik 1085
Ohler, Leon 1363
Olczakowa, Hanna (Mortkowicz) (b.1905) 2073

Olechowski, Gustaw 704
Olitzky, Leib (b.1894) 2347
Olszewska, Maria 990
Opas, Tomasz 991, 1275, 2399, 2452
Opatoshu, Joseph (1886-1954) 992
Oppenheim, Israel 1419
Oppenheim, Mika Falk 4
Oppenheimer, Franz (1864-1943) 1276
Oppman, Artur (pseud. Or-Ot) (1867-1932) 1086
Ordyński, A.P. (pseud. of Antoni Potocki) 1820
Orlicki, Józef 420
Ormian, Haim 421
Ormicki, W. 1483
Ortner, Nathan 774
Orzeszkowa, Eliza (1842-1910) 1087, 1088, 1089, 1090, 1091, 1582, 1583
Osherowitch, Mendel (1888-1965) 1277
Ostersetzer, I. 2669
Ostrowski, Antoni Jan 1680
Ostrowski, Krystyan Józef (1811-1882) 1092
Ostrowski, Wiktor 1821
Otiker, Yisrael 1420
Ozher, Mauritzi 1364

Pakentreger, Aleksander 2321, 2322
Papajski, Leon 114
Paperna, Abraham Jacob (1840-1919) 635, 705
Paprocki, Stanisław J. 599
Parkes, James William (b.1896) 1822
Parnas, H. 543
Pasmanik, Daniel (1869-1930) 1421
Patkin, Abraham L. 1319
Paulewicz, Marian 2239, 2240
Pazdro, Zbigniew (1874-1939) 636
Peczenik, M.L. 1952
Penkalla, Adam 170, 528, 2482, 2518, 2523, 2587
Pennell, Joseph 1953
Penzik, Abraham (1891-1945) 1823
Perelman, Jakob 1422
Peretz, Adolf 544
Peretz, Isaac Leib (1852-1915) 1954, 1955
Perl, Joseph (1773-1839) 786, 787
Perl, Leon 545
Perles, Joseph (1835-1894) 2509
Perlov, Yishak (b.1911) 2524, 2555
Perski, Jakub 2769
Peter, Egon 115
Piasecki, Henryk 1320, 1537, 1538, 1539, 1540, 1541, 1542, 2021, 2022, 2023, 2084, 2091, 2134
Piattoli, Scipione (1749-1809) 1681
Piechotka, Kazimierz 878
Piechotka, Maria 878
Piekarz, Mendel 788, 789, 2113, 2114
Pietkiewicz, Kazimierz 1543
Piłsudski, Józef (1867-1935) 245, 1544
Pinson, Koppel Shub (1904-1961) 1824
Piotrowski, Jan (b.1885) 2074
Piotrowski, Nicholas L. (b.1863) 116
Pitlik, Samuel 2087
Pizem-Karczag, Ida 993
Pizyc, H. 1365
Plakser, Menachem 1956
Plantowski, Noah 879
Podhorizer-Sandel, Erna 881, 882, 883, 2143, 2149, 2157, 2670
Polak, A. 1321
Pollner, Majer J. 1484
Polonus, Salomon 1683
Ponisz, Piotr 1828
Poradowski, Michał 1829
Porath, Elijahu 2335
Portnoy, Samuel A. 2103
Posner, Arthur Bernhard 2287, 2533
Posner, Stanisław 2045
Prager, Moshe 790, 1998
Pragier, Adam (d.1976) 1957
Prajs-Brystygier, Julia 1713
Pranaitis, Iustin Bonaventura (d.1917) 1830
Prawin, Jakub 1958
Privat, Edmond (b.1889) 2176
Próchnik, Adam 1545, 2024
Prowalski, Abraham J. 546, 547
Prus, Bolesław (pseud. of Aleksander Głowacki) (1847-

1912) 1584
Pruszyński, Ksawery (1907-1950) 1093, 1585, 1586
Pryłucki, Nojach (1882-1944) 1640
Przedpełski, Jan 529
Ptaśnik, Jan 171
Pulzer, Peter G. 1832

Rabin, Dov 2373
Rabin, Haim 2383, 2428, 2581, 2586, 2735, 2750
Rabin, Israel Abraham (1882-1951) 2190
Rabinowicz, Alexander Siskind 1959
Rabinowicz, Harry M. (b.1919) 422, 791
Rabinowicz, Osker Kurt (1902-1969) 1174
Rabinowicz, Sara 247
Rabinowicz, Sz. 1366
Rabinowitsch, Wolf Zeev (b.1900) 792, 793
Rabinowitz, Zvi Meir 2054
Rabinson, Markus 2528
Raczka, Jan Władysław 2362
Radliński, Ignacy (1843-1920) 1094, 1834
Radomiński, Jan 1684
Radt, Jenny 423
Rafes, Moses (1883-1942) 1367
Raisin, Jacob S. (1877-1946) 708
Rajzen, Zalman 17
Rak, Elimelech 1964
Rakowski, Puah 1424, 1965
Ran, Leyzer 2721, 2722
Raphael, Itzhak (b.1914) 794
Raphael, P. 326
Rapoport, Solomon Judah (1790-1867) 1967, 2082
Rappaport, A. 709, 2115
Rappaport, Charles (1865-1941) 1966
Rappaport, Jacob 637
Rappaport, Zenon 994
Rappoport, Salomo Leib 1968
Rappoport, Solomon (pseud. S. Ansky) (1863-1920) 995, 996
Ratman, A. (pseud. of Gershom Ziebert) 1368
Ravid, D. 2250
Rechtman, Abraham 884
Reich, Leon 638
Reich, Nathan 508

Reicher, Aniela 1213
Reinharz, Jehuda 108, 2170
Reisen, Zalman 2723
Rejduch-Samkowa, Izabella 885
Remba, Issac (1907-1969) 2337
Rey, Sydor 1095
Richards, Michael D. 2097
Rimon (Granat), Joseph Zevi (1889-1958) 2585
Ringel, Michał (b.1880) 118, 600, 601, 1641, 1835
Ringelblum, Emanuel (1900-1944) 172, 173, 174, 175, 176, 327, 886, 1687, 2463, 2672
Roback, Abraham Aaron (1890-1965) 2130
Robinson, Jacob (b.1889) 602
Rochaway, Robert A. 1485
Rohling, August (1839-1931) 1836
Rojchflajsz, J. 887
Rojter, Pinkas 1322
Rolicki, Henryk (pseud. of Kazimierz Gluziński) 1837
Ropelewski, Andrzej 2284
Rose, Norman 2119
Rosenberg, Henryk 1487
Rosenberg, Leo 248
Rosenfeld, Max (1884-1919) 119, 120, 477, 603, 604
Rosenman, Gedalia 711
Rosenstadt, B. 328
Rosenthal, Judah (b.1904) 121
Rosenthal-Schneiderman, A. 1714
Rosenthal-Stopnicka (Heller), Celia 2568
Rosiński, W. 560
Roskies, David (b.1948) 997, 1278, 1279
Roskies, Diane K. 1279
Rostański, Karol 1486
Rostworowski, Karol Hubert (1877-1938) 1096
Roszgold, Mosze 2397
Rotbaum, Jakub 1143
Roth, Cecil (1899-1970) 18
Roth, Leon (1896-1963) 888
Rothschild, Joseph 1642
Rovner, D. 2736
Rowe, Leonard 1369, 1838, 1839
Rozenbaum, M.M. 1969
Rozenfeld, Morris (1862-1923) 889
Rozenowicz, Ch. 2673
Rubin, Elias 122
Rubin, J. 2379

Rubinstein, Arthur (b.1886) 1970
Rubinstein, Aryeh 795, 796, 797, 798, 891
Rubinstein, Helena (1871-1965) 1971
Rudnicki, Adolf (b.1912) 998
Rundstein, Szymon (1876-1942) 605
Ruppin, Arthur (1876-1943) 478
Russell, Charles Edward (1860-1941) 2148
Ruta, Zygmunt 2595
Rybak, P. 1715
Rywes, M. 1323

Sabatka, H. 2442
Sadan, Dov (b.1902) 999
Sadykiewicz, Lucja 40
Safrin, Horacy 1000, 1972
Sajkowski, Alojzy 2137
Sakowska, Ruta 2075
Salit, Salomon 2311
Samuel, Maurice (b.1895) 1280, 2131
Samuel, Sir Stuart Montagu (1856-1926) 424
Sandauer, Artur (b.1913) 1097, 1973
Sandel, Jozef 893, 894, 895, 2041
Sandrow, Nahma 1144
Sarnicki, Klemens 1001
Sasson, Haim Hillel Ben 1281
Satajczyk, J. 2004
Satanower, Mendel 1688
Sawa, Bogumiła 2759
Sawicki, Aron 2674
Sawicki, M.P. 123
Schall, Jakób 124, 125, 2423
Scharf, Rafael 126
Schatz (-Uffenheimer), Rivka 799, 800, 801, 802
Schauss, Hayyim 712
Schechter, Solomon (1847-1915) 713, 2031, 2169
Schechtman, Joseph B. (1891-1970) 1430
Schenk-Rink, A.G. 1176
Scheps, Samuel 1098
Scherer, I.E. 606
Schiper, Ignacy (1884-1943) 127, 249, 250, 251, 252, 253, 329, 330, 331, 479, 480, 530, 548, 549, 550, 551, 562, 639, 640, 714, 897, 898, 1002, 1003, 1145, 1282, 1427, 1428, 2679
Schneersohn, Joseph Isaac (1880-1950) 803, 1974
Scholem, Gershom Gerhard (b.1897) 715, 716, 717, 804, 805, 806, 807, 1177
Schorr, Moses (1874-1941) 425, 607, 608, 2051, 2515, 2516, 2676, 2677
Schultz, Bruno (1892-1944) 1004, 1975
Schulze-Wilde, Harry (b.1899) 2098
Schutzman, Mark 2341, 2706
Schwartz, Bezalel 2333
Schwarzbard, Isaac Ignacy (1888-1961) 426, 1976
Schweikert, Kurt 561
Schweizer, J. 2583
Seailles, Gabriel (1852-1922) 1099
Segal, Aryen 19
Segal, Benjamin Wolf 1488
Segal, M. 2650
Segal, Simon 427
Segel, Benjamin Wolf (1867-1931) 128, 1977
Segel, Harold B. 332
Seidman, Hillel 609, 718, 2400, 2678
Seidman, J. 641
Semah, Sh. 2498
Semiatitzki, Mordechai 642
Sempołowska, Stefania (1870-1944) 1588
Seraphim, Peter Heinz 428
Sevela, Efraim 2727
Shaiak, G. 2445
Shamri, Arie (b.1907) 2464
Shapira, Meir (1887-1939) 2402
Shapiro, Chaim 2028, 2443
Sharon, Nathan 2446
Sharvit, Elazar 2542
Shatzky, Jacob (1894-1956) 41, 254, 255, 256, 333, 334, 335, 336, 337, 429, 481, 719, 1100, 1147, 1215, 1978, 2080, 2120, 2162, 2457, 2680, 2681, 2682, 2683
Shayari, Abraham 2227
Shayn, Israel 20
Shazar, Shneur Zalman (1889-1974) 808, 1178, 1429, 2571
Shefner, B. 643

Shemen, Nachman (b.1912) 2401
Shener, M. 2444
Shimri, A. 2324
Shinar, Mordechai 2485
Shmeruk, Chone (b.1921) 257, 1285
Shneiderman, Samuerl Loeb 2684
Shohat, Eliezer (1874-1971) 2489
Shohetman, Baruch (1890-1956) 2064
Shtern, Yekhel 720, 2611
Shtift, Nahum (1879-1933) 1979
Shtokfish, D. 2279
Shulman, Abraham 129, 1005
Shulman, Victor (1876-1951) 1370
Shulvass, Moses Avigdor (b.1909) 721, 722, 1489
Shunami, Shlomo 21, 22
Shuval, Dov 2543
Shuzman, M. 2253,
Siegelman, Yitshak 2224, 2317, 2334, 2458, 2588, 2606
Simon, Sir Leon (1881-1965) 1997
Simon (Shemen), M. 2296
Simon, Solomon 2235, 2236
Simonson, Emil 130
Sinclair, Clive 2155
Singer, Bernard (pseud. Regnis) 1980
Singer, Isaac Bashevis (b.1904) 1006, 1007
Singer, Israel Joshua (1893-1944) 1008
Singer, Mendel 2187
Singer, S.D. 2254
Skarbek, Jan 338
Skierko, Adam 131, 431, 1840
Skimborowicz, Hipolit (1815-1880) 1179
Słonimski, Antoni (1895-1976) 2685
Słowacki, Juliusz (1804-1849) 1101, 1102
Słucki, A. 976
Slutsky, Yehuda 899, 2210
Smith, Gus 2156
Smolar, Boris 1841
Smoleński, Władysław (1851-1926) 177
Smolka, Franciszek 1589
Sohn, David 2199
Sokół, Zofia 2200
Sokoler, Sh. 2596
Sokołow, Nahum 1431, 1432, 2012, 2126, 2686
Sokołowski, Jan Optat. 1842
Sokolowsky, M. 2538
Soloveichik, Leontii Albertovich (d.1953) 1324
Sommerfeldt, Joseph 42
Sopicki, Stanisław (b.1903) 432
Soroka, Sh. 2324
Spivak, Sh. 2763
Sprecher, N. 482
Stańczyk, Jan 433
Stand, Adolf (1870-1919) 900, 1433, 1643
Stankiewicz, E. 1009
Stark, Rodney (b.1934) 1757
Staszic, Stanisław (1755-1826) 1843
Stecka, Marja 132
Steiger, Stanislaw 1981
Stein, A. Sh. 2559
Stein, Abraham Samuel 2179, 2283, 2374
Stein, E. 43
Stein, E.S. 2331
Steinberg, Hannah 2576
Steinberg, O.N. 2728
Steinman, Eliezer 2220
Stendig, S. 434
Stępień, Marian 133
Sterling, K. 1216
Stern, Norton B. 1490
Sterner, Henryk 1434
Stocki, Edward 339, 340, 2009
Stoeger, Michael 610
Stojowski, Andrzej 1590
Stokfisch, David 2749
Streit, Leon 2565
Strobel, Georg W. 435
Stryjkowski, Julian (b.1905) 1010, 1011
Strzelecki, A. 2510
Studnicki, Władysław (1867-1953) 134, 436
Styczeń, Jan 901
Sulima, Zygmunt Lucjan (Przyborowski, Walery) 1180
Sułowski, Zygmunt 483
Summer, N. 2222
Sutor, Gustav 2242
Świerczewska, Krystyna 2018
Świętochowski, Aleksander (1849-1938) 1110
Swironi (Drutz), Hanoch 2579
Świtkowski, Piotr 1691
Szabad, C. 2729, 2730

Szacki, Jerzy 509, 1283
Szajkowski, Zosa (1911-1978)
  1325, 1491, 1519, 1520, 1521,
  1522, 1523, 1524, 1717
Szajn, Izrael 437, 438, 439,
  440
Szaniawski, Franciszek 1103
Szaniawski, Klemens (pseud.
  Klemens Junosza) (1849-1898)
  1104, 1105, 1106, 1107
Szczepaniak, Marian 1284, 2323
Szczepański, J.A. 1148
Szczepański, Jerzy 2523
Szczypiorski, Andrzej 135
Szechter, Szymon 1982
Szenwald, L. 1844
Szeps, Zew 1012
Szerer, Barbara 1718
Szerer, Emanuel 136, 1371, 1492
Szlamowicz, L. 552
Szpet, N. 2107
Szpidbaum, Henryk 484, 1286
Szretter, A. 1645
Sztajnberg, Chaim 1435
Sztokfisz, David 2243, 2262,
  2267, 2286, 2327, 2377, 2519
Sztrem, Krystyna 1108
Szulkin, Michal 44, 441, 442,
  1013, 2002, 2007, 2050, 2076,
  2077, 2145
Szurowa, Bogumiła 533
Szwalbe, Natan 443
Szymański, Adam (1852-1916)
  1109
Szymański, Stanisław 2255
Szyszka, Bogdan 2760
Szyszko-Bohusz, A. 902

Talmi, E. 2553
Tamari, Moshe (b.1910) 2701,
  2761
Tamir, Nachman 444, 2490
Tapuach, Shimshon 534, 535
Tarnowski, Stanisław (1837-1917)
  2063
Tartakower, Arieh (b.1897) 45,
  127, 445, 446, 447, 485, 903,
  1287, 1288, 1326, 1461, 1493,
  1494, 1495, 1496, 2688
Tash, Eliezer (Tur-Shalom)
  2552, 2558
Tatarzanka, W. 258
Taubler, Eugen 2230
Taylor, Alan 1436
Tchorsh, Katriel Fishel (b.1896)
  2737

Teitelbaum, Abraham 2689
Teitelboim, Dora 1014
Tenenbaum, Arazi Abraham 2440
Tenenbaum, Joseph L. (1887-1961)
  137, 138, 259, 510, 2424
Tenenbaum, Samuel 2237
Tennenblatt, M.A. 2316
Tenzer, Morton 1497
Terlecki, Tymon (b.1905) 2014,
  2125
Teslar, Tadeusz 1591
Tetmajer, Kazimierz Przerwa
  (1894-1953) 1111
Themerson, Stefan 1996
Thon, Ozjasz (1870-1936) 448,
  1437, 1647
Thon-Rostowa, N. 2164
Tilleman, O. 1015
Tishby, Israel 724, 809
Tobias, Henry Jack 1373
Tokarz, Wacław (1873-1937) 260
Tomaszewski, Jerzy 46, 449,
  450, 486, 511, 563, 1289,
  1498, 1648, 1649, 1845, 2221,
  2425, 2690
Torchalski, Ryszard 2047
Torres, Tereska 1983
Traub, Michael 1499
Trautman, Andrzej 2053
Trunk, Isaiah S. 23, 47, 48,
  1374, 1846, 1847, 2497
Trunk, Yehiel Isaiah (1887-1961)
  1016, 2132, 2691
Tryman, Maurycy 1546
Trzeciak, Stanisław 725, 1848,
  1849, 1850, 1851, 1852, 1853
Trznadel, Jacek 1112
Tsimbalista, Israel 2520
Tsirlin, Shalom 2277
Tsurnamal, Zeev 2430
Tugenhold, Jakob (1794-1871)
  341
Turkow-Grudberg, Isaac 1149,
  1150, 1151, 2527
Turowicz, Jerzy 1593
Turowski, Stanisław 139, 1592
Tuwim, Julian (1894-1953) 1113
Tych, Feliks 2692
Tygel, Zeling 1525
Tyloch, W. 140
Tyrowicz, Marian 261

Uchitelle, Daniel J. 24
Ujejski, Józef (1883-1937) 1114
Ulam, Stanisław M. 1984
Ullmann, F. 2447

Unszlicht, Julian (pseud. Wacław Sedecki) 1716, 1719
Urbach, Efraim Elimelech 726
Urbach, Janusz Konrad 342
Urbański, Zygmunt 451

Vago, Bela 1217
Vago, Bela (1888-1963) 141
Valentin, Hugo 1854
Vaykhert, Mikhal 2693
Vereta, Meir 1500
Vincenz, Stanisław 1115
Vishniac, M. 1855
Vishniac, Roman (b.1897) 904, 905
Vital, David 1438, 1439

Wachstein, Bernhard (1868-1935) 1985
Wagschal, Pinhas 2202
Wajner, M. 1547
Wajsberg, Moshe 2601
Wajsbrot, Jakub 1375
Waks, Szymon 2525
Walden, Aron (1838-1912) 727
Waldman, Morris David (1879-1963) 452
Walichnowski, Tadeusz (b.1928) 1856
Walski, K. 644
Walzer, Michael 2429
Wander, N. 810
Wandycz, Piotr (b.1923) 142
Wańkowicz, Melchior (1891-1974) 143
Wardziński, Mieczysław 1594
Warmiński, Jan 343
Warschauer, Adolf (1885-1930) 262, 2517
Warschauer, Jonathan 1218
Warshawsky, Dov B. 2268
Warszawski, Isaiah (1815-1860) 163
Warszawski, S. 2694, 2695
Washinsky, Emil 2382
Wasilewska, Wanda (1905-1964) 1595
Wasilewski, Leon (1870-1936) 264
Wasiutyński, Bohdan (b.1882) 265, 487
Wasserman, Abraham 1376
Wasserman, P. 453
Wasserman, Rudolf 266
Wat, Aleksander (1900-1967) 1986

Wawrzykowska-Wierciochowa, Danuta 2037
Web, Marek 1526
Wein, Adam 564, 612, 613, 2276, 2459, 2460, 2696, 2697, 2698
Weinberg, Joseph 1440
Weiner, Leo (1862-1939) 1017
Weinlos, I. 2038
Weinlos, L. 1987
Weinrach, B. 565
Weinreich, Beatrice 25, 1021
Weinreich, Max (1894-1969) 1290, 1441, 2732
Weinreich, Uriel 25, 1018, 1019, 1020, 1021
Weinreich, Uriel (1925-1967) 25, 1021
Weinryb, Bernard Dov (b.1900) 144, 512, 513, 514, 645, 811, 1181, 1219
Weinstejn, L. 267, 1650
Weintraub, Wiktor (b.1908) 2013
Weisbord, Chana 2733
Weiss, Abraham (1895-1970) 2152
Weiss, J. 812, 813, 814, 815, 2116, 2117
Weiss, L. 887
Weissberg, Max (1856-1930) 728, 908, 1022, 1023
Weissman, G. 2559
Weitz, Emmy 2566
Weizmann, Chaim (1874-1952) 1988, 1989
Wendel, Jerzy 145
Wenig, N. 1024
Werner, Alfred (b.1911) 909
Werses, S. 1692
Werytus, Antoni 1857
Wettstein, Feivel Hirsch, (1858-1924) 146, 2363, 2364, 2365
Whitby, H.A. Morton (b.1898) 2081
Wielopolska, Maria Jehanne (1884-1940) 1597
Wierczak, K. 1859
Wiesel, Elie (b.1928) 816
Wieviorka, Annette 1990
Wigoder, Geoffrey (1864-1934) 18, 26, 910
Wikler, Jerzy 2272
Wilczek, Ignacy 2135
Wilczynski, H. 1116
Wildecki, H. 1860, 1861
Wilensky, Mordechai 817, 818
Wilhelm, Kurt 1182
Winczakiewicz, Jan 1117

Wischnitzer, Mark (1882-1955)
  566, 1501, 1693, 2218
Wischnitzer, (Bernstein) Rachel
  (b.1885) 906, 907
Witkowski, Marek (pseud.
  "Niedowiarek") 1694
Wittlin, Jozef (1896-1976) 2427
Wojcicki, Mieczyslaw 454
Wolf, G. 268
Wolf, Lucien (1857-1930) 614
Wolf, Zeew 1991
Wolfowicz, Szymel 1695
Wolinski, Janusz 2003
Worobeichic, Moise 2731
Wroblewski, Waclaw 1502, 1503
Wudzki, Leon 1992
Wyka, Kazimierz 1118
Wynot, Edward 1862
Wyrobisz, A. 2589
Wyszomirski, Jerzy 1598

Yaari, Abraham (1899-1966) 2455
Yaari, Meir (b.1897) 1442
Yaari-Wold, Moshe 2541
Yahalomi, Solomon 2575
Yahil, Lewi 1504
Yanasovich, Isaac (b.1909) 2531
Yarmolinsky, Avrahm (1890-1965)
  911
Yashar, Baruch 2342
Yasheev, Zvi 2469
Yerushalmi, Eliezer 2462
Yerushalmi, Shimson Dov (b.1892)
  2315
Yishay, Bar 1526
Ysander, Torsten (1893-1960)
  819

Zabierowski, Stanislaw 1119
Zablotniak, Ryszard 1267, 1600,
  2201, 2654, 2655, 2656, 2699
Zaborowski, Jacek 1599
Zachariasz, Szymon 1720
Zaderecki, Tadeusz 1601, 1602
Zagorodski, Israel Chaim
  (b.1865) 2019
Zahorska, Stefania (1894-1961)
  1120
Zajaczkowski, Henryk 646
Zajdeman, M. 553
Zajczyk, Szymon 912, 2328
Zaleski, Wladyslaw Jozef 455

Zaludkowski, Elias (1890-1943)
  729
Zamoyski, Adam 147
Zangwill, Israel (1864-1926)
  1152
Zapolska, Gabriela (1857-1921)
  1121, 1122, 1123
Zarchin, Michael Moses (b.1893)
  269
Zaremba, Zygmunt (b.1895) 1603
Zawidowitch, Y. Ch. 2301
Zborowski, Mark 1268, 1291
Zeevi, Yosef (Wilk) 2449
Zeitlin, Hillel (1871-1942)
  2118
Zelkovitch, Joseph 2405
Zelmanowich, Ephraim L. 1993
Zesler, Sh. 2753
Zglinski, Daniel 1153
Zhabotinskii, Vladimir Evgen'-
  evich (1880-1940) 1377, 1443,
  1444, 1445
Zhitlowski, Chaim (1865-1943)
  1446
Zieleniewski, L. (b.1899) 615
Zieminski, Jan (pseud. of Jan
  Wagner) 1505
Zilbersztejn, Sara 2700
Zimler, Henryk 2657
Zinberg, Israel (1873-1938) 820
Zineman, Jacob 1378, 1447
Ziolek, Jan 345
Zipper, Jacob 2612
Zitron, Phinehas 2330
Zivier, Ezechiel (b.1868) 1292
Zlotnik, Jehuda Leib (1888-1962)
  1293
Zmigryder-Konopka, Zdzislaw 456
Zoref, Efraim (b.1903) 2522
Zubrzycki, Tadeusz 346, 347
Zucker, Morris (b.1892) 2345
Zucker, Nechemias (b.1896) 270
Zunser, Miriam Shomer 1994
Zunz, Jehiel Mattathias 2366
Zych, Franciszek 2172
Zygelboym, Samuel Mordechai
  (1865-1943) 647
Zylberfarb, M. 1379
Zylberstajn, Roman 515
Zarnowska, Anna 1328
Zyczynski, Henryk (1890-1941)
  1124

ABOUT THE COMPILERS

GEORGE J. LERSKI, Professor Emeritus of Modern European History at the University of San Francisco, was awarded a medal of honor by Jerusalem's Yad Vashem Institute for his prewar and wartime activities on behalf of Jews. His earlier works include *Herbert Hoover and Poland* and *A Polish Chapter in Jacksonian America,* and he has contributed articles to *The Polish Review* and *The Transactions of the Asiatic Society.*

HALINA T. LERSKI, an employee of Bechtel Corporation, assisted in the preparation and editing of this and other works by George J. Lerski.